The Two Gospels

By
Daniel Yordy

Christ lives in our hearts by faith.

God will judge the secrets of men's hearts by my gospel.
Paul

The Scripture quotations used in *The Two Gospels* are taken from the *New King James Version of the Bible*. Copyright © 1982 by Thomas Nelson, Inc. Used by permission. All rights reserved.

Published by

Daniel Yordy
7914 Fernbank Drive
Houston, Texas 77049

Copyright © 2013 by Daniel Yordy

All rights reserved, including the right to reproduce this book or portions thereof in any form whatsoever. For permission to reproduce please contact me.

Introduction

Every Christian on earth believes, sincerely, that his or her present knowledge of God and the Christian gospel is the true and correct gospel of Jesus Christ. Thus every Christian could actually write a personal definition of "The Two Gospels," mine, the correct one, versus everyone else's, the false.

But what if?

What if the problem is, in actuality, the definition of God.

What is God? — Don't be too hasty to answer that question.

In John 16, Jesus said that everything said about God is figurative, but that now He would tell us plainly about the Father. Then He stopped talking.

What happened next was not something God did, but God showing Himself in the human realms as He really is, a Man laying down His life for His friends.

Jesus said, **"He who has seen Me has seen the Father."** In other words, the only description of God granted to either heaven or earth is a Man. We cannot know God without knowing this Man.

Then we must ask the next question — what is man?

God says that man is the likeness and image of God.

This is a bit strange, isn't it? The only way we can know God is to know what man is. And the only way we can know man is to know what God is. This is the puzzle the Bible places before us, and there really is no other way to say it.

The core of the New Covenant, the agreement we signed with God and God with us are these words, from 1 John 3.

We shall be like Him (Jesus), **for we shall see Him as He is.**

This is the same circular thinking God places before us in His definitions of God and man.

We imagine that right now, we are not like Jesus. But how can that be? If we are not just like Jesus right now, then it is apparent that we do NOT see Him as He is. But if we do not see Jesus as He is, then what is this imaginative Jesus we think we are "not like"?

If we are not just like Jesus, then we do not see Him as He is, and if we do not see Him as He is, then the Jesus we think we know is not the Jesus of the gospel in Whom we live.

But we are getting ahead of ourselves. If God is required by His own oath in the gospel to conform us to the image of His Son, to make us just like Jesus, what does that mean? Christianity holds a great argument that Jesus is "God the Son," distinct from God the Father, yet an essential Person of "the Godhead."

So, if Jesus is God, and you and I are "just" humans, how on earth could God ever keep covenant with us?

But what if God is so very different from what most people know? – And how can God not be very different since we do not yet see Him as He is?

Most don't understand that the prevailing definitions of God, of man, of Christ Jesus, and of salvation, found in Christianity, were hammered out by powerful intellectuals at the express dictate of a psycopathic killer who intended to use those definitions to cement his absolute control over the Roman world.

That definition is the Nicene Creed, the gospel of the Nicolaitans.

In this book I wage open warfare against the Nicene Creed and the false knowing about God that it perpetrates through every strata of Christianity, historical and present day.

The gospel of Jesus Christ as taught by Paul and John exists in an entirely different realm than what most Christians know.

Salvation is not some place people "go" after their bodies are ripped away from their spirits; Salvation is a Person in whom we live.

More than that, the Gospel of Salvation begins only inside of two questions.

What is God?

What does He WANT?

You will see that God's desire, His heart, is not found in the Nicene Creed, thus all that comes out of that stark absence of God Himself in Person can be nothing other than another gospel.

More than that, you will see that the "gospel" of the Nicene Creed is simply a far worse version of the same lie out of which the serpent spoke. He was talking blither then; he is talking blither today.

This volume is a definitional approach to a number of key terms in the New Testament, words we imagine we know their meaning. However, when recast in the light of a description of God taken from the only picture we have of Him, a Man laying down His life, then these words take on an entirely different meaning, and impact our lives right now in ways many have never considered.

God has an incredible purpose inside all the darkness of this world.

The Father is coming Home.

Table of Contents

1. Another Gospel	1
2. Door	11
3. Light	19
4. God	29
5. Travail	39
6. The Nicene Creed	46
7. Life	57
8. Christ Jesus	68
9. Man	79
10. Church	89
11. Father	99
12. People	109
13. Salvation	119
14. Face	130
15. Church by Father	140
16. Heart	151
17. Voice	162
18. Spirit	173
19. Body	184
20. The Two Gospels	195
21. Victory	207

1. Another Gospel

God will judge the secrets of men's hearts by my gospel. Paul

Paul gave us a knowledge of Christ and His salvation beyond what the other apostles had received from the Lord. John, having been immersed in Paul's gospel for many years, wrote his own rendition of the gospel alongside of Paul's. But Paul warned the Christian church that another gospel containing another Jesus was already pressing against the truth of Christ. For the next three hundred years another gospel and another Jesus warred against Paul's gospel and Paul's Jesus in the hearts and minds of Christians until AD 325, when another Jesus won at the point of the sword.

In AD 325 another gospel containing another Jesus took full possession of what is called Christianity. Another gospel and another Jesus rule Christianity today.

We face an almost insurmountable difficulty. Both Paul's Jesus and another Jesus share the same name, both promote a gospel using similar words, and both use Bible verses to promote their claims.

Here is our anchor. There is no such thing as another Jesus. The other thing is imagination only. The real Jesus is Savior and Salvation. He carries all regardless of the confusion in their minds.

Yet, in spite of that Rock in which we live, most of our brethren, when they use the word, "Jesus," and when they speak of the glorious goodness of the gospel, are not speaking of the Jesus or the gospel we know. Another Jesus and another gospel rules in their hearts and minds, and they cannot see it.

God always turns the ways of darkness upside down. We who are discovering the incredible joy of the real Jesus of Paul's gospel are accused by our brethren of pushing another Jesus of the "last days." They forget that another Jesus was already around in Paul's day gaining all victory over Paul's Jesus within 300 years.

Both Jesus and another Jesus go by the same name. Both Jesus and another Jesus use the same Bible. Both Jesus and another Jesus refer back to the same Man who walked the earth.

Almost all Christians I know reject Paul's gospel without consideration. Almost all Christians I know believe in another gospel.

Another gospel has a name: the Nicene Creed.

Thus another Jesus is the Nicene Christ, the Christ of the Nicolaitans!

Read the Nicene Creed. If every line does not break your heart, then you are quite comfortable with another Jesus, you know only another salvation.

Paul's Jesus lives in our hearts. We do not know of Him in any other way.

Here are the primary verses of Paul's gospel, laid out in an order of understanding. I use the New King James Version. (Feel free to look up the context.)

> And we know that all things work together for good to those who love God, to those who are the called according to His purpose. For whom He foreknew, He also predestined to be conformed to the image of His Son, that He might be the firstborn among many brethren. Moreover whom He predestined, these He also called; whom He called, these He also justified; and whom He justified, these He also glorified. Romans 8:28-30

> But we all, with unveiled face, beholding as in a mirror the glory of the Lord, are being transformed into the same image from glory to glory, just as by the Spirit of the Lord. 2 Corinthians 3:18

> My little children, for whom I labor in birth again until Christ is formed in you... Galatians 4:19

> That Christ may dwell in your hearts through faith; that you, being rooted and grounded in love, may be able to comprehend with all the saints what is the width and length and depth and height—to know the love of Christ which passes knowledge; that you may be filled with all the fullness of God. Ephesians 3:17-19

> Now hope does not disappoint, because the love of God has been poured out in our hearts by the Holy Spirit who was given to us. - For if when we were enemies we were reconciled to God through the death of His Son, much more, having been reconciled, we shall be saved by His life. Romans 5:5 & 10

> ...The riches of the glory of this mystery among the Gentiles: which is Christ in you, the hope of glory. Him we preach... that we may present every man perfect in Christ Jesus. Colossians 1:27-28

> For in Him dwells all the fullness of the Godhead bodily; and you are complete in Him, who is the head of all principality and power. Col. 2:9

> But God..., even when we were dead... made us alive together with Christ (by grace you have been saved), and raised us up together, and made us sit together in the heavenly places in Christ Jesus... Eph.2:4-6

> I have been crucified with Christ; it is no longer I who live, but Christ lives in me; and the life which I now live in the flesh I live by the faith of the Son of God, who loved me and gave Himself for me. Galatians 2:20

Or do you not know that as many of us as were baptized into Christ Jesus were baptized into His death? Therefore we were buried with Him through baptism into death, that just as Christ was raised from the dead by the glory of the Father, even so we also should walk in newness of life. …knowing this, that our old man was crucified with Him, that the body of sin might be done away with, that we should no longer be slaves of sin. For he who has died has been freed from sin. Romans 6:3-7

But we have this treasure in earthen vessels, that the excellence of the power may be of God and not of us. – that the life of Jesus also may be manifested in our mortal flesh. 2 Corinthians 4:7 & 11

And He said to me, "My grace is sufficient for you, for My strength is made perfect in weakness." Therefore most gladly I will rather boast in my infirmities, that the power of Christ may rest upon me. 2 Cor.12:9

For the law of the Spirit of life in Christ Jesus has made me free from the law of sin and death. Romans 8:2

Put on the Lord Jesus Christ – without considering the flesh or its desires. Romans 14:14 (A more accurate translation.)

For this corruptible must put on incorruption, and this mortal must put on immortality. So when this corruptible has put on incorruption, and this mortal has put on immortality, then shall be brought to pass the saying that is written: "Death is swallowed up in victory." – But thanks be to God, who gives us the victory through our Lord Jesus Christ.
1 Corinthians 15:53-54 & 57

Therefore, if anyone is in Christ, he is a new creation; old things have passed away; behold, all things have become new. Now all things are of God... For He made Him who knew no sin to be sin for us, that we might become the righteousness of God in Him. 2 Corinthians 5:17-18 & 21

Now the body is... for the Lord, and the Lord for the body. And God both raised up the Lord and will also raise us up by His power. Do you not know that your bodies are members of Christ? — But he who is joined to the Lord is one spirit with Him. — Or do you not know that your body is the temple of the Holy Spirit who is in you, whom you have from God, and you are not your own? 1 Corinthians 6:13-19

For we are members of His body, of His flesh and of His bones. Ephesians 5:30

But even if we, or an angel from heaven, preach any other gospel to you than what we have preached to you, let him be accursed. – But I make known to you, brethren, that the gospel which was preached by me is not according to man. For I neither received it from man, nor was I taught it, but it came through the revelation of Jesus Christ.** Galatians 1:8 & 11-12

Jesus did not preach Paul's gospel for the simple reason that He could not. Paul's gospel can be received only by those who are first born again and second, have a living relationship with the Holy Spirit. Such conditions did not exist until after the Day of Pentecost. Thus those who reject Paul's gospel and Paul's Jesus do so partly by using words Jesus Himself spoke to a people who could not hear Him. Those words are true words, but they are not the gospel and they cannot save anyone apart from Paul's gospel. Those who use them separate from Paul's Jesus cannot hear them either.

The other apostles understood Jesus as Savior, having done something incredible for us. Paul gave us an entirely different view of Jesus, Jesus as first Savior, yes, but that same Jesus, now, as Salvation. Every argument in defense of another gospel, though it premises itself on Jesus as Savior, leaves out all thought of Jesus as Salvation. But the real Jesus, though Savior of all, cannot be Savior of anyone except He first becomes ALL of each individual person's Salvation.

Paul's Jesus lives in Person in fullness inside of us – by faith. Faith does not make it happen; faith sees what God knows. Faith honors God as a truth-teller.

And Paul's gospel, by which all men are judged, places you and me entirely, in all that we are, our sin, our flesh, our self, entirely into that Lamb, that Person, that Salvation, in all that He is. Entirely into His Gethsemane, entirely into His death, entirely into His burial, entirely into His Resurrection, and then Paul's gospel places that same Jesus entirely into us. Only Jesus is never alone, all the fullness of God in Person comes into us with Him along with the Holy Spirit who already fills our hearts to overflowing with the Love of God.

Paul's gospel is not figurative; it is absolutely literal. We put on the Lord Jesus Christ, Himself in Person, here and now as our very and only life. Our flesh is God's flesh; our flesh is filled with God!

There is no part of Jesus that is not found in us; there is no part of us not found in Jesus, including our sin and our shame. There is no part of us not filled with Jesus Himself in Person; there is no part of Jesus in which we are not found.

This is Paul's gospel; this is Paul's Jesus. Paul's gospel culminates in the defeat of death and our becoming in all fullness just like Jesus.

Whence, then, came another Jesus and another gospel?

Another Jesus and another gospel came entirely out from Adam's rebellion. Adam loves repenting of sin; it makes him feel a god, a judge. "This is sin; that's not sin. I KNOW the difference. I have my fate entirely in control." Adam hates repenting of self; he never considers such a thing.

There is one way alone a man or a woman could ever repent of self. They must have an entirely other Self to call their very own, another Self who instantly and completely replaces their own self, swallowing them up inside Him Self.

His name is Jesus. If Jesus is not our self, we remain in Adam.

Did you notice the center-point of Paul's gospel, the hinge? We are weak. Jesus is perfected in us only as we are weak. Adam hates weak. Notice all arguers for another gospel. Human achievement of God's requirements is the center-point of their gospel. They will not abandon themselves entirely into another Person.

They will not allow Jesus to be their flesh.

But if Jesus in us is not Salvation, then what did salvation become? This is very difficult to understand. As the early church was driven into persecution and death after the passing of the Apostles, out of that darkness, bit by bit, another Jesus was invented, another gospel, another salvation.

Another salvation is not found in the New Testament; it is not found in the words of Jesus or of Paul or of John. It is not found in the words of Peter or James. Another salvation is an invention of human fear and unbelief divorced entirely from Paul's Jesus and Paul's gospel.

It is hard to comprehend another salvation, but here it is; let me spell it out as much as I am able to make some sort of sense out of it.

You see, the Christians of the second century, without the apostles, driven in fear of persecution, began to imagine that Jesus was not in them, that He was not their life. They determined by the evidence of their eyes and by their human judgment, that Jesus was not here, that they were not His body. At the same time the heavens, the spirit realms in which they lived faded away in their imagination. They became convinced that they did not live in heaven as well as earth. They forgot how to walk in the Spirit. Yet they still had the apostle's letters. In them they read about salvation and the heavenlies and Jesus. But when they looked around them, they saw nothing except precious fellow believers dying and then gone!

In their fear and confusion, in their darkness and unbelief, some began to whisper about this word, "salvation." If I am a Christian and "saved," but Jesus is absent and "heaven" is far away, what then? How is it that I am "saved?" If Jesus is not here. If Jesus is not now, if Jesus is not personal in me, then what is "saved?"

Always there were bold preachers, ravenous wolves as Paul said, going around, heading up churches, becoming bishops, who declared with all certainty, *"Jesus is gone; He is absent. Jesus is not here. Jesus is not now. Jesus is not you. But in His absence, He has placed ME in your lives to take His place. Do what I say and you will be doing what Jesus wants. Jesus will speak to you through me."*

Paul said that people weren't going to die. Paul said that our bodies would be swallowed up by life. *Paul was wrong – see, he himself had his head chopped off.*

But Paul wrote the words of God! *Well, obviously, Paul was talking about something else. We are reading his words wrong.*

So, if Jesus is absent, if heaven is far away, if Paul's claim of victory over death was obviously not for us now, then what is this salvation?

Well, Paul also said that when we die, we are "with the Lord." And people who are not Christians (wicked pagans) obviously cannot be "with the Lord" after they die. So, since Jesus is absent and heaven is far away, then SALVATION must mean that we "go to" heaven after we die! And that must mean that people who are not "saved" go somewhere else far away after they die.

By this reasoning, by the rejection of Jesus here, Jesus now, Jesus our very and only life Personal in us, Salvation turned into something God never says, something simply not found in the Bible.

Salvation became something far away, going to some geographical "place" only after the death of the physical body. And this going to some place is based entirely on some sort of continual transaction engaged in with a far-away Jesus, a Jesus back then, a Jesus up there, a Jesus some-day!

Salvation became nothing more than grubbing along inside of Adam's same mess and hoping that maybe someday what God says might become real. Someday and far away.

You can see how strange and senseless another gospel is, yet so many of our brethren, who do know the real Jesus a little bit, who are carried utterly by Him, hold tightly to another gospel, imagining it is the "truth" of God.

༄

Knowing God is NOT an intellectual exercise. Every idea we have in our minds about God cannot ever be God Himself. Ideas about God do more to separate dear Christians from God than anything else. Yet that separation is imagination only, same as all the ideas. Jesus utterly carries them.

Truth is not known by one plus two. Truth is a Person, Jesus, and He, though gentle, is absolutely wild. To know Him as He is, we must be ready to leap with Him upon the mountain-tops. Truth is known by lateral leaps in unexpected directions. Truth never sets up camp, though He is always faithful and true. To know Truth, we must be willing to ride with Him into unending adventure.

Yet this Truth, Jesus, inside of the God who fills us full, is always meek and lowly of heart, gentle and tender and kind.

We love Him. — We love Him.

Here is a difficulty you must face, dear reader. A contradiction to which you must give an answer out of the bottom-line of your own heart. The core of the Covenant we have entered into with God are these words:

We shall be like Him (Jesus), **for we shall see Him as He is.** 1 John 3:2

Are you just like Jesus right now, dear reader, in all ways? Chances are, you will say, "No, definitely not!" But consider your contradiction. If you are not just like Jesus right now, then it is quite clear that you do not see Him as He is. And if you do not see Him as He is, how do you even know who or what He is? How do you know that you are not, right now, just like Him?

If you do not see Him as He is, then the Jesus you think you know must be another Jesus. But rest assured; there is only one Jesus. And He carries you all the way home.

Let me spell that out again. If you are not just like Jesus right now, then you do not see Him as He is. And if you do not see Him as He is, then the Jesus you think you "know" must be another Jesus.

∽

The Nicene Council was ostensibly a "council of the church" in the same manner of the gathering of the apostles in Jerusalem under James, when Paul presented his gospel of the revelation of Jesus Christ to the leaders of the church. Just as that council was a deliberation over critical questions in the knowledge of the Christian gospel, so the Nicene Council, called in AD 325, was a deliberation over further critical questions.

There was a huge difference, however, between the two councils. The Jerusalem Council was held in the fervent reality of a present Christ and conducted by people utterly separate from the power centers of human society. The Holy Ghost was very present at that meeting and all the original disciples of Jesus acknowledged clearly the hand of God upon Paul.

In contrast, the Nicene Council was a gathering of individuals finding themselves in newly ascendant power and place in the world. Christianity was now the official religion of the Roman Empire. Every decision made in this council would be backed by the point of the Roman sword. The men who gathered at Nicaea were not fishermen and tax collectors, but intellectuals and human powerhouse leaders. They were among the most educated of the day, having risen to their places as bishops and scholars of the church by human achievement.

These men were serious about the Christian religion, about codifying its doctrine so that everyone would know clearly "what Christians believe." The primary argument at the Nicene Council was over the question of "who and what is Christ." That is the great question of the church age, as relevant today as it was when Jesus asked, **"But who do you say that I am?"**

The argument was basically two-sided. One group, led by Athanasius, argued that Jesus was God – "God the Son," having momentarily taken upon Himself an outer shell of humanity. This argument then required a codifying of a definition of

God as "the Trinity." These men positioned themselves as the mouthpiece of God, thus they declared their own words as equivalent to the New Testament. "God the Son," and "the Trinity" became Christian concepts by their declaration.

The other group, led by Arius, argued that Jesus was a man filled with God. The first group won the debate, thus we don't really know what Arius actually understood because the winners always write the history books. However, the entire argument was about Jesus back then and Jesus up there, knowing Jesus according to outward appearance, that is, the flesh. No element of Paul's gospel and Paul's Jesus remained.

The Nicene Jesus – God the Son – was the victory of another Jesus. That definition of Christ broke the Covenant. No human can ever be "God the Son"; therefore we cannot ever be just like Him; Jesus cannot be the first One of our kind. Now, everyone today claims that Arius argued that Jesus was "just a man." Thus the argument presents itself, that is, puts on the face of being an argument between "Jesus was God" versus "Jesus was just a man." That is a false face. That is not the question Jesus asked His disciples; that is not the question "Who and what is Christ?"

I have no idea what Arius really said, nor does it make any difference to us.

What we must know is the answer to Jesus' question, "Daniel, who do you say that I am?" Paul's gospel requires only one answer to that question. "Jesus, you are my only life. You are all I find myself to be."

You see, the lie of the Nicene argument is the identical same lie the serpent offered in the garden. *"God is one who knows ideas. If you know the right ideas, you can be 'godly.'"* It is the entire delusion that God is known by human intellect, by mouthing the correct ideas about God.

The same "elephant in the room" that was ignored in the garden is the same huge thing being ignored at Nicaea.

WHAT IS MAN? — If you do not know what man is, then you cannot know what God is or Jesus or salvation. What is man?

The only answer we can give to that question is "the likeness and image of God," or, **"the express image of God's Person."** We must begin with that question and that answer, but then we must ask a second question, "What is God?" Do not answer that question with the Nicene Creed – though you may very much want to do so. Human reason does not know God. There is one answer only to the question, "What is God?"

"He who has seen Me has seen the Father," stated by a living, breathing, bona fide MAN. The only possible way anyone can describe God is to look at a Man.

Of course Jesus was just a man. In fact, He was the very first man to walk this earth. Adam never did become a man. Man is God revealed. The entity that is

MAN is a being who is mostly all of God. A man is filled with all the fulness of God. A man releases God out from himself as rivers of Spirit. A man is the image and likeness of God.

There is one God, the Father, and one Mediator between man and God, the MAN, Christ Jesus. Paul

"Elephant in the room" means that there is something huge and obvious standing there that everyone knows is there, but everyone is trying so very hard to pretend that the thing doesn't exist at all. The "elephant in the room" in the garden was that Adam and Eve were just like God, His image. Adam and Eve already were the only visible representation of God in both heaven and earth. Adam knew that; the serpent knew that. Both of them ignored that point entirely. When the serpent said, "I will be like the Most High," he meant, "I will take man's place." At the same time, Adam chose to define the serpent's words as meaning, "I will be just like this most glorious outward appearance."

The lie was very simple: "Adam, Christ is not your life."

What is Christ? Christ IS my only life.

This is the most important reality in God; it alone is Salvation. Look at the Nicene Creed. Christ my life is ABSENT, shoved out into the cold.

Human reason will never know Christ as our only life. The mind that generated the Nicene Creed is the mind Adam received from the serpent in the garden.

Jesus said, **"My words are Spirit and they are Life."**

Now, the thing to understand is that the entire definition of God, of Jesus, of the universe, and of salvation as hammered out by the Nicene Creed and all of it's expansions is a false face, a mask. That is not really what the Nicene Creed is.

The Nicene Creed is the loathing hatred of man. The Nicene Creed is the fury and envy of the serpent.

Look again at the words spoken against me on Facebook. *God does just about everything apart from you, Yordy. He doesn't need any human consent. Nice that you are freeing creation. I've read about some in prison for Christ that could use your help. Go at it!*

This is such a wonderful illustration, not of the serpent's hatred of man, but his fury against God. You see, it's God who is not doing what He said. It's God who is not showing up and healing people, setting them free, revealing His love to all. If God is love, if God is real, why doesn't He just show everyone that He is love? What is the point in all the continued heartache and pain and grievous loss?

But since hatred cannot get at God, it turns and attacks man. If God is not revealing Himself as love and life and power, then it is man's fault. The purpose of turning the Lord Jesus Christ into "God the Son," far above and far away is not to exalt Jesus. That idea is part of the false face. The purpose is, rather, to denigrate man, to define human flesh, which is the image of God, as low and evil.

At the same time the Nicene Christ was being defined, human flesh was becoming abhorrent to Christian thinking. The story of the hatred of the flesh, hatred of being the image of God, through Christian history is the most horrific and sordid story in the annals of the human race. One could read the Wikipedia account of Simeon Stylites to see but one picture of how far this hatred can go.

As I sit in a secular college classroom, I understand that their rejection of all things "God," comes entirely out from a twisted image of God produced by the sickness of the Christian hatred of God's image, that is, of human flesh.

The serpent could not himself ever become like God. So half of his entire program is to cause the Christian church to hate and loathe themselves as the image of God. "Let Jesus be seen and not you." Why? Because you are despicable – hatred of being the image and likeness of God.

In this book, I explore the differences and the boundary lines between the real Jesus and the real gospel versus another Jesus and another gospel, that is, the Nicene Creed. I show how much of "Christian" thinking is not from the New Testament, but rather from forcing the New Testament to fit the declarations of the Nicene Council and of Augustine's rendition of that Creed.

I apply the ax to the root of that which keeps Christ from being known as He really is in the earth. I also draw out a knowing of God that comes only from the words of the New Testament, things God says about Himself, coming into us as Spirit and as Life.

You see, the same words that come into our brethren as mental ideas are well able to come into us as our very and only Life. As that happens we come to know that God is utterly different in being and in essence than what most imagine.

So few seem to be speaking out from God's interests and intentions. Almost all repeat what they hear from others. But why can't they stop and think? I do not know. Part of it is the power of the Nicene Christ image. It's the same thing Jesus faced, the power of the Pharisees over the minds of all.

The Nicene Creed must be shattered. Every exercise God takes me through is a honing and polishing, seeing more clearly what is the bottom line. God wants that bottom line to be crystal clear so that when He shatters the Nicene Christ the door into the Lord Jesus will be wide open.

I have little reach, and God may choose to do little more with me; I am content. But at the very least, I would clear the path, make the way plain, show a wide open door with the warmth of light shining out. If I can do that, I have done all.

2. Door

To a brother: – It is true that God carries you completely, ever with you, hovering over you with the tenderest of concerns. But at the same time He does not let you know that He is there. You are perfectly safe, perfectly found, perfectly carried, but God does not let you know it.

There is a very good reason for that. We are such devious characters, we humans, always finagling to get an upper hand, somehow. We can say "I am weak," but look what happens when we get one chance not to be weak. We go for it! And soon we are on our face in the mud once again.

God can take us into the knowledge of Christ through only one door.

But first – love. I want to apologize for not being there for you when you needed someone's regard. Please forgive me.

Now, you might think, "Yordy, you did not know me, and you are nowhere near right now." That is true, but still, my apology is true as well. You may find it impossible to forgive yourself, but can you forgive me? When you say, "Daniel, I forgive you," you can begin to know the forgiveness of Christ.

I am a limited man. I am Asperger's, a form of high-performing autism. Thus all my life I have not fit; I have known much pain. Inwardly we may be more alike than you might think. Only in the last few years have I come to understand the things I now teach.

The vision of my heart is to be a part of a community of Christ, a place that one such as yourself could come and walk with people who will walk with you, learning Christ your only life. That vision is strong and full, rooted in full life-knowledge. But alas, I am incapable of making it happen. Though you would find great strength in me, you would also find a weakness that puzzles, a weakness that looks like insensitivity or even arrogance, yet always withdrawing from the face of confrontation.

I was in my late twenties before I began to grapple with the idea that these others in my life were people just like myself. I always gravitated towards other people, but I in no way comprehended them.

Now, however, after living in Christian community for many years, after teaching school in many settings, public, private, and college, I do smile just a bit at your words. "The people that love me, do not really know me. If they did, they would not love me."

I know what it means that people "do not really know me." I know what it means to be utterly ashamed of myself over years and years.

But you are wrong just as I was wrong. The truth is, you don't know yourself, not really. I am convinced that if God allowed us to walk together, I would value all that you are as a dear and close friend.

How can I say that? I am not able to say that of everyone. Those who are self-righteous, who see themselves as superior, as the "man" or "woman of God" sent to condescend themselves to me, I cannot stand before the face of those people. It takes great courage for me to draw them into love inside my heart. Yet God used all my experience with such to burn from me all of my own trust in myself.

Removing self-righteousness from you is one of the greatest gifts God ever gives anyone. You see to what great lengths He has gone to eliminate from your mind and heart any possibility of sitting in your own righteousness, your own doing? God has given you a great gift, this intimate knowledge of face-in-mud; the day will come when you will treasure it.

You see, Jesus knows the face-in-mud experience. He had boasted to His disciples that they should "carry their cross," yet when He, the Messiah of God, had the chance to prove His words, He could not do it. He stumbled and fell into the mud, just like you and me. Someone else carried His cross for Him.

But before we get back to that door, I must say that I know there are actions that bind us outwardly as far as life in this world is concerned. But there is nothing greater than blood. If you cannot find forgiveness, it's because you do not yet know BLOOD. The blood shed for you is greater than you have ever imagined.

The door into knowing Christ is found in these words: **That every mouth may be stopped, and all the world may become guilty before God.**

Most Christians have never passed through this door. Yes, they once may have said, "I have sinned, Jesus forgive me." But they have not stopped their mouths. Nor have you. Look at all the things you say about yourself that cannot be true.

Consider your words: "I am weak, I am miserable, I am desperate, I am lonely, I am a real mess...bla, bla, bla..." You start out speaking the truth, but then you say, "Bla," as if your true words have not brought you to the most important place in the universe, one step away from all the knowledge of life.

How can you go silent before God? You can't do it. Your problem is that God made you just like Himself. You are a voice; you cannot go silent. God is always speaking; we call the always-speaking-of-God the Lord Jesus Christ.

Just like God, you also are always speaking. How can you shut up before Him? You can shut up for a moment, but before you know it you're back to telling yourself things that are not true, over and over, telling yourself things that cannot be true. God made you to be unable to shut up; He made you just like Himself.

For the first time in my life I know how to be silent before God. This has been only in the last few months. But I can testify with all the certainty of Christ, I know this place and I know the way here.

You see, there are two voices in the universe, not one and not many, just two. God's voice we call Christ Jesus; the other voice we call Satan. Both voices are in our own mouth and in our own mind. Christ speaks blessing and life; Satan speaks accusation and curse. You can know instantly which voice you are speaking, they are both so very different.

The accuser is always lying, yet we humans find it so easy to speak his words – BECAUSE we imagine them to be true. Christ is always speaking the truth, yet we find it impossible to speak Christ – BECAUSE we imagine those words cannot be true.

And we cannot stop speaking; we cannot go silent before God. That is an ability God left out when He created us. Yet the only door into Christ is that we stop running our mouth. "But I, but I, but I."

Consider the following three statements of faith.

"I am a miserable loser. I always fail; I'm no good. I am so ashamed of myself. My sin is so great; I cannot forgive myself. I will never make it."

"I am shuckamatoo. I always dibblededoo. I'm no skood. I am so gyre and gimble in the wabe. My rink is so dankle; I will never hoppety-scotch.

"I am the revelation of Jesus Christ. I am with Him in His glory right now and forever. I am altogether clean, as pure as Christ Himself. The love of God fills me to overflowing all the time. Christ is all there is in me."

Shout the first confession at the top of your lungs (in private, of course). It sounds so true and right, so familiar, doesn't it? It is complete rot, far more ridiculous than if you shouted the second confession.

Shout the third confession at the top of your lungs with all confidence. Can you do it?

You see, I inserted the second confession because, though you might feel silly, you could say those syllables. Why, then, is it so hard to say the syllables, the sounds of the third? Why, when you shout the third confession, does it feel and sound all wrong? Why does it sound as if you are lying?

When you speak the first confession, you are lying to yourself and to God; that is, you are being an absolute hypocrite. Yet those words sound so very right and familiar. When you speak the third confession, you are, for the first time in your life, speaking the truth.

Those words are the truth; they are the only thing that is true. When you speak those words, Christ Himself is in your mouth, and He always tells the truth.

You are the master; God made you so. All angels, fallen or unfallen, are at your command. God has even made Christ subject to you – **the word is in your mouth.** You have the power to speak Christ, regardless of all the screams of accusation being hurled at you by very frightened demons who are sick-to-their-stomach terrified of you.

The only thing not subject to you is the God who fills you full with all of Himself, and He utterly possesses you. You can't make that any other way; you have no power to alter His possession of you.

You see, if you will force yourself to shout that third confession, to speak Christ, you will hear a voice strong in your ear saying, "But I, but I, but I..." Finish that line, "But I, not Christ."

That's the shut up God want's from you. He made you guilty, yes – He led you into darkness. Why? So you would shut up. So you would stop saying that most ridiculous nonsense, "But I, not Christ."

And here's the thing. There is no vacuum. You cannot just shut up. No, you MUST SPEAK. And therefore, the only way to silence the voice God never wants to hear is to speak the only voice He loves – speak Christ.

"Not I, but Christ. Not I, but Christ. Not I, but Christ. Christ is all that I am; I am His revelation. Right now, me, as I find myself to be, I am only the revelation of Jesus Christ."

The voice that hates those words is the voice that has brought all the misery and destruction you have ever known. To hate yourself is to hate Christ; you are perfectly free in God to hate the voice of the accuser. That voice is NOT and NEVER HAS BEEN you.

But to the Father, there is no sweeter sound in all the universe than to hear Christ coming from your lips.

Most righteous Christians you know refuse to speak Christ. They believe that by speaking Christ, they are lying. They imagine that by accusing themselves and others they are "speaking the truth in love." Thus Satan is so often in their mouth.

God has given you the most wonderful gift granted to any human being. He has made you guilty before Him. He has led you into the most utter failure you could possibly know. He doesn't typically offer such a gift to most. Now He wants one little thing from you. He wants you to shut up.

But He knows you can't. Therefore He led you to my website. You see, you have nothing left to lose. Shout Christ at the top of your lungs. So what if you are lost, shout Christ. So what if it sounds like total blasphemy, you can't possibly do anything more wicked than you already have – shout Christ. So what if you are "banished forever," shout Christ. Shout Christ. Shout Christ your only life.

"There is no me, there is only Christ! Christ is all there is in me."

The only way you could ever be silent before God is to put another voice in your mouth. The word, Christ Jesus, is in your mouth. It is a complete exchange: life for life, self for self, actions for actions, voice for voice.

Never ever regard your sin again; when you see it, say, "So what." If you ask forgiveness of others, that's not you atoning for sin, that's Christ flowing out of you as rivers of life. Christ is all that you are.

You see, since you are already such a complete failure, since you already know you won't "make it," then saying "so what" is within your reach. Saying "Christ is all there is in me" can't be worse than anything else you've done, can it? Christians who are righteous don't want to lose their righteousness for His. You who are utterly lost have nothing left to lose.

You have the power to speak. Even the man who was full of 2000 demons, though he could not speak, yet he spoke with his feet. It was not the demons who came to Jesus, but the man.

Only the lost know salvation; only the forgiven wash His feet with tears.

If you were not lost, there would be no hope for you.

Give thanks, give thanks, give thanks for the incredible gift God has given you, complete and utter failure in all things. God is so very good to you.

⸺

Hi Daniel. This was posted on Facebook. It is about the "New False Grace Gospel" being taught.

The New False Gospel - Shepherd Serve

(From the web page): There is a false gospel being perpetrated by MANY in Christendom. A false conversion - false belief, another Jesus. If belief is enough, then even demons would be saved according to this false gospel since the scriptures say that even demons BELIEVE and TREMBLE (James 2:19). If you don't repent, you are not saved. Period. The scriptures are clear. Hebrews says that if you continue in your deliberate sin, there is no sacrifice for sins left and you are crucifying Christ all over again (Hebrews 6). Take HEED "Christians" read the WHOLE Word of God and not only the bits that make you feel better. Your very soul depends on it!

⸺

Most everything the brother says in his article would be true if he lived inside of Salvation. Sadly, he is the one teaching "another Jesus," the far-away Jesus of the Nicene Creed. A Jesus who has left us only a series of transactions through which we must maneuver correctly in order to make it someday into a far-away salvation.

But if grace teachers continue to regard a Nicene Christ (far away) and a Nicene salvation (who gets to go to heaven? – what negotiations with God are appropriate?), they are in exactly the same boat.

I have nothing to lose; if I must negotiate with God, this much repentance, these sins are okay (pretending), those are not; these things are sin, those are not – everyone's list is different, I'm just no good at such transactions. How could I ever know if I have made the right ones, sufficiently?

The writer, of course, is fully confident that he knows exactly which transactions get him in, and that he has fully engaged God with all those correct transactions. He fails to see that pretending is also a sin.

Everyone imagines that God gives us some things, salvation, life, righteousness, heaven after we die, and so on. They just don't get it. God has never given any human any-thing. With the law it's all or nothing; disobey on one tiny point and die. With God it's the same. The only "thing" we get from God is God Himself in Person filling us full with all of Himself. Then, whatever God is, whatever God does, He shows Himself through us. – Almighty Power Exercising Absolute Dominion.

That's the covenant, that's the deal. Our knowledge of God comes in steps, but God Himself in Person is all in us or nothing. Either our body, as it is right now, is His temple, the visible expression of another invisible Person, or nothing. **Put on the Lord Jesus Christ** is 100% literal.

Christ as us is nothing other than our simple acknowledgment that He IS The Almighty. We cannot be "wayward"; He exercises His will in all that we find ourselves to be and in all the ways of our lives.

Salvation is one verse alone in the Bible – John 14:20. The entrance into that salvation is one verse alone – Galatians 2:20. Both are entered by faith alone. Faith is not what most think – believing in an escape from hell and an entrance to heaven someday, holding ideas in one's mind about a far-away God. Thus only those who simply, quietly, and with all finality choose to believe that God is telling us the truth, first in Galatians 2:20, and then in John 14:20, the only place where we live, only those see that Salvation is only Jesus in Person in us.

A sister asked me what I mean by "the tree of life." There is only one answer – John 14:20.

Here, then, is what I find. Living only and entirely inside John 14:20, by faith, that is believing it to be so against everything I see, feel, hear, or even do, I discover that the only way I can see anything is to look out from Jesus' eyes, since I am only inside of Him. Then I see that everything that is God forever comes only and immediately out of John 14:20. Every verse becomes life to us as it comes out of John 14:20. But apart from John 14:20 (the tree of life) every verse is only death, it kills, as Paul said.

So when you see people laboring over verses, as this writer does, unable to see what is so plain and obvious to us, all you can do is point to the door, over and over, point to the door. If you will believe that God is actually telling you the truth, Galatians 2:20 will take you into John 14:20, the only place that IS Salvation and Life, that is, inside the Lord Jesus Himself in Person.

And here's what the brother who wrote the article does not comprehend. He has never repented. Taking all our sin and self and flesh into the Lord Jesus and seeing Him all through all that we are, Him in Person, that we are only flesh of His Flesh, one flesh with Him, is the greatest and only real surrender there is. The more I speak what I speak, the more astonishingly surrendered I find myself to be! Because my self is 100% affirmed inside of God, I find it all joy to see His Self released through me, and always as I find myself to be. I know my true Self; it is He, yet He calls me by name!

I said that Galatians 2:20 is the only doorway into life. Yet the same thing is said elsewhere in a number of different ways. Here is another way to say it: **That every mouth may be stopped and all the earth become silent before Him.** Since "I" am silent, the only thing I speak is Christ.

Then I look out from the tree of life, John 14:20, and see these good people, fellow believers in Jesus, who have never repented, though they prate about it. And it seems that when you try to explain, all you can do is stutter gobbledygook.

An extraordinary phrase we hear is "another Jesus." The horrifying thing is that the "other Jesus" Paul warned about came into the church long centuries ago through the Nicene Creed. "Another Jesus," a Jesus back then, up there, some day, is the only Jesus they know. Thus when they hear us speaking of Jesus as our only life – He is Salvation after all, Jesus in Person in us – then they imagine that we are pushing the "other" Jesus. Well, we are, the real Jesus who really is real Salvation.

And Paul's gospel, by which all men are judged, places you and me entirely, in all that we are, our sin, our flesh, our self, entirely into that Lamb, that Person, that Salvation, in all that He is. Entirely into His Gethsemane, entirely into His death, entirely into His burial, entirely into His Resurrection, and then Paul's gospel places that same Jesus entirely into us. Only Jesus is never alone, all the fullness of God in Person comes into us with Him.

Paul's gospel is not figurative; it is absolutely literal. We **put on the Lord Jesus Christ.**

Have you ever watched someone go into a dark room and work and work at getting rid of the darkness so that someday, someday, they might have light? Most of us simply flip on the light switch.

Have you ever watched someone work and work and work to get rid of their sin and their flesh and all the horror of Adam and the terror of a far-away God? Some of us simply accept Christ Himself in Person in all that is us.

Christ is always all before anything not-Christ could ever vanish away.

And I would caution you to be careful to keep your desire for His desires expressed through you in it's proper place. It is so easy for such desire to cause us to see ourselves separate from Him and suddenly needing to measure up, to "get" something from God we think we need. We already have all of God in Person; as we desire to know Him on the one hand, we rest utterly in Him on the other, both all the time. But desire not found in rest can never be the desire of God; that is, desire that says "I wish" and not "I am." – Calling those things that "be not" as they are is the only proof of true desire. – We must look at ourselves in all we find ourselves to be as the perfect will of God in the present moment, regardless of what we think. We live only in the tree of life.

Abide in Me and I in you. John 15:3

There is no other commandment in the Bible. As we keep this commandment, Christ Himself fulfills the entire Bible in our lives. Those who fail to keep this commandment, though they "keep" all others, live only separated from Christ in their minds and can never please or know God.

Inside of **"Abide in Me and I in you"** we find everything of God. Outside of that place, everything is all wrong, including every word in the Bible.

When I was in college, one of our teachers gave us a "quiz." It was a page of little things to do, such as "write the date on the top left corner of your paper," or "circle the word 'because.'" The test was timed; we all attacked it earnestly. The directions said, "Read all the questions before you begin." Well, I followed the directions. The last item on the quiz said. "Do not do anything except #1, 'Write your name.'" I happily obeyed #1 and sat back laughing at all the other students but one who were busy, busy, busy, doing all that the test said to do.

The rest did all the questions correctly and failed the whole purpose of the quiz.

Paul says that Jesus lives in our hearts by faith. John says that we are in Him by faith. We know that means today; **now is the day of salvation. – Today if you will hear His voice…** 1 Corinthians 6:2 – Hebrews 3:15

Today we abide in Him and He in us.

In that day you shall know that I am in the Father and you in Me and I in you. John 14:20

Today is that day. Today we know, today we see that everything that we are right now in this world is IN the Lord Jesus and the Lord Jesus Christ fills every particle that we are. Absolute and today.

3. Light

I received this question: – Will Jesus come again Himself in His personal glorified body to reign and fellowship with us?

My first response would be: I don't know.

But as I consider such a reality now, I find that it leaves me cold. If it were to be in that way, then very clearly, Jesus is outside of me and I am outside of Him. At this point in my life, that is not something I want to know.

As I become more and more familiar with looking out from Jesus' eyes, carried utterly inside of Him, I also see Him filling you full with His glory. "Christ in you" is no longer a slogan to me; when I see you, I truly do see the Lord Jesus. Thus to look out from His eyes and see Him out there, but not as you, rather isolated and separate, would present a huge question.

If the Father took Jesus' place fully and said, "Okay, I'm the One who fills you full, You live only in Me and I in You. Now, you can get to know outwardly this Man, Jesus," that might be okay for us. But I would find it very strange having gotten to know Him so well, fellowshiping continually with a Person inside my heart, only to discover Him entirely outside my heart.

You see, being filled full with another Person with whom I visit and rely upon on the one hand, but who also lives as me on the other hand, is how I live and think and walk. Even when I have doubts, it's still Jesus as me. Inside of perfect union, the Lord Jesus Christ and I are one, we walk together in pure and joyous fellowship: He inside of me and I inside of Him.

I live in full Salvation. I do so entirely by faith, regardless of any outward sight or momentary feeling.

Thus to see Salvation outside of me and me outside of Him would be, at this point in my life, shocking and incongruous, devastating and lonely. I suspect I would then be ashamed of myself once more. I suspect I would be back to finding others shoving their way ahead of me, securing His attention, while I longed for His recognition of my broken heart in quiet desperation.

You see, in the move (the fellowship I was a part of for many years), we continued to separate the Lord Jesus Christ from "Christ in you," and thus came up with "the Christ within," and other concepts of separation. A big part of my leaving the move was that I could no longer try to "be" a "son of God." It was a burden I simply could not bear. I was very lonely. I so very much needed Someone wiser than me, stronger than me, Someone upon whose breast I might lay my head.

Now I know that Someone was planted in the earth and lives now as me. Everywhere I look, it seems, I see either a lack of communion with Jesus Himself fully in us, or so much limitation of our union with Him, that it is not complete.

I insist that Union is now and complete, with NO limit on that Union. You cannot find anything inside of yourself that is not Jesus, and you cannot find anything that is He that is not also you. That is too much for those who continue to insist that Jesus is "God the Son," far above us lowly humans.

I insist upon full Communion inside that Union with the Person of Jesus living inside my heart and filling me with His glory. I see Jesus in my heart as a Person unique from God the Father who Himself fills me full with all of Himself.

I insist on a third reality as well – full Victory flowing out of that Communion found only inside of Union and made visible right here upon this planet.

Union – Communion – Victory. Each total and complete in absolute fullness made visible, AND none without the other two in fullness. God inside of me and me inside of God. And when I say, "God," I don't mean God in general, but God specifically, God in Person.

And so I walk in unbroken fellowship with this Person, Jesus, my Savior, who lives in my heart. At the same time, I walk knowing that He lives entirely as me, my Salvation.

So if He were to come up to me in another body and say, "Hi, Daniel, I'm here, and not in your heart anymore," that would be so contrary to all I know of Him now as Savior AND as Salvation.

More than that, such a strange scenario would also shatter all of my present seeing, forcing me back into the separated thinking of Nicene Christianity that I have gladly fled from as an unmitigated horror. Everything would shatter back into the separated darkness of Adam's universe.

All that I now see, I see out from this perfect Communion carried utterly inside of complete Union with Jesus Himself. I see all things out from Jesus' eyes.

In seeing all things out from Jesus' eyes, I no longer regard His statement, **"Whatever you do to the least of these My brethren, you do it to Me,"** as being in any way figurative. He was speaking 100% literal. Thus when I see you, I know I am seeing Jesus Himself, in Person. Thus to walk with you and you with me is the fullness of life's delight, because I am, in fact, walking with Jesus, in my heart and as me AND in your heart and as you. What a continual river of joy!

This is not figurative to me as it once was. I have come to know God as a Being utterly different from how all of Nicene Christianity thinks they know Him.

Salvation is one thing alone, the full living reality of John 14:20. **In that day you shall know that I am in the Father and you in me and I in you.** This is the tree of life and it must be lived inside of. And it must be lived inside of by faith.

John 14:20 is the same word as Revelation 3:7: **To him who overcomes I give to eat from the tree of life.** We overcome by faith, that is, we simply come over.

I know what it is to eat of the tree of life, to live only inside of John 14:20. I have tasted by measure, yet I declare all fullness; I speak only Christ. I also know the way into this only Salvation.

Salvation does not exist anywhere outside of John 14:20. The absurd and un-Biblical fable that salvation is a place to which one goes forever is simply vanished. Salvation is a Person, a living reality, here, now, and Personal in us and as us and through us. And we are utterly inside of Him.

I can testify also of a third reality inside this living and thinking, breathing and talking only inside of and out from John 14:20. Everything, that is, everything, looks entirely different.

I know all things as the unregenerate see them. I know all things as non-Spirit-filled Christians see them. I know all things as Spirit-filled Christians see them. I know all things as deeper-truth Christians see them, those living one step away from life, but refusing to enter into it. God took me through all that knowing and all that seeing BEFORE He granted to me to eat of the tree of life. And He gave me an excellent memory.

Everything, that is, everything, now looks entirely different.

I find myself studying literature with and under atheists. The God they reject is the Nicene God pushed by judgmental Christianity. At the same time, it is evident that their atheism is religious impulse with no science in it. True science must say, "I cannot know because science has hardly begun, it is yet in its infancy." True science always doubts its own conclusions, knowing that 500 years from now, children will be taught to laugh at so many of present "certainties" just as they are taught to laugh about past "certainties." On the other hand, atheism has no doubt, thus it is entirely religious.

You see, the foundation of all that I am is a Covenant God entered into with me and I with Him. I have already bound myself to that Covenant, and I have zero inclination to alter that bond. If I go down into blazing insanity, I will do so in all joy, knowing that my heart belongs utterly to Another.

Inside this Covenant, inside this Salvation, inside John 14:20, I now look out ONLY through Jesus' eyes, through eyes of fire. And I testify with all certainty that everything looks different from here.

God is utterly different. Jesus is utterly different. Salvation is utterly different. Heaven/earth is utterly different. I am utterly different. You are utterly different. Knowing fully how all others see, I see now that everything is so different from what all have thought.

Now, this reality is self-evident. Consider this necessary logic.

The core of the Covenant is these words in 1 John 3:2. **Beloved, now we are children of God; and it has not yet been revealed what we shall be, but we know that when He is revealed, we shall be like Him, for we shall see Him as He is.** – But we cannot separate from Paul's gospel any understanding we hold. Thus we never separate 1 John 3:2 from 2 Corinthians 3:18. **But we all, with unveiled face, beholding as in a mirror the glory of the Lord, are being transformed into the same image from glory to glory, just as by the Spirit of the Lord.**

1 John 3:2 seems to be "future"; Paul's gospel says, no, it's right now, a continual transformation from glory to glory.

But let's apply rigid logic to John's statement and in light of Paul's statement. If I am not just like Jesus right now, it is ONLY because I do not see Him as He is. Thus, if I do not see Him as He is, the "Jesus" I think I know cannot be real, it must be another Jesus. More than that, John's statement must mean that ME, as I find myself to be right now, am just like Jesus in all ways.

Yet both of these statements, one from John and one from Paul, are known ONLY inside of John 14:20. Inside that present living reality, we see their full meaning. Outside of that living reality, I am just talking gibberish.

Thus, I cannot answer your question inside the talking points of Christian thinking for two reasons. First, I no longer live there, and second, none of that is real. In saying that, I am not speaking of you in any way. You are utterly inside of Jesus and He fills you full with His glory. However, it is our knowledge of that glory that grows, causing us to see everything brand new.

Thus we bring that same word, "transformed," that Paul uses in 2 Corinthians 3:18, *metamorphosis*, and lay it alongside the other place he used it, Romans 12:2. **And be transformed by the renewing of your mind.**

This is NOT that old way of anti-Christ thinking we once knew – *"Get out of your carnal mind, brother."* Rather, it is the same as being transformed into the same image from glory to glory. We become what we already are. And that becoming happens in our minds, that is, in how we see all things.

Wrapping ourselves utterly inside of John 14:20 by the continual speaking of our mouths, that is by faith, is how our seeing changes.

Our Savior is simply incredible, but His Salvation is extraordinarily difficult. Agreeing to become all our mess was the most difficult decision ever made by anyone, a decision made by a Man rising to His feet the third time in Gethsemane. To be able to make the statements I make in full comfort, I must see all things differently than Christianity sees.

And that brings us back to heart. God is Heart, and we know Him only there.

People want me to read this site or that message. I glance at those things and see mixture only, some truth mixed with false seeing, seeing not out from John

14:20. Anything not spoken out from a full knowledge in present intimacy of John 14:20 cannot be true seeing. But what breaks my heart, over and over, is that no one gives a damn about God. No one cares for His heart.

I say that explicitly; it can be said no other way. God is heart, and one reason He has been slow to show Himself as He is is that people despise His heart. He sent His only Son, and they killed Him. If He sent Him again today, most teachers of the gospel, whether of grace or of jeopardy, of orthodoxy or of "heresy," would turn away from Him just as quickly.

God has sent His Son again, and few desire to know Him.

God is meek and lowly of heart. He never pushes anyone around. He is known only by those who would know Him alone by Heart. Everyone is finding exactly what they are looking for.

I want to talk about the inversion of light.

When light passes through a lens, it inverts, that is, it appears in a different form on the other side of the lens. For instance, light coming into our eyes forms an upside-down image on the back of our eyeballs. The brain reconstructs that image and we "see" it right-side up. In a similar way, when you see a fish below water, you know that the fish is not where you see it, but several inches away. You know that by experience, first, but then science shows you that the light bends as it passes through the water and thus places the appearance of the fish in a different place from its substance.

Appearance and substance are two very different things and must always be understood as very different. Appearance and substance are not always opposite things, like the upside-down image in our eyeballs, sometimes they are just slightly skewered from each other, like the location of a fish under water.

Thus when Paul said, "**The foolishness of God is wiser than men, and the weakness of God is stronger than men,**" he did not mean what most think. Most think that man's wisdom at tops is a ten, and God's wisdom at bottom is a ten thousand. Thus the bottom of God's wisdom (foolishness) is, of course, far higher than man's wisdom.

That is not what God means.

God's wisdom, as it passes through the lens that is the continual boundary-line all through this heaven/earth realm in which we exist, turns into, by appearance, what appears to man as abject foolishness. Thus turned-away man never "aspires" to God's "higher" wisdom. No. He laughs it to scorn – *"Idiocy."*

And God's strength, as it passes into the human experience, is also despised by man as despicable and faint-hearted, *"WEAK, Loser, really, really Weak."*

God's shining glory and power in the heavens is known as a simple man stooping to serve in the earth.

A simple man stooping to serve is the outward appearance of Almighty Substance inside the physical realms. A simple man stooping to serve is the most awesome thing heavenly beings see in all the heavens of God.

When you see heaven's view of the brother sitting next to you in the church service, you will fall upon your face in worship. Yet, he like Jesus, will lift you up and say, "No, look at yourself, you also are all the glory of God. Jesus, the King of Creation, is all that you are as well."

And when I saw Him, I fell at His feet as dead. But He laid His right hand on me, saying to me, "Do not be afraid." Revelation 1:17

And I fell at his feet to worship him. But he said to me, "See that you don't do that! I am your fellow servant, and of your brethren who have the testimony of Jesus. Worship God! For the testimony of Jesus is the spirit of prophecy." Revelation 19:10

(Some people, receiving this revelation from God, go around in church service calling each other "God." But one who truly knows God will always say, "See that you don't do that.")

Light is the first part of God's creation. How we see is most important to God. Light became as God spoke Christ. We see as God sees when we, also, speak Christ.

Sceptics look at Genesis and say, *"See, it says that light came on day one, but the sun did not appear until day four, so it can't possibly be an account of 'creation.'"*

No, light does not come from the sun. If there were no light, the sun would be nothing more than a large gas ball, like Jupiter, only far larger. The sun comes out of light, not the other way around. The light we see blazing "on" the sun, is neither on the sun nor from the sun. That light is a great electrical discharge thousands of miles above the sun's surface. The light comes from all the charged particles flowing through space in great twisted binary currents, discharging upon the largest object in the area. If a larger object than our sun were to come into our solar system, the light would instantly transfer itself to that other object and we would see the sun as it is, just a large ball of gas with no light of its own.

Light comes first, everything that exists in the physical realms is light in its electrical form. Everything that exists in the spirit realms is light in its life form. I suspect that electricity and life are simply a scale of frequency.

Light comes from the speaking of God, thus Word precedes light.

In the beginning was the Word, and the Word was with God, and the Word was God. He was in the beginning with God. All things were made through Him, and without Him nothing was made that was made. In Him was life, and the life was the light of men. And the light shines in the darkness, and the darkness did not comprehend it. John 1:1-5

The Word God speaks becomes Life in the spirit realms and then Light in the earth. Word – Life – Light

Science and the revelation of God are 100% compatible.

It is lying calling itself science and screaming at the top of its lungs that is neither compatible with God nor with science. Science is always meek and lowly of heart. Science always says, "You know, I don't really know."

People do not comprehend light. They study it, finding it fascinating beyond measure, but it still makes no sense to them.

Yet, for us, learning to see is a brand new exercise. We have been blind all our lives; that is, the eyes of our spirit are literally blind. They have not functioned. Thus we don't see the heavens in which we live. Part of the faculty of faith is seeing in the realms of spirit.

"Faith is blind," is said by people who have little faith. "Just be content and don't desire to see heavenly things," is the opposite of the gospel's command.

Faith sees God. Faith is the evidence of things not seen. Faith is substance.

Faith knows where the fish is in the water. Faith turns an upside-down image into it's true form. Faith IS seeing. Faith is the real assessment of light.

When an infant first begins to see, the brain deals with the upside-down images literally. No infant remembers this time of literal seeing, but it takes an infant's brain a period of time to stop seeing by appearance and start seeing by substance. The brain turns those upside-down images into a right-side-up seeing by faith. As the infant reaches out to touch, bit by bit, its brain determines that what it thought was on one side, was actually on the other. By the time the infant is old enough to remember, faith has taken complete residence in the child's brain and he or she no longer sees things as they appear, upside-down, but only as they are.

Yet the continual stream of information coming up from the eyeballs to the brain is of upside-down images. The brain is convinced, that is, it believes, that those upside-down images are incorrect – appearance only, and thus automatically flips them right-side-up without thought.

If you were to see literally, the whole world would be upside down. No one sees literally, everyone sees only by faith.

The exact same thing is true in the Spirit. Appearance and substance are two very different things.

Seeing is a learned response. When people who have been blind from birth because of hard cataracts undergo an operation and thus can see for the first time in their lives, it is always a shocking, even terrifying experience. The images coming into their brain are completely disjointed. A cat sitting still they can deal with, but a cat moving just makes no sense to their brains. It takes them weeks and months to learn to see. Some choose not to learn, but close their eyes and stay in blindness. Some even commit suicide; seeing was just too awful.

The most striking thing about those learning to see for the first time is that things they thought would be beautiful turned out to be ugly. And things they thought would be ugly turned out to be beautiful. — The inversion of light.

Consider the birth of a wildebeest. The infant wildebeest must learn to see the same as any other infant, by trial and error. Yet that little wildebeest MUST be running for its life within minutes of birth. It comes into the world with just a few minutes to learn both seeing and running. Yet it's not happening as quickly as the little wildebeest knows it must. So he fixes his eyes on his mother, who is a confused mess of images and smells, yet instinctively familiar. As the wildebeest keeps his eyes on his mother and runs with her, his seeing rapidly becomes real.

And the dragon stood before the woman to devour her child as soon as it was born.

We come out of the womb running. Only, not from the dragon, but out from God. The dragon is just making his biggest and final mistake.

The change of our seeing is of critical importance to us. We must see things as they are, not as they appear. Yet that seeing is a learned response.

Your brain receives into itself a continual stream of upside-down images. Yet you only KNOW a right-side-up world. How? You know a right-side-up world entirely by the faith your brain has learned. Your brain has learned to take appearance and instantly transform it into substance without thought.

There is no difference in seeing in the spirit realms. The realms of heaven are just as real and substantial as the physical realms. The two realms are always totally integrated. Your spirit is not some little thing deep down inside. Your spirit is the largest part of you; it fills and energizes, gives life to, every single cell in your body. Your spirit is not monolithic like a fog or vapor, rather it is as complex as your body. Every organ of the body has a corresponding organ in your spirit.

The heart is the central organ of the body. At the same time the heart is the central organ of the spirit. For both of those reasons, the heart is the central organ of the soul, of who and what we are.

We learned how to see by faith in the physical realms when we were infants. That is, we constructed our world out of deciphering all the sights, sounds, smells, tastes, and touches coming as mass confusion into our brain. We turned contradictory appearances into substance. We made sense out of our world; we created a story in which to live.

Learning to see in the heavens is the same thing. Things are not as they first appear. We must learn what is really real by experience. Just as we are born a second time, so we must learn to see by faith a second time.

In those who don't know faith, there is the thought that faith is "seeing something that ain't there." No, faith is comprehending the light coming in correctly, that is, by substance and not by initial appearance. Those who see by appearance are the ones "seeing something that ain't there." A person who insists on believing that the fish is where they "see" it is simply deceived. If they hold to that "belief," they will never catch the fish.

Let's bring all this back into the original question. Will Jesus come again Himself in His personal glorified body to reign and fellowship with us?

Yes. My body is His personal glorified body. I put on the Lord Jesus Christ. No, He will not "come again." How can He "do" what He already has done.

Let me explain using portions of an earlier letter, "Meek and Lowly of Heart."

In my last few years in the move, I came close to losing it. One thing held me to a sound mind. One memory gripped like an anchor in my soul that held me steady in the blowing winds of confusion.

I remembered my time walking together with Abel at Bowens Mill (a Christian community in Georgia), with Don at Blueberry and in Oregon, and with Rick at Blair Valley and after. Those times were as different in my life as day is from night. By looking at the difference and figuring out why I was blessed and anointed during those times versus all the other long years of confusion in-between is what brought me to the present place of emotional stability.

Those three brethren treated me as a spiritual equal. They walked in full respect with me, regarding my input as a critical part of their life and ministry. In that light I blossomed. But though it was a long enough time with each to make a marked difference, yet it was only a part of my years in community.

I am a number two man. Without a number one partner, I am out in left field. This has been true throughout my life, both in natural work and in spiritual ministry. There have been five in my life with whom I thrived. First was Jim, who taught me construction, then the three I mentioned, then also, Amos, with whom I installed cabinets professionally in Oregon. What a team we made! Yet apart from him, I am fairly worthless at building cabinets at a professional level.

When I work together with one a little older and stronger inside than I, one who knows instinctively how to maneuver through this world that is so confusing to me, but one who also relates to me with utmost respect, then I can excel in my abilities in this world. The fact that I have known five such powerful relationships in differing arenas of "work" in my adult life is an extraordinary gift. With Jimmy I framed houses and learned construction, with Abel I worked with needy men, with Don I led large construction crews and moved in anointed ministry, with Amos I installed beautiful custom cabinets, and with Rick I learned the deepest meanings of friendship.

With these men, each just a few years older than I, each who regarded me with the fullest respect, treating me as their equal, ignoring my autistic quirks, relying on my strengths and abilities that in some ways were greater than theirs, I excelled. Without them I am fairly useless in the long run.

My life has been the memory of incredible excellence in varied fields – when I walked together with another, all five similar in nature, versus endless mistakes and befuddledness when I try to do the same things by myself.

From the start, the Lord Jesus has always pointed me towards His being that same lead. But the problem is these men were real and Jesus is "not." Jesus is just someone I believe some things about. Jimmy and Amos and Don and Rick were real men with whom I had a real, visible, and continuing connection.

How does Jesus become as real as they? This is the question for all of us.

Jesus is alive, and He lives in our hearts. Yet that is mostly just something we "believe." How does Jesus become as real as what we see and touch and handle?

⁓

Since writing those words a few years ago, Jesus has become as real as Jimmy or Abel or Don or Amos or Rick. Jesus actually lives in my heart. I actually see Him; I actually visit with Him all the time.

How? I have learned to see. I have learned that appearance must be inverted in order to see substance.

God says: **"Christ dwells in your hearts by faith."** It is the Word God speaks that establishes reality.

So I have trained my brain to see and to know what God says. I have done that the same way an infant learns to invert appearance until they see only substance.

My heart once "appeared" empty, but I spoke what God speaks. The day came, almost imperceptibly, when I began to see what is real. I began to see Jesus Himself in Person in my own heart, visible and for real.

Jesus will never appear to anyone until they learn to see. Once they learn to see they will discover that He was there for real, visibly, all along, they just could not see before.

The "parousia" of Jesus Christ is NOT something that happens to Jesus. It's something that happens to our brain. For the first time in our life, we have learned to see what has been so all along.

Jesus is real. This real and visible Jesus IS inside of me. I look down at my chest, "Hi, Jesus. Good to see you this morning."

As Jesus in me has become real for real – I, for the first time in my life, am also real.

4. God

What is God?

First, it is understood that to know someone, we must walk with that person for a time, seeing into their heart. I have learned well as a teacher over many years that outward appearance does not indicate who the person is inside.

Thus God has two parts, that which He is outwardly, and that which He is inwardly, His heart. Those who know God outwardly see a different Person entirely from those who know God by heart.

Many of those who know God outwardly use definitions of God from the Old Testament as the center and core of who and what He is. Then they tack onto that "core essence of God" the elements describing God in the New Testament as outward attachments onto that Old Testament "God."

In complete contrast, we first know God through the writings of Paul and John – minus most of Revelation as it is carnally understood. Then, out from that description of God in His core Essence and Person, we draw in all outward things by which God is described. In doing so, we see that those outward things are ENTIRELY different from what we once thought.

Let's bring in several statements from the New Testament by which to begin talking about God.

I pray. . . that you might be filled with all the fullness of God.

He who has seen Me has seen the Father. – I am meek and lowly of heart.

We shall be like Him for we shall see Him as He is.

God is love. – The Almighty, that is, Unrestricted power exercising absolute dominion.

Whatever is not of faith is sin. – God cannot be tempted by evil, nor does He Himself tempt anyone.

The Spirit Himself makes intercession for us with groanings that cannot be uttered.

Now, let us follow the "Poirot" principle of solving any mystery. Agatha Christy's Belgian detective, Hercule Poirot, always looked for the oddest, most out-of-place clue as the path to solving the question. He did that while the officials followed only the obvious clues to a dead-end. Once he had found the answer to this silly little thing that everyone else ignored, he found the answer to the mystery – and it was always quite different from what all others had imagined.

Poirot put himself into the mind of the perpetrator in order to comprehend motive. Thus I place God's purpose verse as the most important in the Bible. What is God's motive?

Two motives are presented that God might possess. The generally believed motive is Self-protection, that God, far away because of the sin of His creatures, inspects each one and allows into Himself at a future date only those who meet some sort of standard. That standard can be works or grace; God's motive remains the same.

There are many Bible verses, Old Testament and New, that seem to support that motive, but only when certain key verses at the heart of the gospel are violently ignored, especially Romans 8:29 and it's companions.

Now, of all the statements about God in the Bible, which one is the very oddest? – The last one on my list. What is a God who groans in travail? What possible motive is there for such a clue?

Let me suggest that the only way anyone will ever solve the mystery of God is to find the answer, in real and practical experience, to that question. What is a God who groans in travail?

But here is our predicament. This question of travail is God as Spirit, and we will never know God if we seek to define the Holy Spirit. The Spirit of God stays in the background; when we try to look at Him/Her, all we see is a bony finger pointing us straight to Jesus. The Spirit does not speak of Himself.

But if the God we "know" does not groan in travail in His core and essence in our knowledge of Him, even in our knowledge of the One who fills us with all of Himself, then we do not know God.

Yet we will never arrive at knowing the Spirit, knowing a God who groans in travail, without obeying the Spirit by looking first to Jesus, and then, in obedience to Paul's gospel, out from Jesus' eyes.

Thus the first question of knowing God is – What is Jesus? Followed by – What is Christ? Then we must continue on to – What is the Father?

Amazingly, we must pass through – What is Science? And – What is Light/Electricity? And – What is Voice? Before we can arrive at – What is Spirit?

But the confusing thing about knowing God.is that we cannot know Him apart from Jesus' words: **The words that I speak to you are Spirit and they are Life.**

It is only the Spirit who shows us all these things. Thus we cannot know God unless we first know Him by Spirit. And we cannot know God unless we first know Him as our very and only Life, filling us full with ALL of Himself.

It all begins with travail. – **And the Spirit of God hovered over the face of the waters.** No word God could ever speak, no light, no power could ever bring forth anything except it first enters into the travail of God. Only a woman can bring forth life.

What is a God who groans in travail? What is His motive?

And suddenly I see that all other "knowledge" of God vanishes. For there is no possible way we could ever know anything of God outwardly or even near-centeredly, without FIRST knowing in full experience a God who groans in travail.

Last week was another "atheism day" in poetry class, in which all silly Christian "beliefs" about "God" were caused to vanish by waving the magical wand of "science." I said very little. As far as I was concerned, some of the poems we studied were little more than some person filled with hatred vomiting words, and then we gathered around those vomited words, as diviners of old gathered around chicken bones or some such scattered junk, and sought to find meaning in these meaningless words. Yet I did enjoy hearing others share from their hearts.

My point is this – I come away from such a reality of this world with the greatest of groanings inside. God, how can they know You? You see, I could argue the Nicene Creed at these people, and they would rightly laugh me out of the room.

No one knows God. Yet He makes so many claims. How will they know Him? And I groan in the deepest travail.

A dear sister wrote to me in the greatest of distress. She has been hit so hard in so many different directions, including a little grandson who has horrific cancer and just underwent brain surgery. "Why don't I have the power to pray and see healing?"

God, show up!

Christians want to blame either God or us. Atheists want to say, "See there is no God. You are delusional."

What is a God who groans in travail?

What is a God who desires with all of His heart to be known and seen, touched and handled, a God who would place His hands upon little children and BLESS them, yet who does not show Himself as He clearly says?

Is it that God cannot show Himself except through one means alone, through travail, through a woman giving birth?

What is a God who groans in travail?

Oh, please, let this question consume your heart.

Everywhere I read Christians talking about God; I see that they are clearly talking about Someone ELSE, Someone far away, far above. Everyone, including grace teachers, speaks either of how we "get to" this far-away Entity, or which mental ideas extracted from the Bible this far-way Thing, almost, favors. Yes, almost everyone I read treats God as a Thing.

Grace is NOT us going into God. Grace is God going into us.

I simply don't find people talking about the Person who fills them with all that He is. I do not find people talking about knowing this Close One who DESIRES with all desire to bring forth something He does not yet possess. That is inconceivable to everyone including me. To groan in travail is to labor to bring forth something new. What is a God who groans in travail, who labors to birth forth something not yet in creation, not yet in either heaven or earth?

I saw again a familiar statement people make about a God whom they do not know. "God never makes mistakes." Technically, that's true. The problem is they are always talking about Someone far away. There is no far-away God. Is not one of their "ideas" that He is omnipresent? They say it, but they do not know it.

But I do make mistakes all the time. Or do I?

You see, ALL of my mistakes ARE God's mistakes, for I am His flesh. Thus, are they really mistakes? Whatever we say about God MUST be true of the God who fills us with all of His fullness. If not, they are just ideas, straight out of the tree of true and false. Is God not omnipotent? That's another of their ideas, but they do not know it. Almighty-Power-Exercising-Absolute-Dominion cannot need our help to make Himself omnipotent, to make Himself what He is.

I read someone talking about the horrific idea some "latter-rain heretics" have that God is incarnate again in them. But God says that my body is the temple of the Holy Spirit (I thought the Holy Spirit was part of God). "Incarnate" means God in the flesh. Paul prays that we would be filled with all the fullness of God! If all of God is in me, including in my body, if I am of His flesh and of His bones, then is that not INCARNATION?

Someone said, no, we are not yet filled with all of God, not until we prove a certain level of obedience. Let me see if I have this correct. Right now, we are empty of God, that is, we are un-God-ly. But in our un-God-ly state, we must perform a certain level of transaction, maybe we must obey all voices and all verses completely without hesitation, 1,623 times in a row? Or is it 1,625 times in a row? Then, after, that, we will have "earned?" being filled with God? Then, after that, we will finally become God-ly? Being filled with God is something we purchase out from not-God?

> – God comes first before there is any God-liness
> and before anything not godly could ever vanish away. –

I read of the idea that there cannot be "apostles" today because an apostle is one who knows the risen Christ. Hello! Does not the risen Christ Himself in Person live in my heart? And I do know Him, literally and actually. The risen Christ is my best Friend. I look in my heart and see Him all the time, every moment. We visit continually. I am a direct eye-witness of the risen Christ. He has become as real in me as any good friend I have ever known in life.

Listen, being the Incarnation of God, being an eye-witness of the risen Christ IS the NORMAL Christian life. It's what the gospel is all about! Being the Incarnation of God, being a continual eye-witness of the risen Christ, being continually commissioned by Jesus Himself as His full witness, as His sent-one (apostle), does not make us in any way "special," it just means we are finally NORMAL humans! And rivers of living water DO flow out of us all the time. We are all apostles! Everyone of us can and should be speaking as the oracle of God, as Peter said we should, as divine Scripture.

We have finally, for the first time in our lives, become ordinary.

Every created being empty of God is weird.

A human empty of God is more than weird, he or she is the most dangerous entity in creation, far more dangerous than any fallen angel. Christians who imagine themselves empty of God create horror and call that horror "the gospel."

A Christian who is not speaking of God as the God who fills them NOW and HERE with ALL that He is, that Christian is not speaking of God. They are speaking only of some imaginary construct in their brains, an image built by themselves using ideas as its building blocks. What horrifies them is for you and me to declare that this God they think they possess as their own invention fills us with all that He is, and we commune with Him moment-by-moment, and that He, in fact, lives as us in this world.

You see, we have dirtied their "God," and that is "blasphemy."

And that is exactly why they killed Jesus. In their eyes, Jesus had dirtied "God." He had placed FLESH (the image of God) upon this "purified" image (brain imagination) they called "God."

As Hamlet said, "Horrible. Horrible." I am laughing. Why don't they just stop all the stupidity and get to know this Guy who loves them and who lives in them and who shows Himself through them? Why don't they just accept the Blood? Why don't they just accept the Cross? Why don't they just accept the reality that Jesus, the resurrected and ascended Christ, lives in their hearts?

The Covenant is that God gives us hearts of flesh. Jesus lives in our hearts. God Incarnate – God in meat! It's just the gospel.

What is God?

Let me say the exact same thing three different ways.

Jesus sits at the right hand of the Father. – Jesus is ascended above all the heavens. – Jesus lives in my heart.

Some have the incredible idea that these are three different "places." They think that if Jesus is at the right hand of the Father right now, that means He is not walking the earth right now. They think that "Jesus in my heart" and "Jesus above the heavens" means some geographical distinction, two different places! At this point in my life, I find that way of thinking to be so incredibly weird – ignorant.

Jesus in me and Jesus at the right hand of the Father and Jesus above all the heavens ARE the SAME thing.

My heart is as much in heaven as God is (I am speaking literally, not figuratively – the "throne" John saw in Revelation 4 is figurative); my heart is His throne. Where He dwells is the center of all Holiness. The King of all is my best friend. He lives in my heart; we visit all the time. More than that, the King of heaven lives as me right now; He is all I find myself to be. This reality is 100% literal; I am speaking of no "deeper meanings."

I am speaking of being human, being just like Jesus, the first One of our kind.

What is God?

The Nicene Creed and Augustine say that God is Three Persons in One, and that these Three Persons are co-equal together as God. They don't know that. God never says any such thing. Three in One is a construction of human reason, a staked-out position of the human mind.

Paul said, **"There is one God, the Father, and one Mediator between God and man, the Man, Christ Jesus."** God is One Person who reveals Himself through many persons.

We know Jesus by John 14:20, and that is Salvation. But we can only know God by Ephesians 3:19. Where is **"filled with all the fullness of God"** found in the Nicene Creed or in Augustine? The knowledge of God in Person in them is absent from all that they write.

God can be known only by Word coming through Spirit and birthing Life inside of us. "Knowing" something about "God" in any other way ain't God.

There is no purpose whatever in having any ideas about God. All human ideas about God CANNOT ever be God. So what do we gain by having ideas about God? We gain death, exactly as God warned Adam in the garden. The very exercise of reasoning out ideas about God IS the tree of knowledge.

Modern literary criticism states that there are three ways to approach the human in literature or poetry. One is the ideal, what humans ought to be. A second is the ridiculous, let's laugh at people. The third, they say, is people as they are, the real. They call this "realism." They say that all present writing, to be considered by them as "literature" must be about humans "as they are." Thus Tolkien, even though he wrote the greatest literary work of the twentieth century, committed the cardinal sin; he wrote a fable. Fables deal with humanity as we "ought to be."

To them, a chemical reaction "ought to be" nothing other than what it is. In one sense they are correct, but not the way they think.

There is no such thing as "realism." A book is not a human being. No author has created a living, breathing human by writing words on a page. All so-called "realism," including biography, is as much a fiction as any fable. That is not a human person you are engaging with in the story, but the imagination of the author. If an author takes his or her character into damnation, that is neither God's "fault" nor is it "real." The author is always the god of his or her creation, moving the fate of every character in the story.

The problem with realism is that it is lying to you. Realism is as fabulous as "fable." The advantage of fable is that it does not pretend to be real, thus we are more able to draw truth out from a fable than we are out of any lying "realism." Their so-called realism only mocks and makes ridiculous both God and humanity.

All you get when you read "realism" is depressed. That's why these "literary experts" are so angry and judgmental; that's why they are drawn to the red-faced anger of Marx, the bloodiest killer in history. When I read literary experts, I read people who sound like they are sitting on the toilet, trying their hardest and not succeeding. Karl Marx would scream in rage at his allies so ferociously that he would turn bright-red and then purple before collapsing from lack of breath; Lenin was almost as bad.

And this sick mind, whose followers bloodied the world over the last 100 years, is the favorite philosopher of the people who rule modern education.

Realism is not real. Ideas in a book are not a living human being.

The Nicene Creed cannot be real; it matters not what true ideas are in it. Ideas people have about "God" cannot be a real living God in Person inside of them. All ideas push God far away.

What is God? I don't know. And neither does ANYONE else in heaven or on earth, except Jesus. God is not yet known.

No man (or angel) **has seen God, nor can see God. – He who has seen Me has seen the Father.**

The question cannot be – What is God? The question MUST BE – What is a God who groans in travail?

Can we know the Heart of this Incredible Person who fills our hearts full with His deep, agonizing DESIRE to be known, to be seen, to be touched, to be handled? This God who will not rest until He has a man after His own heart, a many-membered man, many sons in glory, through whom, finally, He can be forever known.

What is a God who groans in travail? What is a God who fills finite, tiny, bumpkin humans with ALL of His Fullness?

(I pray) that Christ may dwell in your hearts through faith; that you, being rooted and grounded in love, may be able to comprehend with all the saints what is the width and length and depth and height—to know the love of Christ which passes knowledge; that you may be filled with all the fullness of God.

God is Love. – Rooted and grounded in love.

Here is my increasing present joy. I am filled full with Love in Person, and I, me, my heart of hearts, I live entirely inside this Love inside of me. This Love is not me, thus I am not responsible to maintain it's expression. This Love is Another Person, my Friend, my Savior. Yet this Love is also me, Love as me, thus I rest utterly in my continual envelopment deep inside this Love-One. We visit whenever I think of Him. Wherever I am, I know Love in Person is there fully in me, filling all of me, body, soul, and all the way out to wherever my spirit goes.

How many times over the years have I stood in front of the mirror, my hands pressed to my chest, tears streaming down my face, saying, "Oh Father, if it be possible, if it could somehow be, please, place Your heart right here inside of me." – Oh, the sorrow that I could not know He already had.

Now that I know that I do, every moment and forever, fully share Heart with God, I am so content. I possess all I have ever desired.

Rooted and grounded in love.

God really likes me. He thinks highly of me; I am His special friend. He confides His deepest secrets with me. (Say this as yourself.) This God, who likes me best, is always filling me full in Person. This God, filling me full in Person, is always flowing out from me, liking everyone I meet.

People are such a delight to me; the fact that they also frustrate me makes no difference at all.

Now, why would I bring Karl Marx into the question, What is God? (That is, why would God have me fuming over Marx while I'm trying to know Him?)

I love literature; I love discussing literature. I love seeing all the foibles of the human inside literature. I understand and abhor injustice. I see clearly how awful it has been for women in the past, being forced to live in a straight-jacket denial of all that they were as intelligent, creative persons. I am so glad my wife is my equal in every way; I would never want to see a return to that cursed way of thinking about women.

That is not what I feel and see in this "graduate level" approach to literature. I've never come across, personally, such a spirit in discussing literature before: now, I must keep my nose in it.

I read somewhere that Marx "really respected people." What kind of delusional denial do these people live in?

Marx's answer to the evil of the ruling class was to be more evil than they. Marx's answer to injustice was to be far more unjust. Marx's answer to lying was to lie even more. This is the thinking, the spirit, of all who drink his opiates. Thus, what bothers me – just bothers me – is not the course asking me to consider injustice, but the course asking me to respond to injustice with greater injustice.

The course wants me to disrespect people, to despise them, to excel at pointing out how despicable all but the chosen "honored victims" really are. The course asks the students to engage in a ritualistic Orwellian "three-minute-hate." Here's the target. Okay novices, everyone together, Hate – Hate – Hate. There, don't we all feel cleansed – empowered? I dared to point out the falseness of the "chosen honored victim" in one discussion, and oh the response I drew. But that is what the course asks, to tear down anyone who dares to blaspheme.

This is a religious cult, not a college course.

When the Marxists took power in Russia, after they had killed all the college professors, they drove around in trucks with machine guns in the back gunning down any farmer who had committed the crime of using hired help on his farm. Tens of thousands of decent, hard-working responsible men were slaughtered by these who, like Marx, so "respected people."

Love – Hate.

Do not be overcome by evil, but overcome evil with good.

I marvel as I see in me, more and more, such a delight for people, for each individual person in all their peculiarities, in all their gifts and weaknesses. I delight in each one of my students. Certainly some of them are more challenging than others, but my love is God, and He is pretty big. God is in my classroom with me, in me, flowing out from me. God.

So-called "realism" finds the worst people, the ones at the bottom, the sell-outers, the despicable, the psychopaths, the coy and deceitful, and presents them as a "case study" of the human race. They never discover the good men and women who hold true in adversity, who love at whatever cost. If they notice such people, they denigrate them as fake. The lowest defines all to them.

They do not see Love arising from beneath the lowest of the low.

Realism is Marxism in literary garb; it is utter disrespect of people. It claims to show people "as they are." Although it does use facts as its weapons, it always leaves in its readers a pervasive spirit of scorn. Realism discovers that none are righteous, no not one, and then mocks and revels in human unrighteousness.

What is a God who groans in travail?

To most, **"bringing many sons to glory"** just means God taking a bunch of losers to heaven even though we all should be cast into hell.

Grace to them is our chance to be happy; they have no thought about God groaning in travail to bring forth.

What if God is so different from what they think? What if God CANNOT do everything? What if God cannot sin? What if God cannot violate faith? What if God MUST treat every individual person with utmost respect? What if God is Love?

What if God wants something He does not yet possess?

What if God groans in travail to bring forth from His own being something so HOLY, something so beyond all, and birth that very HEART of His Heart through His image, you and me?

What if God longs to be known – to touch and to be touched. What if we are God's body – God Incarnate?

What kind of a God is that? And where is such a God found in the Nicene Creed or in Augustine's cold intellect?

Is God the Father in me as He is in you? – Yes. Is Christ Jesus, the Son, in me as He is in you? – Yes. Is the Holy Spirit in me as He is in you? – Yes.

Am I confused as to which One I am visiting with? — Yes.

Do I try to explain God as "The Trinity"? NO! I never kill myself.

Is God the Father most of what I am? – Yes. Does Christ Jesus, the Son, live as me – am I just like Him in all ways? – Yes. Is the Holy Spirit flowing out from me in all directions at all times? – Yes.

Am I God Incarnate? – Yes. Am I utterly weak and silent before Him? – Yes. Am I a normal human being, living the normal Christian life? – Yes.

Do I try to rationalize any of this to myself or to others? NEVER. I do not disobey God's command not to eat of the tree of the knowledge of good and evil. I am content to believe what God says.

God speaks His Word into me by the Spirit. I receive that Word into my Faith (Jesus as me) by that same Spirit. That Word reproduces itself inside of me as my only Life as I speak it with my mouth. God fills me full with All of Himself.

What is a God who groans in travail? What is a God who longs to be touched, to be seen, to visit happily with His dearest friends, to touch little children and to bless them? What is a God who pays every price, casts all of Himself into loss, bears all, weeps with all, carries all, so that He might know His dream?

What is a God who longs to be known?

What is a God who shares heart with me?

5. Travail

In the previous letter, I suggested that comprehending God requires that we deal with the question, – What is a God who groans in travail? Again, I do not write because I know anything. I write because I must know this God who fills me with all that He is. How can anyone think about anything else?

Writing is how I contend with God.

I have the thought that I seem to be turning God into a mamby-pamby cry-baby. On the other hand, the Nicene God snuffs the life out of untold billions, cutting short all their dreams and hopes and casts them forever into screaming agony of torment without giving it a thought. The Nicene God stands aloof from all human suffering, blames man for his own stupidity, and justifies Himself in keeping His distance. The Nicene God sees a sparrow fall to the ground, yes, but does nothing to bring an end to the death and the suffering.

The Nicene God sent His Son once to share in human suffering, yes, and will send Him again to punish all sin, intended or unintended, and takes us out of this damnable place only by death, but does not walk the earth today, carrying all sorrow, grief, sin, and death inside Himself.

The Nicene God is absent and derelict.

What if the God of the Bible is utterly, utterly different from what they claim?

What if the entire creation is the travail and sorrow of God?

What if my pain IS God's pain? What if I am filled with God?

I am writing this because I am reading an essay about Mark Twain in which the writer explains the irrelevance to human life of any notion of a "God." He uses these very arguments that define the Nicene God as if that God is the "Christian" God. Sadly, that is the idea "God" that "Christians" have argued at the world.

Let me quote from one of Twain's books.

> I (Satan/Christ) am but a dream—your dream, creature of your imagination. In a moment you will have realized this, then you will banish me from your visions and I shall dissolve into the nothingness out of which you made me. . . . I, your poor servant, have revealed you to yourself and set you free. Dream other dreams and better!
>
> . . . Strange, indeed, that you should not have suspected that your universe and its contents were only dreams, visions, fiction! Strange, because they are so frankly and hysterically insane—like all dreams: a God who

could make good children as easily as bad, yet preferred to make bad ones; who could have made every one of them happy, yet never made a single happy one; who made them prize their bitter life, yet stingily cut it short; who gave his angels eternal happiness unearned, yet required his other children to earn it; who gave his angels painless lives, yet cursed his other children with biting miseries and maladies of mind and body; who mouths justice and invented hell—mouths mercy and invented hell—mouths Golden Rules, and forgiveness multiplied by seventy times seven, and invented hell; who mouths morals to other people and has none himself; who frowns upon crimes, yet commits them all; who created man without invitation, then tries to shuffle the responsibility for man's acts upon man, instead of honorably placing it where it belongs, upon himself; and finally, with altogether divine obtuseness, invites this poor, abused slave to worship him!... You perceive, now, that these things are all impossible except in a dream." (Twain 1916 – The Mysterious Stranger, 73-74)

May I suggest to you that Twain's portrayal of the Nicene God is accurate and just. May I suggest that it's not just for these reasons that we must break from the Nicene definitions of Christianity and return to the God who speaks His Word, Christ, first through Paul's gospel, a God who is entirely different from how Christianity has painted Him.

Miracles are for getting people's attention. But once God has people's attention, what do they see? Yes, God longs to do good things for all, but that goodness must come out from God through their faith. God cannot sin; He cannot violate faith. God cannot impose goodness on anyone any more than demons can impose badness. Both God and demons are restricted entirely to coming through human consent, that is, through faith.

Jesus did not do any miracles until He was sent forth by the Father to gather a people for the Day of Pentecost. Then, from turning water into wine on, the miracles He did came through the faith He Himself inspired in the hearts of those who saw Him.

What did they see? The miracles were to get people's attention; once Jesus had their attention, what did they see?

First, they saw a man. There was not the slightest indication, NONE, that they were "seeing the Father." Isaiah says that they saw no beauty at all, nor anything desirable. (Isaiah 53)

Then Isaiah says this: **Surely He has borne our griefs and carried our sorrows.** But he says more than that: **For He shall bear their iniquity – and He bore the sin of many.**

"Borne" and "bear" are the same Hebrew word meaning "to bear a heavy load." "Carried" and "bore" are the same Hebrew word meaning "to carry."

When people looked at Jesus, they saw only a man, and not an attractive man at that. But they saw something else as well. They did not understand what they saw; if you had asked any, they could not have explained it to you except with simple words. The best way to say this is personal, that is, first person.

I saw One who bore every grief I've ever known in life, my own griefs, as if I were the only person in the universe, just this Man and me. I saw One who carried every sin I have ever committed without any condemnation of me. I saw One who simply loved ME with all tender love.

But it is by Paul's Jesus that we now say, "I see One who carries me." — God.

Look at everyone talking about "God." It seems that almost all talk about Some-Thing far away. Thus they discuss this Thing rationally; that is, they present ideas about this Thing they call God.

Jesus said, "**The Words that I speak to you are Spirit and they are Life.**" What is Life?

I read a speaker on a forum who said he had gone to my site, but did not care for it because I spoke too much about Bible symbols that "could mean anything." He also claimed that I disdained "science," pulling in some rant I made totally out of its context. No, I highly regard science, that is, the study of facts, attempting to understand them; what I despise is boastful lying based on no-facts or on contempt of facts declaring itself to be "science." I despise religious beliefs that call themselves "science."

But the issue is "Bible symbols that could mean anything."

Yes and no. The bottom line is "What do you want?" Everyone finds exactly what they seek; everyone receives from the realms of spirit precisely what they want. Man is the master, and there is no way of getting around that reality.

I am very clear about what I want. I let you know all the time what I seek. I am not afraid of challenge, of those who would say, "Yordy, you're in denial, your stated 'desire' is not really 'what you want.'" First, God has proven me to the uttermost, not for Him to see what is in me, but for me to know my own heart. Second, and far more important, I am so thrilled with my present ever-growing knowledge of this One I love, close and real. I have never been so content in the God I presently know than now.

I find what I seek; I receive what I ask. It has ALWAYS been so.

I want to be the revelation of Jesus Christ. Thus, I want to know the full measure of what God means in these words, "**Christ in you the hope of glory – we shall be like Him – conformed to the image of His Son.**"

This is my bottom line; it's what I want; it's what I look for. Therefore, when I discuss all the "symbols" of the Bible, guess what? I find exactly what I seek; I find the Lord Jesus Christ revealed through me.

The entire Bible, every verse, is written out from one word – LIFE. Anyone who does not know what "life" means cannot grasp the intent and meaning of the Bible. Very few people teach out from a knowledge of "life," thus most teach the Bible as a series of partially connected ideas.

No symbol in the universe is as prolific and all around us, speaking to us from every direction, than this most important of symbols – Life.

Nothing in the Bible can convey its real meaning to anyone apart from knowing exactly what Jesus means when He says, "**The Words that I speak to you are Spirit and they are Life."**

Everything I write, I write ONLY and ALWAYS out from the full application of the two parts of this all-defining symbol God uses, LIFE.

Let me be more clear. Yes, LIFE is the word that describes the matter of heavenly substance. But that same word shows itself in the physical realms in two specific ways. Life is heavenly reality coming into the earth, yes, but it is known only by two specific symbols.

In other words, because I am always speaking out of these two symbols, many don't have a clue what I'm saying. They never see that God also is always speaking out of these two symbols in every word in the Bible. All other symbols in the Bible are simply extensions of these two representations of LIFE.

We cannot begin to know God without knowing in our brains – first, and in continual experience second, what LIFE is and means.

I said this earlier: – Look at everyone talking about "God." It seems that almost all talk about SomeThing far away. Thus they discuss this Thing rationally; that is, they present ideas about this Thing they call God. –

Let me explain further. People think that when James said, **"Demons see God and tremble,"** he was speaking literally. No! Demons and all heavenly beings see only an outer form of God's expression. What they "see" is entirely symbolic. To "see" something in a literal sense is to define that thing from all other things. In other words, if I see a chair, I have separated that chair in my knowledge from all other things. The chair is now monolithic. It is a thing. I can measure it and define it. I can sit down in it or get up and walk away from it.

God does not have a form that can be "seen" or defined or measured. You cannot "enter into" God nor walk away from Him.

Everything exists in God, and God fills everything. Christians say, "omnipresent," but they actually do not believe it. They say "omnipresent," but see SomeThing outside themselves inspecting them.

The most incredible, mind-blowing reality about this God in whom all things exist and who fills all things is that He is Personal. What that really means, in it's essence, is that God is Heart. The fact that I think, feel, and decide does not really make me the person I am. Those things are essential parts of personhood, but not its core. Person means heart.

The universe is utterly, intensely Personal, utterly, intensely Heart.

And here I want to throw back in the SCREAMING Contradiction!!!

Go back up and read Twain's complaint; do not avoid the justice and RIGHTNESS of his agony. What about it, God?

I rip wide-open the heart of this Guy who tells us that He created us and is our Father. I get right at the words, **"He bears our griefs and carries our sorrows."**

I give God no peace until He makes Jerusalem a praise in all the earth.

I contend with God until I have out-wrestled Him, until I have won.

In my last letter, I worded the "motive" almost all Christians impute to God in this way: – The generally believed motive is self-protection, that God, far away because of the sin of His creatures, inspects each one and allows into Himself (and into happiness) at a future date only those who meet some sort of standard. That standard can be works or grace; God's motive remains the same. –

I will keep trying my best to turn you around. Stop looking at heaven, you already live in it fully. Stop looking for a "heavenly body," you possess your heavenly body fully in all ways, your spirit. Stop waiting for "another life"; another Life has already seized you for His purposes.

You are not going into God. God is coming now through you.

You can know Him no other way. Those who imagine that physical death takes us into "God," "life," "salvation" are NOT in the present knowing of God that we must know. Heaven is not the new creation.

You ARE God's invasion of earth. You are an alien. You are the greatest threat the powers of earth and Hades have ever encountered. You are more than a threat; you are ALL the Victory of God.

MOTIVE! What is God's motive?

We deal with the present reality of life on this earth filled with unending horror, heartache, and sin. We deal with the present reality of a God who simply seems absent, a God who says mighty things in His Word and then just does not do them. In our frustration with this present reality, we create all the excuses for God that is called "Christianity," and then we define "faith" as this wimpish, meaningless thing that "just believes" what so obviously ain't so.

Is God's motive to protect Himself? Is God's motive to place large barriers against us to keep us out until we "whatever"? Does God put us through this hellhole called life on planet Earth just because it's "good for us?"

Self – self – self! – God-for-Self and our own self-benefit.

What if? What if God CANNOT just do whatever He wants? What if God is limited and bound? What if God CANNOT sin? What if God cannot violate faith? What if God is Love and must respect all? What if God is Life and must bring forth life?

Look at Twain's accusation. "Who mouths justice and invented hell—mouths mercy and invented hell—mouths Golden Rules, and forgiveness multiplied by seventy times seven, and invented hell; who mouths morals to other people and has none himself; who frowns upon crimes, yet commits them all."

This is NOT Twain's accusation; this IS the accusation of "Christianity." This IS the accusation out of which the Nicene Creed was penned.

Let's go back to reality. Four thousand years, then Jesus. Two thousand more years, then Jesus again. Fifteen billion human lives of hopeless sorrow and purposeless agony. — Why?

If Jesus could come after four thousand years, why could He not have come at forty years? If Jesus could come again after two thousand years, why could He not come again forty years later, AD 69, just as all the apostles expected. (Not the year, but in their lifetime.)

If it was right for God to save man, why would it not have been right for Him to do so right away, before all of us were born?

Don't blame man for the misery of our lives; not one of us asked to be born into this world. As Twain insinuated, had we been given a choice, we would all have chosen to be angels – or even humans – happy "in heaven."

We did not have a choice. Here we are in misery through life and, according to Nicene Christianity, damned to be tortured in hopeless unending pain forever.

And most of those who know that judgment is for an age and not forever, still see everything by Nicene definitions. They say, "God is love," all the while accepting the present agony of the human race as whatever. They still substitute this lame excuse, "Oh, we'll be happy in heaven, when we rise into the 'higher' life."

I reject the "dream" of "heaven," a dream rooted in unbelief. Turn around.

You are in God; you are heart of His Heart. Your whole focus is upon planet Earth. You want God's WANT with all that is in you, that is, with all the fullness of God.

MOTIVE! — Four thousand years of agony and failure, then Jesus. Two thousand more years of agony and contradiction, then Jesus again. Why? What does six thousand years of wickedness and shattered dreams "do for" God?

At the center of that question we place the question – What is a God who groans in travail? And we define that question by these words: **Surely He has borne our griefs and carried our sorrows.**

I do not "explain" God; I wrestle with Him. It is travail.

Does God want something He CANNOT obtain any other way than through six-thousand years of human misery? Is God utterly different than the Nicene Creed has known Him?

Is the agony of the human the agony of God? Does He bear our griefs and carry our sorrows? Have we ever experienced anything that has not been utterly inside this God who always carries us?

The miracles turned people's attention to Jesus. What did they see?

All the WANTING of Almighty God is to be seen, to touch and to be touched, to be known all through His creation, heaven as much as earth, life laid down, love poured out. Does the wanting of God require the appointed 6,000 years? Is this the only way?

Do you WANT the WANTING of God? Do you WANT God through you?

If there is ever a thing called "paradox," its apex, its ultimate is an unknowable God known. The ultimate paradox is man; man IS an unknowable God known, Jesus the first One of our kind, we just like Him.

—to know the love of Christ which passes knowledge; that you may be filled with all the fullness of God.

We do not share the sufferings of Christ, bearing all grief, carrying all sorrow, because it's "good for us" or to "earn" some future thing. We share the fellowship of His suffering that God might be known through us. Love suffers long.

To love is to create a lover. To love is to lose everything. To love is to bear all the agony of loss and sorrow, of sin and darkness. To love is to win it all back in return through one means alone. God must win their hearts!

Surely He has borne our griefs and carried our sorrows. Christ become us. Love suffers long.

Creation is the suffering of God Himself. Makes no sense, does it? Good, we can now begin to know God.

We know God only as we know ourselves, that is, God through us. God in Person through our persons, seen and known by all. Man, the image and likeness of God, the visible expression of a forever invisible Person.

I write in this way to batter your heart that you also would contend with God until He proves all that He speaks through you upon this earth. We're not looking at miracles, but at God revealed, that is, man. Your own contention with God is God Himself in travail.

And out of our belly flow rivers of living water.

6. The Nicene Creed

In this letter I want to take a close look at the Nicene Creed and its expansions into all Christian thinking, Eastern Orthodox, Roman Catholic, Protestant, Evangelical, Charismatic, Deeper-truth, and yes, even "union with Christ" and present grace. So much of what I read by present grace and union with Christ teachers is rooted in the Nicene definitions of God and salvation.

Yet I have referred to Nicene and Augustinian thinking so much, people wonder what's the big deal. People don't understand that their minds, their definitions and thinking of God and salvation and what they "read in the Bible" are ruled absolutely by the declarations of a particular group of men 1600-1700 years ago.

And so it is necessary for me to go through Nicene thinking and show how the revelation of Jesus Christ as Savior and Salvation, coming out from what God actually says in the New Testament is something entirely different.

There are many versions of the Nicene Creed, slight variations. I will present a present-day version used by the Catholic Bishops of America.

I believe in one God, the Father almighty, maker of heaven and earth, of all things visible and invis-ible.

I believe in one Lord Jesus Christ, the Only Begotten Son of God, born of the Father before all ages. God from God, Light from Light, true God from true God, begotten, not made, consubstantial with the Father; through him all things were made. For us men and for our salvation he came down from heaven, and by the Holy Spirit was incarnate of the Virgin Mary, and became man. For our sake he was crucified under Pontius Pilate, he suffered death and was buried, and rose again on the third day in accordance with the Scriptures. He ascended into heaven and is seated at the right hand of the Father. He will come again in glory to judge the living and the dead and his kingdom will have no end.

I believe in the Holy Spirit, the Lord, the giver of life, who proceeds from the Father and the Son, who with the Father and the Son is adored and glorified, who has spoken through the prophets.

I believe in one, holy, catholic and apostolic Church. I confess one Baptism for the forgiveness of sins and I look forward to the resurrection of the dead and the life of the world to come. Amen.

It is Augustine who wrote out the strict definition of "the Trinity" from these original ideas. This version adds Augustine's words to the original Creed.

The first words we must break are *"I believe,"* or, in many versions, *"we believe."* First, no you don't, and second, so what! Idolatry, that is the image people construct in their minds which they call, "God," is formed by the human mind by using the words, "I believe."

Faith connects directly with a Spirit Word. Ideas constructed by "believing" have nothing whatsoever to do with faith. *"I believe"* is a poor substitute for faith; When I hear someone say, *"Well, I believe,"* I know that they really don't. And I know that they are building a citadel of pretending with their ideas behind which to hide. *"I believe"* is an effective shield against God.

Let's bring in the words spoken out from the lie.

Then the serpent said to the woman, *"You will not surely die. For God knows that in the day you eat of it your eyes will be opened, and you will be like God, knowing good and evil."* Genesis 3:4-5

These words are not the lie; these words come out from the lie. The lie is the unstated assumptions behind these words. The Nicene Creed is the same. The lie is the unstated assumptions behind the Nicene declarations.

Deceit ALWAYS works by sleight-of-hand; what is said is never as important as what is not said.

There is a difference between the Nicene Creed and the serpent's words, however, a difference that makes the lie hiding behind the Nicene Creed more powerful. The serpent's words are all baloney and hot air. Each idea presented in the serpent's words is a lie, complete nonsense, with no true ideas. In contrast, the Nicene Creed contains many true ideas intermingled with ideas God never says, forcing God into a box separated from the speaking of Christ. The field of Christianity is filled with serpent seed growing alongside the truth.

No one will ever know God by believing in ideas, in the same way that no one will ever obtain life by keeping the law, even keeping it to perfection.

Here is the direct connection between the serpent's words and the Nicene Creed, however. "You, Adam and Eve, will be like God by knowing ideas."

As I read over versions of "What We Believe" on Christian websites, I become sadder and sadder. What breaks my heart is the thought of refuting ideas with ideas, a wearisome, pointless task.

You see, most people, in reading my claim that I intend to break the Nicene Creed's hold over God's people would imagine that I will argue why the ideas in it are "wrong" by using my own "correct" ideas. Therefore, they would read such a letter as this expecting to find point-by-point "disagreement."

In other words, everyone expects tree of knowledge versus tree of knowledge, tree of ideas versus tree of ideas. Anyone who says *"I believe"* and then presents an idea is living in the tree of ideas, the tree of knowledge.

Life is something so entirely different. The tree of knowledge, the Nicene Creed, can be broken only out from the tree of Life.

When I read those What-We-Believe's, whether from a Spirit-filled church or from a progressive church or even the earliest rendition of the Creed, I am struck first and foremost by the absence of two fairly important entities.

Now, in spite of the dissimilarity in wording between the Nicene Creed and the serpent's words, the two big entities missing are the same.

God Himself in Person, His Heart and intentions, is simply not there. Words containing ideas about God do not bring God in Person into the immediate picture. Then, the second thing is absent because of the absence of God's Heart, and that is MAN. What is man? is never mentioned, let alone addressed.

The serpent's second lie is the biggest: ***"God knows."***

Now here is the fascinating thing. The word, "to know" has two completely different meanings. "To know" has one meaning inside the tree of knowledge, but it also exists inside the tree of life with a very, very different meaning. In actuality, they are two completely different words, yet they take on the same appearance as they present themselves to man.

In the tree of knowledge, "to know" means to "believe in" a set of "correct" ideas.

In the tree of life, "to know" means sexual intimacy whereby we receive into ourselves Seed from God that we might carry that Seed, Christ, inside our womb as it develops and forms until that Seed is birthed out from us that God might be seen and known by all. My next letter addresses God's definition of Life.

Ideas in the mind versus marriage union, two opposing definitions of the word, "to know."

Now, I wrote a "What I Believe" when I first started my website. I was not trying to be succinct; rather, I wanted to spell out a reasonably complete version for the sake of honesty. Here are the first four points on my list.

1. That God is sovereign and that all things are subject to His pleasure.

2. That God is invisible and unknowable, yet desires to be seen, heard, and touched.

3. That God created man in His own image and likeness uniquely for this purpose, to be God's "body," God's dwelling place, that God could be seen, heard, and touched through man.

4. That man was created with the capacity to contain God, to fit God, and to release God in a river of life to the entire universe.

First, I am not attempting to "define" God, but to place Him as God first, and then proceed directly to God's heart: DESIRES. No Creed I have found considers

God's desire from the beginning. No Creed considers motive. But here's the deal: leave out motive, leave out heart, and God Himself in Person is also left out in the cold.

Two things happen immediately, however, with the word, desire. God becomes a present Person on the one hand, and man must appear as he is on the other hand.

Man is the fulfillment of God's desire.

Jesus said, **"He who has seen Me, has seen the Father."** You cannot eliminate man from the picture without in full measure banishing God. You cannot bring God in Person into the picture without immediately seeing Him revealed through man. Jesus said in John 17, **"I desire – man."**

To separate God from man is to know neither one. You cannot know God except through man; you cannot know man except by God.

The moment the serpent said, *"You shall be like God,"* those words created instantaneous overwhelming Static Friction as in the largest screeching-of-brakes, finger-nails-on-chalk-board imaginable. Grating, horrendous disconnect.

Those were the words that severed man from God.

Man was already like God; but he was not yet complete. Adam must eat of the tree of life to be filled with all the fullness of God, to enter into full marriage God, that God Himself might flow out through Adam to transform the proto-universe into the real deal God has always intended.

As those words entered into Adam's consciousness, he did a full double-take; they spun him completely around. In the split-second before, he had been contemplating the full meaning of the tree of life, of being filled with all of God. Now he saw the other.

Adam could be godly or he could be God-ly, one or the other. Every Christian that chooses to push **"filled with all the fullness of God"** into the future has already chosen to be godly instead of being God-ly. They prefer their own achievement over being a vessel containing God.

They say, "Grace"; they really mean, *"It's okay to live with 'no-God-now.'"*

Now, look back at the words of the Nicene Creed. Does that Creed maintain the separation established by Adam, or does it restore the union won by Jesus? Since the Nicene Creed savagely maintains that separation, it cannot be God speaking. If it is not God speaking, then what is it?

Let me give a God-speaking, that is, making what God actually says personal and real in us – faith.

I am filled with all the fullness of the Father. – Christ is my only life. – Rivers of Spirit flow out from me.

That you (man) might be filled with all the fullness of God. – I (man) am crucified with Christ . . . Christ who is my (man) life. – Out of his (man) belly will flow rivers of living water . . . the Holy Spirit.

To separate God from man and man from God is to depart from the gospel. ("Man" means male and female.)

God cannot be known except through man; man cannot be man except to be filled with God.

The largest problem with the Nicene Creed is centered around Christ. Who is Christ? What is Christ? Here is what this present version argues.

> *I believe in one Lord Jesus Christ, the Only Begotten Son of God, born of the Father before all ages. God from God, Light from Light, true God from true God, begotten, not made, consubstantial with the Father; through him all things were made. For us men and for our salvation he came down from heaven, and by the Holy Spirit was incarnate of the Virgin Mary, and became man. . . He ascended into heaven and is seated at the right hand of the Father. He will come again. . .*

Let's start with the second half. This is the gospel as understood by the Apostles before Paul received his gospel, the revelation of Jesus Christ. Thus Paul's gospel is totally absent; this is "another" gospel. These words establish Jesus entirely as back then, up there, some day. Notice that *"became man"* is an incidental part of a momentary transition. By these words, Jesus Christ is ABSENT from the earth right now. It is this second half that RULES all comprehension of the first half.

Notice the assumption of purpose; a purpose that, because it stands alone, eliminates all possibility of any other purpose. *"For us men and for our salvation he came down."* That's what everyone says. Define "salvation." It's not stated here, just assumed. Yet we cannot know God except first by MOTIVE, that is, by heart. This salvation means to all one thing alone – after death, we go to heaven and not to hell.

Separation continues on, right on. No consideration of – What is Man? Well, yes, actually, there is. By these words, man is defined entirely by the serpent's hatred. *Man is despicable and low. Look at how ridiculous and weak man is. God hates weak; yet He has disdained to save a few of us miserable creatures.*

The stated purpose of the Nicene Creed is to define Jesus as fully God, co-equal with the Father, and fully man, sort-of, for a short period of time. That is a false assumption. What is really happening in the Nicene Creed is the hidden definition of SALVATION. Everything pivots on this un-Biblical definition.

The Nicene Creed assumes that Salvation means one thing ALONE: that all humans face a split in the road after death. Death normally drops people into all the misery of hell; but after death, there is also a gate through which one arises into all the bliss of heaven. Salvation is to have the right ticket for that gate in the road. Some say the ticket is works; others say the ticket is grace; others say the ticket is the correct church and the right rituals; others say the ticket is asking Jesus into your heart. It matters not how you get the ticket; the idea is all the same. Get the ticket now so that after death you can enter the gate and "go to" heaven.

This salvation has two parts. The first part is the ticket; the second is the deification of heaven, that all that God speaks, all that salvation is and means, finds its reality only in that place called heaven which we know after we lose our physical bodies. God is as absent in people's knowledge of heaven as He is right now.

When I read grace teachers laboring over the meaning of grace and faith, I see so clearly that they are NOT speaking of Salvation but of having the right ticket.

And everyone is convinced that physical death is the door to salvation.

All those who have died in Christ remain entirely inside the present life. They are NOT found in any *"next life."* They continue in this present life of in-part-ness; they continue in the chrysalis that must be cast off. Heaven saves no one. Heaven is passing away. Heaven is under the curse. Heaven is old, and it is finished.

The Salvation of the Gospel is something entirely different. The Salvation of the Gospel is living inside of John 14:20 now and forever. Death takes no one into John 14:20. If Christians who have lost their physical bodies and exist only in their spirits, their heaven-bodies right now had the faith to take them into Salvation, then they would be back here on earth in their glorified physical bodies, incorruptible and manifesting all the revelation of Jesus Christ out from heaven/earth. Faith and Salvation begin only in the earth; that is, in the full, God-filled union of spirit and flesh.

Salvation is God in us now. Grace is God in us now. Faith is God in us now in ALL that God in us now could possibly mean.

Then, the rigid, outwardly true ideas of the second half of the definition of Jesus in the Nicene Creed, absent any consideration of Paul's gospel, then rule all thought of the first half of this definition of Jesus. The first sentence is an interesting mix of things God says with things God does not say, void of other things God says.

Here is what God says: . . . **Lord Jesus Christ, the Only Begotten Son. . .; through him all things were made.**

The in-between stuff God never speaks inside the gospel. To those who live in knowledge knowledge, those ideas mean something. But to those who live in life knowledge, no word not spoken by God could ever bring forth God-life. The more I speak what God speaks concerning Christ personal in me, the more I hear phrases God does not speak as abrasive and without life.

We will never know Him in that way.

But even the words here that God does speak contain a lie. That lie is not found in what is said, but in what is NOT said. Deceit is always sleight of hand. The lie is never stated, just implied.

"Only Begotten Son," *monogenes*, is a phrase used to refer to Jesus only by John, and only five times. The fifth time John used it, in 1 John 4:9, he turns this Nicene declaration entirely on its head. But there is far more than that left out. The interplay, the positioning of *monogenes, mono,* and *prototokos* (also used five times to refer to Jesus) in the gospel is enough to blow everything right out of the water. Alas, that explanation must wait for the article: "Christ Jesus."

By saying *monogenes*, only begotten, but leaving out *prototokos*, firstborn, is to lie. It leaves MOTIVE entirely out in the cold, and with Motive, God.

Those who will not have God's heart, will not have God.

In a recent letter, I quickly whipped out what I then titled "The Anti-Nicene Creed." As I look at it, I find nothing much to change except the title.

My Creed of Christ

I know God the Father who fills me with all of His fullness. He creates and fills all things, but He is known in both heaven and earth only as a Man laying down His life for His friends.

I know Jesus-Sent who is my very and only life. I live only in Him who carried me inside Himself all the way through death into life. His Gethsemane is my Gethsemane, His death is my death, His resurrection is my resurrection; His blood always cleanses me. This same Jesus is now seated upon my heart, the throne of heaven. Inside of Him, seeing out from His eyes alone, I know God.

I live always in the Holy Spirit of God who reveals God in the heavens and who reveals Christ in me and who flows out from me as rivers of living water bringing life to all.

I am a member of the one body of Christ in which Jesus walks the earth today. Our flesh is His flesh. Together, He in us and we in Him, we defeat death and all the curse, casting them off human experience in heaven/earth, spirit and flesh. God judges all things by our revealed union with Christ. This same Jesus, as our very and only life, will subdue all things by love, by our lives laid down, and will restore all creation back to the Father.

∽

Only life can defeat ideas.

You see, we can never be like the Nicene Jesus Christ, thus that Creed breaks the Covenant and turns the most important verse in the Bible, Romans 8:29, into a discussion of who goes to heaven and who goes to hell.

The gospel is that I am filled full with another Person, and that Person is God. Every particle of me is found ONLY inside of God Himself in Person, and God Himself in Person fills every particle of me with ALL that He is, and God Himself in Person flows out from me at all times and in every direction. I share heart with this God who fills me full and that shared heart is the very throne of heaven, the Mercy Seat of God. I am seated always upon that throne inside of God and God inside of me. Together, He and I draw all into love upon that throne by a life laid down, by love poured out.

Salvation is not anything else.

Salvation has no connection to time or place. Salvation is always Here and Today. Salvation is Christ Jesus.

Notice that the definition of the Holy Spirit in the Nicene Creed is that He *"proceeds from the Father and the Son."* Those are Roman Catholic words and are the largest split in church history, when the Roman and Greek churches pulled apart completely, one thousand years ago. The Greek Orthodox Creed says, *"proceeds from the Father through the Son,"* not *"and the Son."* Of course, splits are never about ideas, but about power-over.

But where is the third most important verse in the Bible? **"Out of his belly will flow rivers of living water."**

You see, we know the Holy Spirit as the One who abounds in our hearts as the love of God first, and we know Him as the One who proceeds out from our bellies, second. If the Holy Ghost ain't proceeding out of your belly, it ain't the Holy Ghost, no matter how precise and high falutin' one's words might be.

The Holy Spirit is found only in the words that say, "The Holy Spirit, who proceeds out of me."

Then this: *"I believe in one, holy, catholic and apostolic Church."* Of course, this is a modern Roman Catholic rendition, but all other versions are similar. May I suggest that "I am a member of the one body of Christ" is a far better way to say it. More than that, only the Spirit immersing us into that one body of Christ is that unity; no outward form, no sect, no group is that unity.

Finally, all versions of the Nicene Creed end with someday, someday.

To-morrow and to-morrow and to-morrow. – Shakespeare (Macbeth)

The life of the age to come is to know God in us now. It has nothing to do with "someday" except as it flows out of us setting all creation free.

Many versions of "what we believe" also contain a section on the Bible. Here is an example.

We believe that "all Scripture is given by inspiration of God" (2 Timothy 3:16). We understand this to mean that the whole Bible is inspired. . . We believe that this divine inspiration extends equally and fully to all parts of Scripture as it appeared in the original manuscripts. We believe that the whole Bible in those original manuscripts is, therefore, without error. We believe that all Scripture centers around the Lord Jesus Christ in His person, work, and in His first and second coming . . .

Hogwash. I simply do not think those who proclaim this are being honest.

"*I believe*" is the defense of unbelief. The person who wrote this always takes Augustine's ideas in *On Christian Doctrine* above anything God says in the Bible. The person who wrote this will reject many, many things God says, pushing those things off for *"heaven someday,"* but not God in us now.

There is a verse in the Bible that says the verses in the Bible will kill us unless they come into us entirely through the Holy Spirit and not as ideas in the mind. Most Christians who "believe in the Bible" do not believe that verse. In fact, this "*I believe*" positions the Bible as a set of correct ideas.

Notice this statement centers the Scripture around Jesus back then and Jesus someday. Thus none of the Bible is Jesus in us now as our very and only life. The Bible is not the Word of God; though it certainly can be. Ideas on the page cannot be God. The Bible becomes the Word of God as it comes into us by the Holy Spirit becoming Christ our only life.

I have a high regard for the Bible; God speaks to me through the Bible all the time. But I neither deify the Bible nor turn it into a fact-book. Yes, I believe that the Bible is true facts, but that doesn't make it anyone's life.

More than that, God in me can speak Bible out through me just as easily as He could through Moses or Paul. Christ is in my mouth, as Paul said. Peter said we should all speak as the oracle of God, as divine Scripture.

The spirit of anti-Christ is the spirit that says that God could speak back then, but He sure does not speak through you now. The spirit of anti-Christ severs God from present flesh. God in past-flesh is only a deified idea; God in present-flesh is not allowed. God Himself is banished from the earth.

Yet if a person is speaking only ideas, no matter how good and true those ideas might be, if they are not speaking Christ, God filling them full and flowing out here and now. God Personal and real. God now and here. Christ as me. If they are not speaking Christ, then they are not speaking life or salvation. Their words draw people close, yes, but then bar them from actually entering in.

I read this comment on Facebook.

> Question: Pertaining to the Return of Christ, are we waiting for Him or is He waiting for us? Most of Christianity would rather wait for Him, but then consider the parable of the ten virgins awaiting the Bridegroom. While we wait, we rest to be ready.

The brother's response to his own question is excellent; I want to refer to the question itself. – Pertaining to the Return of Christ, are we waiting for Him or is He waiting for us? –

In actuality, both sides of this question come out of the Nicene Creed. What if God has nothing to do with either option? What if neither option is referring to the most important thing happening upon this earth right now today?

What if, contrary to the Nicene Creed, Jesus walks the earth today.

What if we are His body?

What if He is living as us, filling us right now with all of His glory?

What if everything is exactly the way it is supposed to be, the travail of God?

What if God is birthing Himself into visible manifestation through His elect, men and women scattered across the earth who are, as a corporate body, the Return of Christ? What if their task is to show to the Bride of Christ the Lord Jesus Christ as He is?

You see, the largest underlying assumption upon which the Nicene Creed is written is that Jesus is, in fact, absent from the earth. Defining Jesus in the way they do serves to create a "Superman Christ" in the minds of those who mouth those words.

Look around. Is there any SuperChrist visible?

So, it is an evidential fact that Jesus is not here!

But what if the only image of God, the only seeing of God, the only picture of God ever given to either heaven or earth apart from symbolic images or figurative language IS a man stumbling from Gethsemane to the cross?

What if that man IS God revealed?

What if His strength is revealed only in weakness?

What if Almighty God in the heavens appears as a meek and mild man or woman in the earth, looking just like you and me? What if God Almighty in the heavens appears in the earth right now as you and me?

What if "waiting for the return of the Lord" is open unbelief and a refusal to allow God to fill us full against the sight of our eyes and the judgment of our self?

What if "waiting for the return of the Lord" is living according to the flesh? What if it is idolatry?

What if John 14:20 is the only reality in the Bible; what if everything else in the Bible viewed from outside of John 14:20 is death?

Put on the Lord Jesus Christ. — Put on the Lord Jesus Christ. — Put on the Lord Jesus Christ.

This command is **"Abide in Me and I in you"** in a slightly different form. It is the one thing we do. It is John 14:20. **Put on the Lord Jesus Christ.**

We do so only by faith; that is, by our confidence in God that He is telling us the truth, and thus seeing Christ as our only outward appearance contrary to any sight of the eyes or judgment of the self.

Put on the Lord Jesus Christ IS Salvation. Salvation is nothing, nothing, nothing else. Almost everyone who says, "Salvation" is NOT talking about salvation, but about fantasy. The moment someone knows Salvation, the Nicene Creed is abhorrent and must become "My Creed of Christ."

When we clothe ourselves with another Person for real, that is the Person is real, we clothe ourselves with Him by faith, then outwardly we are that other Person. We have a totally new identity. We, ourselves, are tucked away inside. We don't have to "get out of the way"; we are entirely in the Way.

Do you see how stupid *"Get out of the way, brother; let Christ be seen and not you"* really is?

I am entirely IN the Way. When others see me, they are seeing Jesus.

I am clothed entirely with Christ Jesus, Himself in Person, here and now.

That is the only Creed I know.

Jesus walks the earth. All you need to do is look in the mirror or at me to know that it is true.

Ideas about God versus Jesus as you. Creed versus Christ.

I refute the Nicene Creed utterly and more than defeat it by this reality.

Put on the Lord Jesus Christ.

7. Life

The words that I speak to you are spirit, and they are life. John 6:63

Augustine, in *On Christian Doctrine*, the guiding document of ALL Christian thinking from then until now, raised the question – How do we interpret the Bible? How do we understand God's words as they are found in the Scriptures? In fact, he raised that question as the proper entry point into any consideration of "what Christians believe." As I was agreeing fully that this question is the entry point, I eagerly anticipated some rendition of John 6:63.

You can be assured how stunned I was when I saw no such answer to the question Augustine had raised. In fact, Augustine postulated the very opposite of John 6:63 as the only entry point into Christian "truth."

Augustine's answer was not stated, otherwise it would not have worked so effectively. Deceit operates by sleight of hand. But Augustine's answer was forcibly clear – *"Embrace with all your thinking this 'correct' doctrine FIRST, then, when you read the Bible, you will know how to deal with what you find there."*

Let me give all of John 6:63: **It is the Spirit who gives life; the flesh profits nothing. The words that I speak to you are spirit, and they are life.**

It makes no difference if "true" ideas are found in Augustine's rendition of "correct Christian doctrine." By ignoring Spirit and life, Augustine made the Christian reading of the Bible to be by intellect only, that is, by the flesh.

I know personally the mind-set and thinking of Mennonites, Baptists, Pentecostals, Charismatics, and deeper-truth Christians. I am acquainted with Methodist, Catholic, Church of Christ, and Jesus-only thinking. I have looked at Universalist, Eastern Orthodox, and present-grace/union-with-Christ thinking. Where there is the baptism of the Holy Spirit, there is an awareness of **"the words that I speak to you are spirit, and they are life,"** but invariably, when push comes to shove, ALL fall back on Augustine's required approach to the Bible.

► The mind of the flesh insists that the Bible presents to us ideas to understand, that, since those ideas are contradictory and confusing, "good Bible teaching" is needed first for any one of us to "get the ideas right." Since the words of the Bible and all the ideas people find create such a mishmash of confusion and argument in the church, it's better just to "believe" these correct ideas you are told and not think you can "know" the real purpose of all that is found in the Bible. ◄

I live in Jesus' words, **"the words that I speak to you are spirit, and they are life."** I read the Bible by those words and have done so for years. Everything I teach, I speak out from those words. That's why many Christians do not recognize what I teach; it's too bizarre for them, to outside the "reasonings" of Augustine.

I suspect they are astonished by how rooted in Scripture I am, but they just do not read those verses the same way I do. They require every word in the Bible to fit itself under Augustine's *On Christian Doctrine*, which is the underlying doctrine, that is, list of ideas, of every group I mentioned above and more besides.

Consider the brother who objected to my claim that I am filled with all the fullness of God now. He suggested that no, such a reality is not now. First, we must "learn obedience," then, after that, at a certain point, we will, someday, be filled with all the fullness of God.

But right now, God is ABSENT. I am un-God-ly. And in my un-God-liness, I must please this absent God. How must I please this absent God? By the right ideas (grace), yes, but also by the right performance.

If grace is an idea we can define, then we are living in the mind of the flesh.

Grace is one thing alone, grace is God in Person now in us.

That you may be filled with all the fullness of God. There it is, sitting quietly on the page. God would not have said such a thing if He had not designed us to be filled with all of Him – that is, if it was impossible. So what does the preacher say? No, that's future, that's not for now.

Really? Then what is for now? Being empty of God? God not filling me full? If I am made to be filled with all of God, but not being filled with God is okay for me. If I can continue on my "way to heaven" by grace, Amen, hallelujah! But empty of God – just because, well, I guess. COME ON!!!! That's the rejection of God bought by Adam, spoken out from the empty thinking of grace preachers!

Grace is one thing alone, grace is God in Person now in us.

So-called "godliness," absent of God, is exactly what Adam bought in the garden. "I can be 'like God' without God." This godliness without God is iniquity. *Doing great without You, God! On my way! Being filled with all of Your fullness now just doesn't interest me.* Better to be silent before Him than to speak a rejection of what God says.

I will write on the Holy Spirit last, because that is God's order. The problem is, of course, that without the Spirit first, we cannot know anything real. That also is God's order. You see, without God present, it's all a bunch of confusion. God present in us Personal and now in all fullness is the only thing that makes sense.

We know such a thing ONLY by the Spirit.

I am positioning before us the utter importance of **the words that I speak to you are spirit and they are life.** There are five things of utmost importance in this line: 1. Words. 2. I speak. 3. To you. 4. Are Spirit. 5. Are Life.

Let's start with life. Life is the nature of substance in the heavens, life is the *energia*, the matter of spirit being. Our physical bodies know life only as our spirits transfer the life that they are into our physical bodies. But the life of Spirit is explained to us by God through two earthly symbols.

For since the creation of the world His invisible attributes are clearly seen, being understood by the things that are made, even His eternal power and Godhead... Romans 1:20

Life is an invisible attribute coming out from God. We understand life by looking at the things that are made. The things that are made are part of God's language to us as He communicates to us His reality.

The primary visible reality, the primary symbol God gave us to comprehend Jesus' words, **"My Words are LIFE,"** is reproduction – sex. Reproduction of life is everywhere, the most prolific symbol in the creation all around us, staring us in the face, shouting God to us.

The central element of the reproduction of life is sperm, or its more generic term, SEED. Seed as sperm is the central defining reality of the entire Bible from Genesis 1:1 to Revelation 22:21.

Life! – The reproduction of life!

When Jesus said, **"You must be born again,"** He was talking entirely about sex in all of its ramifications.

I am not speaking of smut, but of God. The reason God places sex only into marriage is because it is holy, as Hebrews says.

Seed is found in the Nicene Creed – "only-begotten," but that Seed is left fruitless, cut-off by the savageness of its isolation from ever reproducing itself, totally contrary to the gospel.

Everything in the Bible is written around the metaphor of how life brings forth life. You separate that metaphor from the Bible and nothing in the Bible makes sense. You see that metaphor as the basis of the construction of the entire Bible and suddenly you see it all the way through, that the Bible is nothing other than a vast opening up of this one thing, the reproduction of life.

The Words that I speak to you are Spirit AND THEY ARE Life.

The seed is the Word of God.

The words God speaks are God's sperm. We understand what that means by studying both human seed and plant seed. Both types of seed are 100% contributive to our knowledge of God in experience.

It's all about God reproducing Himself; many sons to glory is literal.

In the beginning was the Word and the Word was with God and the Word was God.

In the beginning was the Sperm and the Sperm was with God and the Sperm was God.

When God speaks, He does not give us ideas to know or commands to obey; rather, He plants His Seed into us, that it might bring forth in us the Life that it is.

This is the work of God, that you believe in Him whom He sent.

Everything in these words of Jesus speaks of the female part of the sexual act, from beginning to end, from foreplay that awakens desire to bringing forth a child. Faith is the female part of sex.

You know, when we beat around the bush, dressing up God's reality with Victorian blushing we only prevent ourselves from seeing and knowing God clearly.

To the pure all things are pure, but to those who are defiled and unbelieving nothing is pure; but even their mind and conscience are defiled. Titus 1:15

Worship without preaching after is like foreplay without consummation; desire is awakened, yes, but no life can come forth. Preaching without worship first is like sex without romance; it gets the job done, but not inside of love. More than that, preaching without worship first means much of the seed sown will not find faith.

It's all about God; – the whole Bible and all creation are all about God reproducing Himself.

Life MUST bring forth life.

The drive for sex is life's most visible characteristic in all realms, human, animal, plant, fish, insects, even creatures under the soil. Why do salmon beat themselves to death to arrive back, somehow, to the place where they were spawned? They must bring forth life.

Life Must bring forth life. – God MUST bring forth Himself.

To those who do not know this reality, the Bible cannot be what it is.

You know, I must put it bluntly because this IS God's reality as He has crafted the universe: **His invisible attributes are clearly seen, being understood by the things that are made.** Human reproduction reveals God.

We do not read the Bible in order to know things about God. We do not read the Bible in order to obey what God says. We read the Bible in order to "have Spirit-sex" with God, that He might plant His Sperm, Christ, inside of us, inside of the female egg, our faith, that we might birth the revelation of God into the universe.

In an earlier letter I said this: – God speaks His Word into me by the Spirit. I receive that Word into my Faith (Jesus as me) by that same Spirit. That Word reproduces itself inside of me as my only Life as I speak it with my mouth. God fills me full with All of Himself. – the same thing, the reproduction of life.

Now, the New Testament did not exist during the early church. Thus word, that is *logos*, did not refer to the "written word" contrary to what some teach. Over and over, the apostles said, "**The *logos* that was preached into you.**"

God plants His seed in us through the foolishness of preaching.

You know, we dress reality up with euphemisms, and that's okay. Most people are not pure; most people see evil, that is, double, flesh AND Christ, and thus possess defiled minds.

We love God, therefore we give ourselves to Him that He might have His way with us, that He might procreate Himself in us, that He might plant His Seed, the Lord Jesus Christ, inside of us, that we might bring forth to God His very own sons and daughters.

My children are everything to me. I would trade all that I am at a moment's notice for their sakes. I love with all my heart the precious woman God gave to me that I might know and behold these most precious children of OURS.

God is all about SONS, many, many sons. God must bring forth God. Where is that in the Nicene Creed?

My children are as much out of my wife as they are out of me; yet each one stands completely as his or her own person. I have no children not of my wife.

No son of God can be non-human. No son of God can be non-divine.

Fully God and fully man.

We can bring forth God because we are of His same species, created in the likeness of God.

A human empty of God is all contradiction, that is, all speaking-against.

It is entirely in this context alone that we can understand the full implications of **"Did God indeed say?"**

The serpent was deflecting God's Seed, that it might fall upon the ground, useless. The serpent deflected God's Seed; Adam and Eve cast it useless to the ground. The tree of life contained God's Seed; Adam turned his back on it.

Do you see the horror of Adam's rebellion?

It is only when we see the obvious about life, that life MUST bring forth life, can we then see the full meaning of the first three things Jesus said: "**The words that I speak to you.**" – "My Seed that I plant in you that it might bring forth its life through you."

"I" the male; "speak" the act of procreation; to "you" the female; "words" the seed.

Did you know that the Feasts of the Lord in Israel's religious year follow the pattern of the growth of the fetus in the womb exactly, to the day – in a "normal" progression of that development? It's a fascinating study.

Now, NONE of this procreation of God can take place outside of Spirit. And when I say, "Spirit," I don't mean spirit generally, but Spirit specifically. And what that means we must also know.

But first, there is a second aspect to life; Life is STORY. Most of the Bible is story, human story, and the parts that are not story are built around the parts that are story. Story imparts the meaning of life at a gut level, at a level of Seed.

Let me give an example. As an autistic man, certain social settings terrify me, specifically, hard-browed people who are absolutely certain of themselves and who speak down at me from their lofty perch, but who also have the authority to cause harm to my life. Out from that reality, I have been frightened in one of my present college courses, at the level of a child's fright. Yet I must bear this thing out and win at least a B; I must have these credits I have already purchased.

I asked for prayer and a number of people shared good things, which I read and acknowledged. Jesus said, **"Do not be afraid."** Peter said, **"Cast all your care upon Him for He cares for you."** Sorry, those nice ideas have never helped me. (God moved through your prayers, however. Thank you.)

Last Sunday I was facing a gauntlet; I did not know if I could survive it; I was terrified. Then, I watched *After Earth* with Will Smith and his son. As I watched a real father playing a pretend father speak to his real son playing a pretend son, I heard the father's instructions on fear. Then I watched the son, in the hour of greatest need, draw that instruction into himself. I watched that boy lie under terror in utter peace, knowing the demon could sense only fear and nothing else; I watched that boy kill his demon.

In that moment I was set free in a way I have never known in my life. I went out the next morning without fear and slew the big test, not missing one question on the part relevant to me. I inserted my disagreement into the college course without fear, I chose not to do one assignment, something I have never done, and suddenly I now know how to slay the big one yet coming up. I know how to turn Thomas Hardy on his head.

STORY. – God's seed is much more than just a Word, it is STORY.

The most important stories in the Bible to us are the life of Abraham, the journey of Israel, the life of David, the life of Jesus, and the acts of the Apostles. Intermingled with these are many other stories, great and small.

How can anyone walk with God without knowing every single tiny detail of the life of Abraham? I don't think it can be done. I can praise the Lord in my fear because David praised the Lord in his. I can walk around a shattered church weeping because Jeremiah walked around a shattered city weeping. I can wrestle with God until I win because Jacob wrestled with God and won. I know these things in my darkest moments.

Story is the impartation of God. Story means many things including purpose and a journey, companions and an enemy.

I read because I love story. To my great horror, I have discovered that literature "study" in the secular college despises story with all the hatred of the serpent for Christ. And that hatred is real and very visible. Story means purpose; purpose has no basis in "science." "Scientism," that is the worship of knowledge, hates purpose.

"YOU HAVE NO PURPOSE AT ALL," they scream.

Thus I am finding that these people "study" literature as a biologist dissects a frog. They simply cut everything to pieces and leave you feeling torn up and depressed. They then call their spirit-driven accusations "realism" and consider themselves "scholars" and "scientists." Underlying their words I see great purpose all the way through. They have a continual desperate need to prove that they are SUPERIOR to all those stupid people out there. I sometimes feel like I'm in kindergarten, and all the highly-educated scholars are sitting on top of their little hills beating their chests and feeling mighty pleased with themselves.

Human beings empty of God are empty indeed. Being so empty inside, they build all around their empty souls this mighty fortress of bluster and pretending out of powerful boastful words. For their sakes we lay down our lives, that they also may know the God who carries them with tender concern.

I will go no more into story here; rather, I want to look more closely at Jesus' first words in John 6:63: **It is the Spirit who gives life. – The Words that I speak to you ARE Spirit.**

The procreation of God, the story of God, takes place ONLY inside the life-giving Spirit. Apart from the immediate presence of the Holy Ghost, the words of the Bible, the words of the preacher, remain either ideas or commands only. Without the immediate presence of the Holy Ghost, no life of God can ever be known. Without the immediate presence of the Holy Ghost, all seed of God falls useless to the ground.

Spirit/Word, Word/Spirit can never ever be separated.

Truth is known by lateral leaps in unexpected directions. I want to go in an entirely different direction now, hoping that Truth Himself will cause what He wishes to be life in you. I want to talk about "the anointing."

Also Moses took the anointing oil, and anointed the tabernacle and all that was in it, and consecrated them. He sprinkled some of it on the altar seven times, anointed the altar and all its utensils, and the laver and its

base, to consecrate them. **And he poured some of the anointing oil on Aaron's head and anointed him, to consecrate him.** Leviticus 8:10-12

"I still have many things to say to you, but you cannot bear them now. However, when He, the Spirit of truth, has come, He will guide you into all truth; for He will not speak on His own authority, but whatever He hears He will speak; and He will tell you things to come. He will glorify Me, for He will take of what is Mine and declare it to you. John 16:12-13

. . . **partakers of His promise in Christ through the gospel, of which I became a minister according to the gift of the grace of God given to me by the effective working of His power.** Ephesians 3:6-7

But you have an anointing from the Holy One, and you know all things. – But the anointing which you have received from Him abides in you, and you do not need that anyone teach you; but as the same anointing teaches you concerning all things, and is true, and is not a lie, and just as it has taught you, you will abide in Him. 1 John 2:20 & 27

The Spirit is life, *energia*, power. The "anointing" is not something from God. The anointing is the Holy Spirit Himself, but in a very, very specific manner and for a very, very specific purpose. Grace and anointing are two sides of the same thing. Grace is the phenomenon of God within filling us full; anointing is the phenomenon of God flowing out. Yet we see New Testament verses switching those two around just as easily with the anointing as God within and grace as God flowing out. Such is the Spirit.

There is no such thing as birthing God into visibility that all might see and know Him without POWER.

Christ is a Spirit of Power.

The entirety of procreation, carrying, and bringing forth life is enabled by, bathed in oil. Without the immediate presence of the Holy Spirit, none of it can be. People who read what I write apart from the Holy Spirit receive nothing. Yet that Holy Spirit attends my words, to those who will hear.

I came across a statement: "God will anoint that word (preached) which is from Him." I have been pondering this reality since. "God, I know that what I write is from you. What about that anointing?" Yet I KNOW that anointing is not something we drum up or pretend.

I know what is a man anointed by God in the demonstration of the Spirit and power, preaching a word that opened the heavens wide open to our understanding. Sam Fife, an apostolic ministry I once sat under, was such a man.

There have been others, including William Branham. In fact, there seems to have been a number of such men and women to varying degrees from the 1930's into the 70's, about a 50-year period. Some of these were rough and hoary men like the prophets of old. All established in a segment of the church something powerful and utterly in-part.

Today, God has a different kind of servant speaking to His church, men like Joel Osteen, the most influential pastor in church history, and Bill Johnson. These are gentle men, of impeccable character and integrity, pointing God's people towards hope and love and power. Don't ever speak against these men and women (I think of Joyce Myers, much the same) God is using now. They are perfect in their place. We owe them much.

The church is one; don't ever think of her any other way.

Joel Osteen could not possibly fulfill my calling in God, and I could not possibly fulfill his. Let's not lay the wrong tasks on our brethren.

But as I ponder this word I read, I see, almost as a vision, the curtain going down on the present scene. As it goes down, I have this thought. God is FINISHED with the William Branham's and the Sam Fife's. They filled their place; they did their part, but God will not have such again.

When the curtain comes back up on the final scene of this present in-part church age, there will be there standing, scattered all across the earth, as if they have just sprung full-grown and brand-new out from the woodwork, a ministry more powerfully anointed by the Spirit of God right from the moment they "appear" than any ministry before now in human history.

They will be more anointed by far than Sam Fife or William Branham, but there will be nothing of control or self-exaltation coming through their impact on others. They will be more anointed than Moses and Elijah.

They will even be "more anointed" than Jesus.

Please understand what I mean. The "anointing" is divine enablement for specific ministry. God flowing out from us is always for specific purposes and in specific directions, differing entirely from one member of the body of Christ to the next. There is no generalization in God; everything of God is unique and specific.

God anointed Jesus primarily for two very specific and limited ministries. Yes, Jesus enjoyed the Spirit without measure, as do we right now. But He did not use that Spirit without measure; that is, Jesus did not by the Spirit transform the whole earth.

The first specific and limited task God anointed Jesus to accomplish was to prepare a people for the Day of Pentecost, a people who would hear His apostles and enter His church with joy. The second focused and specific task God anointed Jesus to accomplish during His time on earth was to walk the path of the Atonement and to obtain eternal redemption for us. Every element of the anointing Jesus expressed was directed entirely to the accomplishing of these two tasks.

On the Day of Pentecost, God anointed Jesus for a third task, the task of becoming us, of being the mono-Seed, which having been planted in the earth, now becomes the plant out of which many new seeds will come, each individual and unique, yet each just like the original seed that was planted.

This ministry appearing suddenly (you and I know God has been hammering our hearts for years, teaching us of His ways in the secret places, in the lonely seasons of our lives) will also be anointed by God for specific tasks, five, in fact. That anointing will be like the continual crackling of lightning, like St. Elmo's fire, almost. In the presence of these ministries, God will instantly become known to people by power and by word, that is, by the gospel.

Those five tasks are these:

1. Get people's attention (Jesus also had this task).

2. Preach the gospel of the Kingdom, a gospel that few have ever heard.

3. Establish the church in righteousness, that is, in the Tabernacling of God, out from a Melchizedek priesthood. (Of truth, this is the positive side of defeating the beast.)

4. Cast every demon out from the experience of mankind, the positive of which is to demonstrate the highest respect and the tenderest of compassion for each individual person – life laid down, love poured out.

5. Defeat death, the positive side of which is the release of the River of Life across the whole earth. They will do so by 1 John 3:16.

Look again at Jesus' words. **It is the Spirit who gives life; the flesh profits nothing. The words that I speak to you are spirit, and they are life.**

Word/Spirit/Life. These three can never be without the other two in fullness. Word/Spirit without Life is not. Word/Life without Spirit is not. Spirit/Life without Word is not. The gospel is and has always been only WORD/SPIRIT/LIFE.

Christianity never has been humans sitting around telling each other ideas and then attempting to live some sort of "life" out from those ideas. Christianity has always only been God reproducing Himself through us into all creation, both heaven and earth.

You cannot know anything of God without the present *energia*, the immediate, miraculous presence and power of the Holy Ghost resting upon you. POWER. Apostles show you what that means.

Words without Spirit cannot bring forth Life. Spirit without Words cannot bring forth Life. Words and Spirit that do not bring forth God-Life are, in the end, fruitless and wasted.

Ministries such as Joel Osteen and Bill Johnson are preparing God's people for the final act of God upon the earth. When God anoints us with power, we will find millions eager to know Him. Both men move in Word and Spirit, but neither brings forth God-Life in the church.

That task is given to us. I draw freely from both men with all honor because my ministry is to complete that which comes to me through them. My ministry is to birth God-Life in you; that is, my ministry is to cause you to know the God who already fills you full.

When I read brethren who know God in Tabernacles sharing that they see God speaking through what I write beyond what they find anywhere else, I am so grateful, so deeply grateful for all the total, mind-numbing failures of my life. How those moments and years of ignominy and ruin shine like priceless jewels. I see how incredibly perfect is my gross inability; that I, a 57-year-old man, attempting to share Christ, would also need to confess a child's autistic fear, and a hearing of the words of a younger father.

Let it all be Him. Yet, beyond all wonder, He shares His glory with me.

Christ IS every Word God speaks. Christ IS a Spirit of Power. Christ IS a many-membered temple through whom God Himself is seen and known by all, a Corporate Body – God-Life.

Christ is the One who lives as me, my Friend, the One upon whose breast I lean my head.

It is the Spirit who gives Life, knowing ideas about God **profits nothing.**

8. Christ Jesus

As I began the *Christ Our Life* letter in late 2008, I connected with some readers who also wanted to call those two something entirely different. One brother posted something I wrote on his website, but replaced "Jesus" all the way through with "Christ."

I accept nothing of large consequence without writing out all that God actually says on the subject from the New Testament. In this case, I started with Romans, thinking that I would write out every verse in the epistles – that is, through Jude, in which "Jesus" and/or "Christ" appears. I needed to know from the actual words how the apostles truly understood the nature of the Lord Jesus Christ.

I stopped my study at Romans 8:11; there was no need to continue.

But if the Spirit of Him who raised Jesus from the dead dwells in you, He who raised Christ from the dead will also give life to your mortal bodies through His Spirit who dwells in you.

It is a simple law of logic. If A is B and if C is B, then A is C. Jesus IS the Christ. Now I see that it is Paul who uses every possible combination of Jesus, Christ, Christ Jesus, Jesus Christ, and the Lord Jesus Christ all the way through.

However, the most important reference there is, Romans 13:14, is very specific. We do not put on Christ, we do not put on Jesus, we do not put on the Lord. **We put on the Lord Jesus Christ.**

What, exactly then, are we wrapping around ourselves? What is it that we are making our only identity? What is this new Self of ours?

If the entirety of our task as believers is to wrap ourselves by faith entirely inside of the Lord Jesus Christ, *enduo*, put on, with what, precisely, are we enclothing ourselves?

In a book discussing poetry, the writer stated: "The universe is organized, but it is not personal." I wrote these words recently, "The universe is utterly, intensely personal," in direct contradiction of this professor's non-thinking claim.

You see, if the universe is not personal, then neither are we. And if we are not personal, that is, just a chemical reaction, then stomping out humans, as the Marxists like to do, is just a-okay.

In the same regard, if Christ is not Personal, that is, Jesus, then neither are we. If "Christ" is just some impersonal "force" that permeates everywhere, with which we connect and learn to arise into, some new "consciousness" that pervades but does not have a heart, then we also are not persons. And, you see, those who want such a "christ" also push "you are dead," or *"you're just a dead man walking."*

I KNOW the debilitating numbness that comes into people's lives by the ever present demand to "just die," by the horrific mutterings of "God isn't making you nothing, you already are."

I can assure you of this: Jesus did not die for nothing. The true death of the cross is entirely **"was dead,"** and entirely **"alive forevermore."**

Value is measured only by the price for which something is purchased, never by the thinking of the seller. I could have a car into which I have put thousands of dollars, but if it's not worth that to any buyer, it cannot be valued by what went into it. Only the purchaser determines the value of anything.

You were purchased with Blood, the highest value in the universe. You are of higher regard inside the Heart of a very Personal universe than all the wealth of creation.

Here is part of what the Nicene Creed says about this Person, the Lord Jesus Christ.

". . . born of the Father before all ages. God from God, Light from Light. . ."

Now, this is very confusing, how do I wrap myself with this?

You see, there is only ONE command in the entire Bible, one command that must be obeyed. All of Christianity, whether works or grace FAILS unless we obey this one command: **Put on the Lord Jesus Christ**, that is, **Abide in Me and I in you.**

"Born of the Father before all ages" places God into the realms of time. The writers of the Creed do not comprehend that all time words in the Bible, when referring to God, are figurative, just as Jesus said in John 16.

The Father is both NOW and HERE. He doesn't exist any other way. There is no God that is not now; there is no God that is not here. They claim that God is eternal and infinite; they just do not believe it.

What is "the Lord Jesus Christ?"

I do not consider Him as *"God the Son"*; I don't think God is known in that way. I don't consider Him as non-Divine, even in His humanity.

Part of the difficulty of the religious human living with his or her back turned to God is this desperate need to drive God and man far apart, to place God in one box over here and man in a totally different box over there, and to require them to be utterly, utterly different.

No one considers marriage.

With my present seeing, I see God as One Person, the Father.

I see that One Person, the Father, revealing Himself through many persons.

I see that the Man, Christ Jesus, is the continual revelation of the Father in the Now, in the Here, in the Personal in us – in the physical realms of earth.

I see that the Spirit, who is the Spirit of the Father sent out as the expression of all heaven's God-phenomena, who is also the Spirit of Christ, who is also my Sspirit and yours, in whom we live and move, who is our breath and the *energia* of our lives, is Gladness. Is that not what David called Him, a Spirit of Gladness? **You have anointed me with Gladness above all my fellows.**

The humanity of Jesus is in me, and that is a divine expression.

You see, if the Man, the humanity of Jesus is in me and if the Man, the humanity of Jesus is in you, that takes a type of omnipresence, which is an attribute of divinity.

Physical bodies cannot be omnipresent. Jesus was confined to one place and one expression when He walked the earth. Yet now, Jesus the Man is not confined to one place and one expression, but He shows up, not everywhere, as the Spirit does, but in many, as in a many-membered body. Jesus is not omnipresent as Spirit; He is omnipresent as Body.

This is all a mystery, but we are talking about Christ and the church.

Jesus' humanity is fully divine; Jesus' divinity is utterly human.

Now how's that for something to chew on? One great crime of the Nicene Creed is the concrete boxes into which God is forced over here and man is forced over there.

In my last letter, I said that Word/Spirit can never be separated from each other and that Word/Spirit can never be separated from the bringing forth of Life. We could say Word is Jesus, Spirit is the Holy Spirit, and Life is the Father. Yet when I read any discussion of *"the Trinity,"* I go cold. It's as if they are talking about something foreign and different, something I cannot know.

If I cannot know the Father as the One who fills me full, it ain't the Father. If I cannot know the Son as the One who lives as me, it ain't the Son. If I cannot know the Spirit as the One who fills my heart with love and who flows out of me as joy and gladness, it ain't the Spirit.

My humanity is fully divine, utterly saturated with all of God in Person; my divinity is utterly human, a kind word, a tender touch, a Man on His knees to serve. Do we know Him thus?

There is no other way to know Him. We cannot speak of God and Man except as total marriage union.

Jesus said, **"He who has seen Me has seen the Father."**

There are two ways only to know "God," one is real, the other is false.

The real way to know God is to see Him through the lens of Jesus, the Man, particularly through His walk of the Atonement, that is, through Jesus' eyes, through the eyes of a Man laying down His life for His friends.

The false way to know "God" is to see through the lens of an angel who thinks highly of his pretty self and who wants everyone to see him as grand, wise, and powerful. Most people see "God" through those eyes.

Everything said about God in the Bible, every one of His attributes can be seen through either set of eyes.

BUT! The same thing of God seen through a life poured out versus seen through self-exaltation appears and is known as something entirely different.

It's as if there are two "God's," two "Jesus's," and two "Holy Spirits."

It's not what we see, but the lens through which we look, that is, the eyes.

But this letter is not about God, but Christ Jesus.

Here's the point. Just as there is one way alone by which we can know anything "about" God, that is, by Jesus Christ walking this earth, so there is one way alone by which we can know anything "about" Jesus. Here it is.

Behold what manner of love the Father has bestowed on us, that we should be called children of God! Therefore the world does not know us, because it did not know Him. Beloved, now we are children of God; and it has not yet been revealed what we shall be, but we know that when He is revealed, we shall be like Him, for we shall see Him as He is. And everyone who has this hope in Him purifies himself, just as He is pure. 1 John 3:1-3

Do you see my point, here in these words? The world does not know us, because it did not know Him.

We shall be like Him, for we shall see Him as He is.

This is the core of the Covenant. It is found in my list of the most important verses in the Bible, entirely inside of #1 – Romans 8:29, to be conformed, symmorphos, to the image of His Son, that He might be the firstborn, *prototokos*, of many brethren. Romans 8:29 is written three different ways. Here is the third way it is written.

But we all, with unveiled face, beholding as in a mirror the glory of the Lord, are being transformed into the same image from glory to glory, just as by the Spirit of the Lord. 2 Corinthians 3:18

If we cannot be entirely like Jesus, then the Jesus we cannot be like ain't Jesus.

"He that has seen Me, has seen the Father." Jesus the Christ.

"He that has seen me, has seen Jesus the Christ." Daniel Yordy

Those who think "blasphemy" know neither man nor God.

I want to get at something so fundamental. Everywhere I read, people define "being like Jesus" as being outwardly powerful. These are the same people who will reject Him utterly when He shows up as just ordinary.

Look at those who knew Jesus, His brothers. They knew their brother; He was an ordinary man. They did not believe Him.

When we think of "being like Jesus," let us think of age 29, not age 32.

Hebrews says that **"He was tempted in all points just as we are, yet without sin."** We are talking about age 29. It is not sinful to be a human; sin is the spirit of the mind, the source out of which people live.

Consider James. Let's assume that James was 26 when Jesus was 29. Now, I was a younger brother and I had a younger brother. Likewise, I have two sons, one older and the other younger, who is also named James. I know younger sons; I know older sons.

But let's get a full picture of this 26-year-old James. In twelve years he will be the unappointed, but fully recognized head of the church of Jesus Christ. He has the carriage and natural authority to which all the apostles, including Paul quietly yield. In seventeen years he will write his letter, James. That letter demonstrates both a keen intellect and a natural wisdom, that is, an understanding of human psychology.

We are not talking about a dunce or a has-been. We are talking about a fully qualified young man.

For 26 years, James has lived with his older brother. Now, there is no question that those 26 years have been filled with squabbles and wrestlings. James has told on his brother, gotten him into trouble when it was James who did the deed. James has "borrowed" his brother's favorite things and then forgotten to bring them back. James has pestered and poked at his brother for 26 years, secretly admiring him, but outwardly putting on a show of disdain.

No one on earth knows Jesus the way James knows Him.

James is 26; Jesus is 29. Let's ask James two questions.

James, is your brother, Jesus, the Messiah of God? — "NO WAY!!"

James, is your brother, Jesus, God in the flesh? — "Are you a blasphemous idiot? Of course not!"

James, who knew Jesus better than anyone, James, of above average intellect and carriage, saw not one thing, not one thing that caused him to think that Jesus was anything more than his big brother.

Except, I suspect we could ask James one more question.

James, is your brother, Jesus, always kind to you? Does he always treat you like you're something special?

– Uh. I guess. Yea.

God in the flesh is always KINDNESS first and alone before anything else is ever added on.

The miracles, the ministry, even the cross and all the rumors of a resurrection, none of that convinced James. Paul tells us, in 1 Corinthians 15, what was the only thing that convinced James. A few days before the ascension, Jesus appeared to His younger brother and showed Himself to him. They likely spent a quiet afternoon together, walking the familiar paths, laughing about childhood pranks.

Then, and only then, did James believe.

DO WE SEE HIM?

Don't make Jesus into a demi-god, into a superman, into a power ranger. Don't treat Him like that. Do not add to the endless abuse of the Lord Jesus.

When God shows up in the earth; He is a man just like you and me.

God in heaven, Man on earth – same thing.

The anointing of the Spirit that came upon Jesus for 3 1/2 years was not "who Jesus is." Yes, that anointing was upon and always flowed out from Jesus, the ordinary man. But that anointing was for a specific purpose and ministry. We can safely say that God will never anoint us to win a people for the day of Pentecost or to walk the path of the Atonement ourselves for the sake of eternal redemption.

Yes, God anoints us for the present ministry appointed to us, just like He anointed Jesus for the present ministry appointed to Him, whether it was being kind to a rascally little brother when He was 29 or whether it was spitting into a piece of dirt and rubbing the mud onto a man's blind eyes when He was 32.

Here are Jesus' words. – John 5. **Most assuredly I say to you, the Son can do nothing of Himself – I can of Myself do nothing.**

But that's not all; here is what else He says.

If I bear witness of Myself, My witness is not true.

Think about that one. (In John 8, Jesus seems to say the opposite, but let His point here sink fully in.)

Then in John 8, Jesus said this. **If you had known Me, you would have known My Father also.**

We CANNOT know God except by a Man.

Then Jesus said this in John 14:10. **Do you not believe that I am in the Father, and the Father in Me? The words that I speak to you I do not speak on My own; but the Father who dwells in Me does the works.**

I have paced us through these statements of Jesus slowly because I want their full impact to fill us full. In fact, as I read through just now the words of Jesus in John's gospel, I see so differently, such wonder and glory, such precious treasure; I see, now, out from Jesus' eyes.

The gospel is that I, Daniel Yordy, am in the Father, inside of Christ, and the Father is in me, inside of Christ my only life. Whatever there might be that could be called "miraculous" is the Father who dwells in me doing whatever the Father does. I am just an ordinary man, filled with God.

We will never know Him in His power until we know Him first as our weakness. Though God does seem to anoint pretenders, He will never show Himself as He is through anyone unreal, through anyone un-human.

People say, "See as God sees." They are close, but still they don't enter in. We do not see "as" God sees, we see only out from His eyes, tucked utterly inside of Him. The difference is the difference between Salvation and every form of pretension.

I am in the Father who is inside of me.

Now that I am just like Jesus (paying ZERO attention to outward anointing for specific ministry), I can know Him. And now that I know Him, for the first time in my life, I know the Father.

I know the God who fills me full with ALL of Himself.

It is a terrible mistake to imagine that one specific outward anointing for ministry is "being like Jesus."

Now, the Nicene Creed says two things true, that God says, in it's definition of Jesus. The second thing is **"by Him all things were made."** Inside the context of the definition of Life as I described in the last chapter, this Word from God shows the nature of that Word. But outside of Spirit and Life, it remains just an idea.

The first thing God actually says, however, is **"the only-begotten Son of God."** *Monogenes Huios Theos*. As I said, *monogenes* is a word used only by John and only five times. Let's pull in two. The other three are just like the first one here; but the fifth and last time John used the term, he said something quite different.

For God so loved the world that He gave His only begotten Son, that whoever believes in Him should not perish but have the life of the age to come. John 3:16 – His *monogenes* Son.

In this the love of God was manifested toward us, that God has sent His only begotten Son into the world, that we might live through Him. 1 John 4:9 – That we might live through the *monogenes* Son.

Monogenes is two Greek words merged together. The first is *monos*, alone or only; the second is *ginomai*, similar to *gennao*, to procreate, to conceive (**you must be born again**). But *ginomai* means "to cause to be."

Here is the telling verse, the truth conveniently ignored in the Nicene Creed.

Most assuredly, I say to you, unless a grain of wheat (illustrating to us *gennao*, seed, the Word God speaks) **falls into the ground and dies, it remains ALONE; but if it dies, it produces much grain.** John 12:24

The word "alone" is *monos*.

Purpose! Intent! Heart! Motive! Desire!

Father, I DESIRE that they also whom You gave Me may be with Me where I AM (in the Father) . . . **– I in them, and You in Me; that they may be made perfect in one.** . . John 17:24 first, then 23.

Monogenes, alone, alone, alone! I will forever be alone, forever alone, forever the only-begotten, unless I, Jesus the Christ, fall into the ground and become the plant, My church, and then, I will be the begotten in many.

FATHER! I WILL drink Your cup.

Seed, *monogenes*, alone, *monos*, into the earth, **you must be born again,** the plant, **you in Me and I in you,** seeds, many, *tikto*, coming out of the womb, **and her child was caught up to God and to His throne.**

Seed – plant – seeds. That's how the whole thing works.

The Nicene Creed and Christianity puts it thus: Seed – ticketed sinners – bliss someday.

Yes, the Seed is the same EXCEPT with His heart ripped right out of Him.

Yes, that is an appropriate picture. Mel Gibson's *Apocalypto* is both a great movie and an horrific one. It is not for the squeamish, but it's a powerful story filled with truth. In that movie, one is presented with a very vivid picture of Mayan priests tearing the hearts out of the human sacrifices.

And so the church has done to Jesus, ripped His heart right out of Him, right out of their whole picture.

It is awful. It is, in fact, the greatest of the Nicene crimes, ripping the heart right out of God by ripping it out of themselves and offering it up to Self-for-self, the appearance of the serpent as God.

We never see the word *monogenes*, only begotten, without its full match, *prototokos*, first born.

I desire. Let's allow (never make) our heart to be Jesus' heart; that is, call it to be so all the time regardless. To rip His heart out of ourselves is to rip His heart out of Him.

Jesus lives in our hearts as DESIRE, desire first to live as us, and by living as us, by carrying utterly all that we are in Himself, and desire, second, that causes us to be – *ginomai* – just like Himself in every conceivable way. That's why Paul said, **"Do not ever lose your heart, but keep it with all diligence."** Our heart and Jesus' heart are the same thing, the throne of heaven, upon which we sit in Him. — Desire.

This interplay of *monogenes* to (not)*mono*, then to *prototokos*, seed-plant-seeds, is very telling.

Prototokos, firstborn. *Proto* is the Greek word meaning first and foremost. *Tokos* is an inflection of *tikto*, to bring forth a child, as in, **Mary brought forth a newborn son** and **the woman brought forth a manchild.**

Here are the uses of *prototokos* as referring to Jesus' resurrection.

For whom He foreknew, He also predestined to be conformed to the image of His Son, that He might be the firstborn among many brethren. Romans 8:29

He is the image of the invisible God, the firstborn over all creation. – And He is the head of the body, the church, who is the beginning, the firstborn from the dead, that in all things He may have the preeminence. Colossians 1:15 & 18 (two times)

But you have come. . . to the general assembly and church of the firstborn who are registered in heaven, to God the Judge of all, to the spirits of just men made perfect. . . Hebrews 12:23

Grace to you and peace. . . from Jesus Christ, the faithful witness, the firstborn from the dead, and the ruler over the kings of the earth. To Him who loved us and washed us from our sins in His own blood. . . Revelation 1:5

Every Greek "dictionary" attempts to define *prototokos*, firstborn, by the prejudice of the Nicene Creed and the opposite of Paul's so obvious context in Romans 8 and Colossians 1. They make it a part of God's definition, separate from "man," and turn their backs on what the context says.

They all assume that "preeminence" means DIFFERENT. Nothing is preeminent except AMONG it's own kind. A large starfish is preeminent over smaller starfish, but it cannot be preeminent over a spark plug. No one would claim that a starfish is preeminent over spark plugs.

That He might be the firsborn, the *prototokos*, among many brethren can mean one thing only. Jesus is the first One of our kind, our *genes*. Jesus, the *monogenes*, the alone Seed, when He walked this earth, did not ever want to be alone, *monos*, but rather chose to drink the Father's cup, becoming us. He did so for one reason only, that He, the *monogenes* in our hearts THROUGH whom we live, might also be the *prototokos*, the first One of our kind, that we might, in all possible ways, be just like Him, conformed, *symmorphos*, become us becoming Him, into the image of *Theos Huios*.

Now where is that in the Nicene Creed? And do you see why I always place Romans 8:29 as the most important verse in the Bible. If we don't have that DESIRE and Heart of God – Motive – as the definition of everything else in the Bible or in the universe, then we cannot know anything as it is.

I want to get at something; that is, I want to take a sword and cut clean through two very different things. Here on one side is Jesus, the Christ of God, the Son of God, a Man filled with God, God revealed, God showing up in the earth. On the other side is the specific anointing for a specific ministry Jesus was given to fulfill. Here is a place where some say, well, the Man is Jesus, but the ministry is Christ. NO!!

The ministry was a ministry, neither Jesus nor Christ.

Here is a little old lady. She is confined to her bed or a wheelchair. She cannot speak. She loves Jesus with all her heart, lying upon her bed, worshipping Him. She intercedes in what she knows for others, but the only sign of outward ministry is the smile upon her face. She is anointed by God for the ministry of loving Jesus, of being an intercession for those she loves, and of smiling.

She is JUST LIKE Jesus in every possible way – except for the nature of her particular outward ministry.

There are diversities of gifts, but the same Spirit. There are differences of ministries, but the same Lord. And there are diversities of activities, but it is the same God who works all in all. 1 Corinthians 12:4-6

This seems so obvious now as we spell it out; the ministry, the activity, is not the man or woman.

IDENTITY! Who we are does not come out of what we do.

We CANNOT know Jesus, who and what He was and is, and thus we cannot know how we are just like Him by looking at any part of that outward ministry of His pertaining to preparing a people for the day of Pentecost.

Yet everyone I know, when they say "like Jesus" creates an image of an outward performer, outward power, outward zapping, outward shebang! It is, in fact, idolatry.

Outward zapping, discharging lightning bolts, healing the sick and raising the dead in an outward, temporal manner, as Jesus did, has nothing whatsoever to do with "being like Jesus."

Jesus did not heal the sick or raise the dead as a performance of outward reality. Everyone whom He healed got sick again. Everyone whom He raised from the dead died again. It was not nearly as awesome as people imagine. Nothing was different; the universe stayed the same. Jesus did those things for one reason only: to prepare a people for the day of Pentecost.

Did God send us into the world to prepare a people for the day of Pentecost? Pentecost already happened, June 5, AD 29. God sent us into the world to prepare a people for the Day of Tabernacles. And that is something entirely different.

We can speak of Passover and Pentecost by personal knowledge and experience, but not Tabernacles. In exactly the same way, Jesus could not speak of either Passover or Pentecost except obliquely; that is, He spoke entirely out from His present purpose, that is, preparing Himself for the first and a people for the second. And that is how we must speak of Tabernacles!

So when we say – What is Christ Jesus? – we must not look at His "gifts," His "ministries," His "activities," as Paul described the various workings of the Holy Spirit, but rather at the God who fills and works all in all. Thus, in knowing what is Christ Jesus, we look only at the Man, not at His particular ministry. And we look at the Man as a growing unfolding; that is, we see Him at age 29, wrestling with his little brother, then we see Him in His human actions, visiting with a Samaritan woman, taking children in His arms to bless them, getting down on His knees to wash His disciples' feet. But that develops much further as Jesus walks across the brook Kidron into Gethsemane. Jesus walked the Path of the Atonement entirely as a Man. That is, entirely as the Revelation of God.

Jesus knew no one could hear Him, including His disciples. He did not waste His time trying to cause something that could not be to happen. He did not waste His time trying to alter God's purpose or present human reality. Jesus did not teach so that the people would understand Him. He did not do miracles so that the people would know He was "the Christ of God." His teaching and His miracles were for ONE purpose alone, and that was to prepare a people on both sides of the Day of Pentecost, to prepare His disciples as those who would speak Him, and to prepare a people who would hear the apostles speak Christ. No one heard Jesus until the Day of Pentecost, and Jesus did not ever imagine that they did.

I now understand God's purpose through us as never before; we come out of the womb running. Christ Jesus is one thing alone to us: our life, and as our Life, our Salvation. **We are saved by His life.**

Those who insist on defining and separating God and man, as if they are two divorced and irreconcilable things live only in their intellects, in the imagination of minds turned away from Him. We see Jesus alone, and in seeing Jesus, we see that, by His very nature, in His essence and being, God and man are forever married. As God and man are married, fully and without outward distinction, in Jesus, so we are just like Him.

When you see a Man, you are seeing God, God revealed. And if you ever get a chance to see God? Surprise! You are seeing a Man, God revealed.

Look in the mirror, see God and yourself, married fully and forever, and by so doing you are transformed into all the glory and image of Christ Jesus.

9. Man

There is one God the Father and one mediator between God and man, the Man, Christ Jesus. 1 Timothy

I received an email recently; someone must have read a line I placed on Facebook saying that anything we say about Jesus, we must also say about us. Of course, I was speaking entirely out of marriage union, out of Christ as our new and only Self, out of **put on the Lord Jesus Christ.**

The man said, "Jesus is God; I am not God." (I do not have his exact words because I will not allow darkness to speak at me.) But then the man said something like, "I must know; do you say that Jesus is God or not?"

I did reply to him, saying very briefly. **"You are dead – Christ who is our life."** I told him I will not play intellectual tiddlywinks with anyone. I received an immediate reply, then erased all of it without opening the reply. I am neither Savior nor Salvation, though He lives through me; I am so glad that I am not responsible for anyone's darkness. Nehemiah's story holds me in good stead; I will not leave my place on the wall to come down to the temple to discuss "truth" with people who love their imaginative construct they call "God," but who would also kill the real God should He show up again in the earth.

Normally, I wait to reply to anything, for good reason. I never judge myself, there is no "myself" to judge. But I am seeing more and more the vital reality of **"He opened not His mouth to speak."** Even though my reply was brief and "true," I would, now, maybe, have replied with only one line.

"Sir, you try to drive a wedge between my Savior and me, something you are incapable of doing."

The title of this article is "Man."

What is man? There is only one possible answer to that question. The Lord Jesus Christ. If it ain't the Lord Jesus Christ, it ain't man.

People sometimes call Jesus the second Adam. God does not want a second Adam. God had enough of Adam and will have no more. Jesus is the last Adam, rather, and the second man. Here is how I understand that reality as God meant it through Paul in 1 Corinthians 15.

The first man [the first Adam – the last Adam] the second man.

Look carefully at that first bracket. That first bracket is the very moment Adam's teeth pierced the fruit of knowledge. Look carefully at that last bracket. That last bracket is the very second Jesus departed from His body of the likeness of sinful flesh.

Adam is no more. Adam lasted almost exactly four thousand years; he is no more. Those who live as if they are still Adamic live in that which already is not.

Now, look at the entire space found between the two brackets. No man is found there except Jesus in His transitional role. Yet that transitional role is not the Man Paul describes in 1 Timothy. The Man, Christ Jesus, Paul refers to there is Jesus as He is now, the resurrected Christ, filling our hearts with His glory. It is the fullness of Man, Christ Jesus, that He, living as us, is causing us to become.

We have the hopes of becoming, very very soon, real human beings in outward manifestation, the new man.

I do not like the phrase Jesus *"had to"* die. It is incongruous with the word God speaks. Jesus did not *"have to"* die, but Adam did. Jesus' death was not "Christ dying," but Adam dying. Christ Jesus was not born "to die"; He was born to bring an end to Adam.

At the very second that Jesus **"gave up the ghost,"** Adam ceased.

Man, the second man, is Who came out of the grave, that is, you and I inside of Jesus. Our humanity has ZERO relationship with Adam; it cannot. Therefore, if we are humans, we are entirely of the Man, Christ Jesus.

What is Man?

It is clear to me that in this series, especially, I have gone far beyond the pale of accepted Christian thinking. I am not ignorant of my folly; I know that I am beside myself for Christ's sake, as Paul said of himself.

Therefore let us go forth to Him, outside the camp, bearing His reproach. Hebrews 13:13

But you know what? The world is mad. I see raving madness everywhere I look. Christians are insane. A "Christian" Texas congressman warned the nation that the "curse" of Genesis 12 will come upon America if we do not support Israel in every possible way including its lust to murder Iranians.

Say what??!!!

One third of the Bible is written against the government of Israel in its wicked deeds. John the Baptist got his head chopped off, and Jesus crucified, because they openly opposed the wicked deeds of the government of Israel. Yes, there is a curse, but it's not from the blessing of Abraham, but that of Jeremiah against a nation that rejected the Lord Jesus Christ, that the nation and government of Israel would be a curse to all the world.

And where, in the Bible, does God ever suggest to Israel that they should rely on weapons of war and on Egypt (or the United States) for their deliverance?

Madness; they're all mad. Let us also be as bonkers as the rest of them.

Let us accept ourselves, as we are right now, as the revelation of Almighty God. And in the joy of that acceptance, in the knowing of the Holy Spirit, God reveals Himself through us.

God designed me as an interesting marriage of imagination and reason. At the same time that I lived in endless fantasy worlds of imagination, I also designed and built buildings of many types, leading crews large and small in the utterly practical arena of construction. I have never been subject to addiction. I know the difference between wondrous fantasy and specific reality and have never confused the two.

I am a weak and vulnerable man, desperately in need of both Savior and Salvation. I will not create my own religion; what mindless folly that would be. I cannot stay in "Christianity"; what emptiness of soul, void of God present, here, and personal in me.

But I find now that the "mind" that once created endless fantasy worlds in which to live, no longer connects with such. Now, that same mind sees the heavens all around us, sees the realms of Spirit, sees God who is invisible. In complete contrast, these secular college courses require me to drop into a strictly rational mind void of personal interest. I can do that, with minimal effort and time to spit out what I must, but I hate it. Rather, I find the rational side of my brain would far rather contend with what God actually says in His Word concerning Christ my only life.

And so the two minds are fused together in me now, on the one hand to know the realms of Spirit as they exist all around us, working always on the outward realities of earth, on the other hand to know all that God actually says in the Covenant I signed with Him concerning Christ my only life.

Word and Spirit always together as One, with Life pulsing continually inside of me, groaning to come forth.

I am saying these things about myself for a very definite purpose.

What is Man? **The Man Christ Jesus**: what is Man?

Therefore let us go forth to Him, outside the camp, bearing His reproach.

By striking such a blow against the Nicene Creed, I have severed myself from "Christianity," though "Christians" think that because I engage myself with the Lord Jesus Christ, they have a right to some sort of control over me.

Thus, when I see dear believers in Jesus, you who read these letters, whom I love, witnessing to what I write, I know that God has led you outside the camp as well. I know that I have had nothing, really, to do with that. You find yourself outside the pale because you love Jesus, because you say, "Yes," to Him, and because He led you here.

But as a rational man, I must share with you the reality of where we stand. Look around. This is the place of sacrifice; it is the killing grounds.

No one tolerates God in the flesh.

Bearing His reproach. Christians, typically, do not bear His reproach, not in our world. Those who say, "Jesus and I are one," do.

As a boy, I grew up with my dad's copy of the Mennonite book, Martyr's Mirror. As a young boy, those stories and the black and white pictures accompanying some of them entered deep inside of me. I want to combine a picture and a line from a martyr of Jesus. The picture is of John, banished to Patmos. The line is from one of John's disciples,

John, banished to Patmos.

Polycarp made this comment to his persecutor, just before he was burned at the stake. "I have now served my Lord Christ Jesus eighty-six years, and He has never done me any harm. How can I deny my King, who hath hitherto preserved me from all evil, and so faithfully redeemed me."

This image and this line have come to me as I contemplate the present reality of where we now find ourselves, outside the camp, here in the killing grounds.

Now, let's come at Man from a different angle.

For years, I was taught to "hear" from God and to obey His voice. I was taught to yield myself to His will and to follow Him. This all sounded very Biblical EXCEPT – God was completely other. God was over there, I was over here; this God over there was "above me," looking down on me and testing me to see if I would prove myself worthy, or whatever this distant God expected of me.

I followed this "God" into mind-numbing ruin and loss.

Now, it is true that the God who loves me and who always carries me had great purpose in all He allowed me to go through, and I give Him all thanks. But it is also true that He wanted to alter my knowing of Him.

God is not out to prove us – what a ridiculous endeavor. I mean really, how stupid of an idea can people come up with? We are proven unmitigated failures. We can't do it. Yes, God wants us to learn that, so He allows us to beat our heads bloody against brick walls until we just stop.

Until we shut up and just stop it.

But God is not out to prove us; He is out to prove Himself in all that He speaks.

When I left move community in 1998, moving into Fort St. John, British Columbia, I made a firm resolve inside myself. My resolve was simply to direct my own life without "trying to discover the will of God." I hardened myself against witness for or against or any lack thereof. I followed what was in my heart, stepping through doors that opened and turning away from doors that closed, trusting that God directed my ways without my needing to go through any contortions of – *"am I missing God?"*

That resolve was very much a part of God rescuing me from mental illness.

For fifteen years, now, I have completely avoided the question, "God, what do YOU want me to do; where do YOU want me to go." A huge part of why I have avoided that question has been the underlying terror that "God" would make me go back under move covering in a move community where I will be required to *"just die, brother,"* including a complete repudiation of my knowledge of Christ as me and all of my present ministry. You see, the entire environment in which I ever knew *"seek the will of God and not your own,"* was inside of *"submit to the ministry and just die."*

It is fall again, here in Houston. Autumn, with the browning of the leaves and the nip in the wind, always carries a deep nostalgia for me, a sense of wanderlust, a need to see mountains again. My family and I are in an untenable situation as are most of you who read this. When the system shuts down, and it's on the verge of doing so, there is no food, but there are millions of people all around who will need food now, whatever it takes.

Meanwhile I am attempting to find a way to support my family completely separate from my own true heart. I live always in God, and Christ lives as me, in all I find myself to be. But I would rather be in the midst of all that my heart knows is God than in the empty shadows of this empty world. Some have a ministry to others to sustain them; I do not except sending out what I write.

So, this morning I'm looking at properties again, all of which cost millions against the $250 in my bank account. I pause, saddened by the emptiness even of properties that do not contain the present Spirit of God (I love to explore, though, even if only on Google maps). In my pause, the thought comes, "God where do YOU want me to go?" Followed by, "God, what do YOU want me to do?"

It has been more than fifteen years since I have asked such a question from the depths of my spirit. BUT! What a world of difference. A universe of difference.

What is (male/female) man?

This God to whom I am addressing myself is entirely in me, in full communion with me utterly inside of full union with me. The full union is Christ as me;

thus I am utterly tucked into Him. But God is also in me as Himself, that is, as communion. And as Himself, this God who fills me full is utterly responsible for all things, especially all things concerning me.

We walk together, God and I, in sweet communion inside of Christ as me.

"Pre-eminent" means that He is in underlying essence the lead; "of His same kind" means that I am just like Him, Christ as me. "Love" means we highly regard one another in all ways, eye to Eye, heart to Heart.

God has no intentions of forcing me back under move covering. Yet in my present place, I am not singing in that which God made me to be. When I am in the place of His singing, I will be in the place where I sing.

It is inside this knowledge of God, then, that I look at the words of Jesus in red text in the gospel of John. Oh, how my heart sings by those words. It is like harmonic ringing, like the same DNA. I know those words, they speak of me. They speak of all that I am in God and all that God is, now, in me and flowing out from me. Yet they are never divorced from Jesus, my Savior, upon whose breast I always lean my head.

We sing those words together. They speak of me as they speak of Him; they speak of Him as me; they speak of Him in me; they speak of me. I say them as myself; Christ is in my mouth. — I am a man.

Then I look over at the tree of knowledge and understand the killing grounds.

The two things spoken against me recently are of particular note. The first, which I shared earlier, *"Yordy, God does just about everything apart from you. He needs no human consent. Nice that your setting creation free; got some people who need a miracle. Go at it."* And the second, which I presented at the start of this letter, both of these are of a very specific spirit.

The harsh accusation is identical in spirit and in word to the voice of the Pharisees against Jesus as He hung from the cross. The second, a whining question, is identical in spirit and in word to the questions the Pharisees and others threw at Jesus in order to trap Him.

Look at the question. *"Is Jesus God? What do you say? I need to know."*

Do we pay taxes to Caesar? What do you say? We need to know.

It's a simple trick, used by all pollsters. Phrase the question so that any possible answer will go in a pre-desired direction, each of which is a wonderful trap.

So, if I say, "Yes, Jesus is God." Then they say, *"Okay, you CANNOT be like Him, blasphemer."* If I say, "Jesus is not God, thus I can be like Him," then they say, *"Heretic and false teacher, you are damned to hell."* If I refuse to answer, they say, *"See, Yordy knows he's a liar; he knows we're right. He can't give a straight answer; he's hiding his denial and emptiness."*

The point, of course, is not the foolish psychological trap, but the spirit that demands that its speakers set up that trap against me. This is the importance of **"He opened not His mouth."**

The world does not know us because it did not know Him. 1 John 3

Peter said, **"All who live godly in Christ Jesus will suffer persecution."** I have always wondered at that, since we, who do our best to be good Christians, have been completely tolerated by the world and are not persecuted. Now I know that Christianity has always read it wrong. Peter really meant, **"All who live God-ly in Christ Jesus will suffer persecution."** Those who try to be godly fit right into the world's mould.

When we say, "I am filled with all the fullness of God," when we say, "I am just like Jesus in all ways right now," when we say, "I am one with the Lord Jesus Christ – He that has seen me has seen Jesus the Christ," suddenly we have become a terrifying, deadly threat. We have become the lights turning on.

No one allows God in the flesh. No one tolerates God showing up on planet Earth.

If you want to see full and completely unity in this world, just be God in the flesh. Everyone will come together to be of one heart and purpose – to send God back to "heaven" where He belongs.

Don't be fooled. The spirit behind these two recent accusations is a spirit of murder.

These things I command you, that you love one another. If the world hates you, you know that it hated Me before it hated you. If you were of the world, the world would love its own. Yet because you are not of the world, but I chose you out of the world, therefore the world hates you... But all these things they will do to you for My name's sake, because they do not know Him who sent Me... that the word might be fulfilled... 'They hated Me without a cause.'" John 15:17-23

Even though I seem to be jumping all around in this letter, I really am driving hard at one very specific thing. — Purpose. We cannot know – What is man? – without knowing purpose.

You see, it's not me; it's the God who lives in me. He's the One sneaking into this present scene. People have no problem with me; it's God they're tracking down with pitchforks and torches in hand. If I say, "Hey, it's just me, God's nowhere around," they'll leave me alone. I'll be okay.

But if I say, "He that has seen me has seen the Father," the pitchforks go through me to get at Him.

So, you see, now when I say, "God where do YOU want me to go? God, what do YOU want me to do," I am speaking to this God who fills me full. And He is

One determined Dude. At this moment in human history, this God who fills me full, this God who has seized me in His grip to reveal Himself through me, is, shall we say, as narrow-minded as One can be. He has one purpose, one focus, one intent, and He will have what He DESIRES.

There is one way only by which we can know – What is a man? We must look at Jesus. In my last letter, I posited that Jesus KNEW that not one thing He did or said would have any present results, that is, not anything real, not anything that would actually change people's lives.

Jesus knew that before Him was a set path. He knew that the real results, that is the birthing of His church, would not come through Him but through His disciples. Yet in the present moment they were a weight and liability only, bumbling, foolish, and wrong.

A woman, when she is in labor, has sorrow because her hour has come; but as soon as she has given birth to the child, she no longer remembers the anguish, for joy that a MAN has been born into the world. John 16

More than once, Jesus insinuated to His disciples that He could not tell them what we now know as Paul's gospel. He could not tell them, because they were not born again, they were not filled with the Holy Spirit, and He could not yet live as them.

Jesus faced a definite path ahead of Him; we face a similar path. If Jesus had not traversed His *monogenes* path, then the outcome, that is, the birthing of His church on the Day of Pentecost, could not have been.

For 2,000 years, Jesus has been the Plant, His church, living as us in this world. Outwardly, nothing has changed in the world. Demons continue to scream, wicked men continue to rule, and people continue to suffer.

On the third day, He will rise again, this time as a many-membered body, many sons to glory. He will do so through us by a second, very similar and very definite PATH.

I'm getting right at – What is (male/female) man? WHAT are you?

Jesus did not *"have to"* die.

Why am I trying to get a full-time job as a college teacher? Because I must provide for my family. Why does this prospect feel so empty to me? I can do it; I will do it. Unless. Yet I must get my family into a real place; I would not have my children continue one more day in the public school if I could but provide.

I am a teacher; I am filled with Word and a knowledge of the revelation of Jesus Christ. God's people by the millions NEED to sit under the teaching that LONGS with ALL desire to flow out through me. Why could this not provide for my family?

Yet I am so foolish, and I don't know how. And I so easily get all bent out of shape when my brethren say or do such foolish, non-Christ things. I have to bring everything into rest inside of me, but sometimes it takes hours of sleeplessness.

"God, what do YOU want me to do; God, where do YOU want me to go?"

Jesus did not *"have to"* die. He died so that He could become me. He died so that I could become Him.

Jesus laid down His life for me. I am His close and dear friend.

What is Man? — A Man lays down his life for His friends, just like God.

What is man? — A man lays down his life for his friends.

There is no knowing of these words except by those who live utterly in the God who fills them with all that He is in Person. We do not know the outer perimeters of our path, but we know its heart.

My brethren will NOT get it. No matter how much they read my letters and say, "Amen," they will not get it – until I lay down my life for them. I am not speaking of physical death, but of something Holy in God.

This goes in both directions; I do not raise myself superior to you. I will not "get it" until you lay down your life for me.

All the other stuff is worthless, meaningless, and going nowhere.

Now, I do not say the above because of any desire for an outward ministry of teaching these things I write; the writing is sufficient. I say it, rather, out of the travail of my soul and out of my present very real need. My real desire is to provide a particular type of school for children (parents are welcome to) as a place of safety and the full expression of their hearts.

But no church, no enterprise will be God in the earth unless the core leadership is always laying down their lives for the brethren. And that does NOT mean telling people what to do. It means always willing to lose everything, always willing to allow, even to encourage Christ to be who He is through others, even if that means continually letting go of personal hopes and expectations.

Almost all humans cannot be a guide while refusing to be master. There is something in the judge God created us as that wants to insist that my "wisdom," my hearing, my "in" with God is "God" to you and that since I am the leader here, you must submit to me and thus submit to God.

Read *A Tale of Three Kings* by Gene Edwards.

When a man has a vision of "the city of God," he will seek "volunteers" who will help him fulfill that vision. At first the volunteers are willing, because everything is exciting and new, but before long Christ asserts Himself as them, and the leader now has a choice. Almost all choose to call those who have a different idea, "the devil" and not Christ; they then use every trick known to man to coerce their "vision," that it might not fail or be sullied by these "rebellious heretics." The most evil trick in the church is to claim that *"obeying me because I have the vision,"* is obeying God.

In the world, it always ends with murder.

Very few will allow Christ to be who He is in others or will quietly walk away from all the labor of their hands and all their substance and dreams and hopes if they know the thing has become wrong, without casting any blame on anyone.

David did. — And Jesus. — Few others.

But here's the thing. A laid-down-life and love-poured-out does not happen when the challenge comes. It is God in us now; it is present from the start, as rivers of life.

A few days ago, I happened upon a conversation among precious brethren with whom I associate. They were attempting to control another brother in the Lord, a man with whom they have no association, by their critical words and by their pronouncement of what Jesus ought to do through this other brother, if He were just as smart as they. I know this way of thinking; it is that which puts its hand to the vision to force others to obey it.

Needless to say, I was deeply distressed by this conversation. And that is where life-laid-down proves itself. I have three options in response.

1. Attempt to control these brethren who are, in my estimation, "acting wrongly." And control has many devices at hand; I certainly thought of a number of such devices.

2. Ignore it and walk away, washing my hands of these brethren and having nothing more to do with them.

3. Lay down my life for them, for my friends, that is, be a man.

But how do I do that? — A man is filled with God.

You see, if they are "wrong" for declaring that their brother is NOT Christ as him, then how am I "right" by seeing their actions NOT as Christ as them?

Jesus drew all wrong into Himself, causing it all to cease upon the cross; Jesus is now our Life forevermore.

The revelation of Jesus Christ begins at home. Since I am filled with all the fullness of Love, the very Mercy Seat of heaven, I draw them into love upon my heart, seeing Christ as them in spite of my own judgment. I do not correct them; I do not ignore them; I love them.

That is, I draw them into Love, into the One who fills me with His glory.

I would be a man; I would lay down my life for my friends.

10. Church

Except a grain of wheat fall into the ground and die it abides alone. But if it die, it brings forth much fruit. John 12:24

It is true that we are light in this world and in the church; our desire to know God turns the lights on. Light and truth are for showing things as they are, exposing what IS.

Thus, this series, in exploring the meaning of "Church" in the context of defeating the Nicene Creed, must ask the most basic of questions. We have asked, "What is God," "What is Man," "What is Christ Jesus," but we have failed to ask the most pertinent question.

What Is? – Light reveals what IS. To expose means to place things out where they can be seen. What Is? – If we are caused to see all things as they really are, what do we see?

If I look at myself, at my flesh, to see myself as I really am, in all honesty of heart and sobriety of conscience what do I see? If I look at you, at your flesh, to see you as you really are, in all honesty of heart and sobriety of conscience what do I see?

What IS? – I'm actually trying to get right at "What is Church?"

The Nicene Creed says this: *"I believe in one, holy, catholic and apostolic Church."* That's good as far as it goes, but words on paper and ideas in the brain are not real. Only Spirit reality is real, that is, God in Person here and now, and only what God actually says.

What is Church? Let me give the short answer. Church IS the Lord Jesus Christ, in substance Himself in all fullness, in appearance as many in weakness.

The Church is One Person for real – the Lord Jesus.

This One Person, the Church, APPEARS as many persons in outward form, yet at no point is any tiny particle of the Church, any least little member, anything other than the Person of Jesus. We ARE His body, the visible appearance of His Person, and members in particular.

Now, we understand the laws of physics as science. And when I say physics as science, I refer only to those practical, well-known by continual use, laws of the physical sciences. In exactly the same way, we understand the laws of spirit as science. Just as there is no whimsical judgment in physics, so there is no whimsical judgment in spirit. If you violate the laws of physics, you die. If you violate the laws of spirit, you die. No one blames God if someone dies because they were driving drunk, tried to beat a train, and got creamed. The person violated the laws of physics and suffered the consequences. There was nothing "personal" taking place.

The laws of spirit are the same. Many of the things Jesus said in particular were not religious, but scientific. A huge misconception of religion is that God up there arbitrarily makes whimsical decisions by judgments no one understands as to what happens to individual persons, who goes up and who goes down.

For instance, **"Seek and you will find."** God does not sit up there somewhere and decide whether you have "sought enough," or "sought in the right way," before He "allows" you now to find. God is not like that at all. Jesus was simply stating a scientific law of spirit. Everyone finds precisely what they seek. What have you found? You have found exactly what you are seeking; you are receiving precisely what you want. There is nothing personal involved. Those who expect God know God. Those who don't expect God know everything else but God.

Jesus said, **"Many are called, but few are chosen."** John saw those who were called, chosen, and faithful. This is absolutely true; the question for us then is, – HOW is it true. This is not a religious judgment, but a law of spirit science. Yet most people approach it as a religious judgment. In other words, most think one of two things. Some think, *"Well, I guess I just don't know whether I'll be one of those who are faithful; I just don't know if I'll make it."* Others think, *"Got it, God, watch me, I'll prove to you that I am FAITHFUL."*

Both these have turned Jesus' words into performance, the second as self-righteousness, the first as unbelief. Yet it has nothing to do with performance, but rather, what do you want? Faith comes only out of desire.

There is a third response. That third response says, "I know already that I cannot measure up, but I cannot be anywhere else, Jesus, than with You, in that last category of faithful. And so, Lord Jesus, by Your Word in my mouth, I declare that I AM faithful and true, with You now in all of Your glory. I simply cannot be found anywhere else." You see, in this third response there is no thought of performance or of falling short. Only faith coming out of true desire. And that is the only thing that pleases God. Everything else is sin.

But right now I am concerned with Church. What is Church? Church is found for us in the seeing of the eyes. Church is Christ Jesus, yes, but for us, Church or not Church is found in the seeing of our eyes.

Jesus said something that sounds like arbitrary judgment on the part of God, a judgment applied entirely to – what is Church. But we remember that He later said that all of His talk about God was figurative.

And his master was angry, and delivered him to the torturers until he should pay all that was due to him. So My heavenly Father also will do to

you if each of you, from his heart, does not forgive his brother his trespasses. Matthew 18:34-35

This is, of course, the parable of the unforgiving servant, the one who was forgiven much, then turned and punished his neighbour for owing him little.

I do not want to fill this letter with verses on seeing, but I will give an explanation of the laws of seeing based entirely on specific verses; you will likely think of some of them.

The first law of seeing is simple: the complete acceptance in all humility and in all certainty that we are blind, we cannot see. Those who say, *"I see,"* are sealed in their blindness. Only those who rest in the utter certainty of being blind will ever hope to learn to see.

The reason we cannot see is we are blind, literally. Our spirit eyes are covered over with a thick skin similar to a cataract. That is the skin God put upon Adam and Eve in the garden. Yes, it is taken off in Christ, but we must understand what "in Christ" means. I am convinced that "in Christ" has one definition only. "In Christ" means being inside a Person, Jesus, and seeing out only through His eyes in the full knowledge of being "in Him" in all ways. The greatest honor given to Jesus is those who believe that He is true even when they are blind.

So, we are blind because there is a heavy obstruction over our spirit eyeballs. Thus when we "see" in an outward manner, we see ONLY a reflection of ourselves. You and I have never SEEN another person; we have only ever seen ourselves as we "look" in the direction of other people.

Thus, when Jesus said, **"Judge not lest you be judged,"** He was not speaking of arbitrary decisions of God based on our performance. He was speaking of a simple, but absolute, law of spirit science.

When you and I look at others to "see" them, we cannot see anything but ourselves. Thus, if we don't like what we see, we speak judgment against our brother and sister. We speak at them concerning our own failings, yet we wrongfully assume that our own failings, the only thing we can see, somehow belong to our brother or sister, when in fact, what we see has zero relationship with them. We speak only of ourselves, yet we call our own condemnation of our self "them." They are just busy tootling along, and our description of our self with their name forced on it, hurled at them, completely sidelines them. Wow, where did that come from?

The gift of discernment is a discernment of spirits, not a source of information, the "low-down," on other people.

So, when Jesus said, **"My heavenly Father will do to you,"** I simply cannot read that as God sitting up there doing arbitrary things at people based on their outward performance. Rather, I see it entirely as a spirit law.

And this should not be a strange concept. Heaven and earth are continually and intrinsically related at every point. We learn and are taught as we grow up to respect and to use the laws of physics by which to live; spirit is a realm just like physical is a realm, closely related, sharing great similarities, though also great differences. Thus to learn and be taught to respect and to use the laws of spirit by which to live should be the same. No one becomes religious because they leave the pan on high heat and the soup is burned. In the same way, we should not become religious about the simple laws of spirit.

But this law goes in both directions. I see Christ living as me, I see me carried utterly in Him, I see Him revealing Himself through every nuance of the human me, stumbling, foolish, and so often wrong. If this is true, then, in looking "at" you, I also see me. That is, I also see you so wonderfully tucked into Jesus, so much so that, by gum, I have to keep myself from falling on my face to worship you, because you are altogether glorious. Yet we walk heart in heart, comfortable and close, knowing Who it is we both really love.

Those who reach out to "correct" others by outward appearance are doing nothing more than groping their own false self. Jesus said, "**You judge according to the flesh.**" You judge by outward appearance and NOT by real substance. He meant, "You are judging only your false self."

It is astonishing. When a corrector begins to "correct" others in a fellowship of believers, those who truly know the Lord are simply amazed. It is so plain that this corrector is talking only of him or herself, yet foisting their own judgment of self upon others as if the problem is the others and not the false self.

Let me give the absolute law of all church. **Whatever you do**, say, see, feel, or do **to others you ARE doing it to Me.** Notice the "doing to." Church is doing things with each other; not-Church is doing things to each other.

My next letter is "Father." Part of Father is these words of Jesus, "**In My Father's house are many dwelling places.**" Father is so big and He has so many, many, many different appearances.

There is one sin in the church, one sin that you and I could commit, even though we subscribe to the testimony of Christ as me. That sin is to say with one breath, "Christ as me," and then to turn and, seeing Christ as someone utterly, utterly different from me, not recognize Christ, but see only our own false self and thus declare, *"Hey, you have to be like me, you have to fulfill my calling, you have to find my expression of God BEFORE I will accept that Christ is as you."*

That sin will turn every part of "Christ as me" into lying in our mouth.

Now I see that I must write about the nature of scorn as it works inside every gathering of believers. Yet I can write such an account only by tears of sorrow, by life laid-down, and by love poured-out.

In this world of vanity into which our Father has placed us, we cannot know **Father,** except we also, in full measure, deal openly with scorn. Scorn is insidious; it hides itself in common human talk. One of the several specific and deliberate reasons why I chose to leave move community is that I came to the place where I could no longer walk with scorn. I could not walk with scorn as others because I could no longer live with scorn in me.

When I see scorn, not as human foolishness, but as deep-rooted theology, then I can only get as far away as I can as fast as I can. It is not any judgment of others; it's simply God.

~

Jesus IS Lord. We ARE His body.

What is? — Jesus IS. We do not make Him so. The idea that we could *"make Jesus Lord"* is part of the package Adam bought from the serpent, trading his identity as the image of God in weakness for the outward appearance of the serpent. The idea that we are *"to make ourselves His church"* is in the same package.

John 12:24 does not refer to us, but rather to Jesus alone. Yet, as we abandon all thought of *"our needing to die,"* we discover that Jesus our only life reveals Himself through us in a special way, a God-way, in a laying down of our lives for the brethren. This measure of life poured out comes only out of ALL Fullness now.

What is Church? – Church is NOT a group. One of the destructive forces preventing God's people from knowing the full joy of Church is the idea that church is a group.

Church is not a group; it is the connection between one individual and another individual, eye to eye, heart to heart, in mutual respect and honor. No matter how many people are in a room, all interaction is one person interacting with one other person. The fact that someone speaking is being heard by several at the same time does not remove the simple reality that every single one of those connections is one with one, even though there are several or hundreds of such one-with-one connections happening at the same time.

The one speaking is Christ, the one hearing is Christ, both hearts are Christ; Christ sharing life with Christ.

There is something else that requires a group, that requires an impersonal relationship, replacing the eye to eye with a stream of words separate from a relationship of mutual respect and full recognition of the other. But that something else is not church, and thus not the question of this letter, though it bears upon our experience.

This connection, then, between two individuals, this connection we call, "Church," is Spirit. Think of cell phones. One cell phone cannot communicate with another cell phone except through the "bath" of microwaves filling the atmosphere. Inside that very bath are thousands of separate individual cell phone connections, filled with communication. But your cell phone picks up only those signals sent to it from that one other cell phone, yet entirely inside the larger bath of microwaves containing all.

Thus the Church is that connection happening entirely inside of Spirit. Christ as me is not the connection; Christ as you is not the connection. While the connection, as Spirit, is Christ, it is not Christ as, but simply the Spirit of Christ. Christ as me stops at my perimeter. What goes beyond my perimeter, then, in connecting with others in the Church, can be Christ or it can be something else.

There is one sin that breaks Christ. That sin is manipulating others as if they are not what Christ ought to be. It is sin, straightforward and unforgiven.

You see Church, since it is Spirit, is entirely the nature of Spirit. Spirit is wind; Spirit is dove. A dove leaves the moment there is any sign of commotion. Church leaves the moment it does not exist in the connection between two people. In complete contrast, Christ as my only life is a rock. Rocks stay put; they do not move. Rocks are sure and certain anchors. Regardless of my callous disregard of another person, Christ still carries me.

Thus, manipulation of others, in all of its forms, as it moves out into the pathways of connection from one individual to another, the pathways that are Spirit in which alone Church exists, instantly create not-Church taking place between the one manipulating and the one allowing him or herself to be manipulated. Allowing one's self to be manipulated is as sinful as manipulating. Both are not of faith because both do not come out of Christ.

Now, I must say that I am not speaking of normal bumbling human interaction, normal human frustration and misunderstanding. I am speaking of another spirit. So, the next time you get frustrated and say things to others you shouldn't have said, and then go back and ask forgiveness, all of that is just part of Church. I am speaking of that which never says, "I am wrong," that which never appears in a place of needing forgiveness.

Church is 100% real to the human experience. But there is another spirit that shows up where it does not belong. If you want to see a real example of what I am saying, read Gene Edwards, *A Tale of Three Kings*. Read the Bible account of Absalom and David as well. David would NOT manipulate others; David would NOT allow others to manipulate him. Thus David acted entirely as Christ; he walked away. More on this later.

> **But, speaking the truth in love, may grow up in all things into Him who is the head—Christ—from whom the whole body, joined and knit together by what every joint supplies, according to the effective working by which every part does its share, causes growth of the body for the edifying of itself in love.** Ephesians 4:15-16

Paul gives, here, one of the purest expressions of Church in the Bible. You see that every joint and every part are operating fully as individual to individual before the larger entity of "body" can exist. And inside of this reality called Church, at its core, is the word "speaking."

What do we speak in order to know Church? – **Speaking the truth in love.** What is the truth? You see, it is apparent that we cannot know in experience what is Church unless we know what is truth and unless we actually speak that which is truth inside of and out from the love of God abounding in our hearts.

So, what is truth? Let me bring back in some questions I asked at the beginning of this letter. What Is? – Light reveals what IS. To expose means to place things out where they can be seen. What Is? – If we are caused to see all things as they really are, what do we see?

If I look at myself, at my flesh, to see myself as I really am, in all honesty of heart and sobriety of conscience what do I see? If I look at you, at your flesh, to see you as you really are, in all honesty of heart and sobriety of conscience what do I see?

Now, let's go back to our present reality. When I look at you, all I can "see" is outward appearance. Outward appearance is deceptive, that is, the real fish ain't where you "see" it. The light has bent and the real substance is something entirely different. Substance is entirely in the heavenlies, yet our spirit eyes are quite blind, covered over with cataracts that have a reflective surface on the inside. Thus, what I "see" is entirely my own view of myself as I catch my reflection on the back side of my cataracts. Yet I CALL what I "see" you.

(Again, the Holy Spirit gift of discernment cannot be seeing things "in" another person, but in the heavens. Thus we do not "fix" people, but war in the spirit for others. The most powerful element of that war is the Mercy Seat, our hearts.)

All I have to do is see Christ as me and thus I call you by Christ as you. If I see Christ when I look at me, then, by the same measure, I see Christ when I look at you! Jesus' words could just as readily be translated thus: You judge others by how you judge yourself; you measure others by your measurement of yourself.

Very simply, when I look at myself, at my flesh, to see myself, I see either one of only two things. Either I see Christ by honesty or I see not-Christ by pretending.

Now, not-Christ has a split personality, good and evil, that is, not-Christ is schizophrenic, Gollum and Smeagol, but it's still only one other thing. And Gollum/Smeagol (J.R.R. Tolkein) is a great example. One requires itself to be in control; the other always draws "control me" from others, and you never know which one will show its face next.

Truth is Christ; we speak the truth only as we speak Christ. But truth is Christ in a specific way, that is Christ says, "I am the Truth." Thus we also speak Christ.

As we speak Christ to ourselves, we know the God who fills us with His fullness now. But something different happens when we speak Christ into each other. — Church. — Has there yet been a Church upon this earth? A valid question.

Any form of "you do not measure up to Christ" is speaking not-Christ. Every form of speaking not-Christ is simply self-sight, the judgment of self against self. We say, "self for self," and that has a valid application, but there is just as certainly, "self against self," which might be more descriptive of Adam, in actuality.

What is Church? Church is the Song of the Lamb. Church is one person speaking truth, Christ our only life, into another person and entirely inside of Love, that is entirely inside of GOD who, in His entirety, is inside of us.

Then, inside of speaking Christ into one another, singing the Song of the Lamb, we walk together as foolish and bumbling humans, that is, the image of God in the earth, highly regarding one another, fully compassionate, forgiving one another, and sharing a joy of fellowship, *koinonia*, communion, that is unknown to all other created beings save those honored few who truly know Church.

Friendship, the deepest, deepest of friendship between two, does not create "elitism." And it is here ALONE that Church begins.

Because you see, here's the amazing thing. Church is not Words. Church is not the flow of Spirit. Yes, real Church comes by those things, but it is not those things. Church is not people as in "the group." Church is not form or structure. Yes Church is found in those things, but it is not those things.

Church is the deepest of friendship between two. Now, of all words in the Bible, what one word also shares that definition, "the deepest of friendship between two," at the center of its essence? — Father.

I am a friend of God. — You are a friend of God.

So you see, we cannot know Church without also, in equal measure, knowing Father. And Father, I can assure you, is simply, mind-blowingly incredible.

The parable of the prodigal son — how we have always read it so terribly wrong. Everyone sees the issue of the two sons, back and forth, which son is wrong, both, which son are we, back and forth. We have missed the whole point. The parable has nothing to do with either the prodigal son or the stay-at-home son; it has nothing to do with the receiving or the demanding of sons.

It is Father who fills us full. The Father is who we are; the Father is the One who shows Himself through us. The parable is not about how we react to Father, but how Father reveals Himself through us to ALL of the bumbling foolishness of humanity, no matter on which side they fall.

What is Church? – Church is Christ Jesus planted in the earth as us. Church is Christ as the in-between form. Just as a plant is the in-between form by which a Seed brings forth seeds, so Church is Christ appearing now as something that outwardly does not "look like" Christ, yet is the very form or appearance through which Christ as the *monogenes*, the only begotten, becomes Christ as the many.

When you look at any and every other believer in Jesus, anyone who in some way calls upon His name, any one who in some fashion looks to Him as Savior, you are seeing Jesus as the Plant. Yet in our blindness, we demand that Jesus appear in our brother as Seed, not as plant. Thus we see our brother as "falling short of Christ" because he appears as Christ as Plant, not as Christ as Seed.

Christ as Plant is perfect as a plant. A caterpillar is perfect as a caterpillar. Any caterpillar that tries to act like a butterfly is psychotic. Why? Because as a caterpillar, the caterpillar knows what a caterpillar is and does and functions well as a caterpillar. And of truth, the butterfly, every element of that butterfly including the very DNA, the seed that will form the butterfly, is there inside the caterpillar. But the caterpillar cannot know what a butterfly is; therefore any attempt of the caterpillar to "act like" a butterfly is nothing other than a caterpillar being stupid. No element of the butterfly inside the caterpillar, which truly is a butterfly in caterpillar form, has anything to do with that stupid pretending.

The problem is not the caterpillar. The problem is the caterpillars who, having caught a glimpse of a butterfly through murky eyes, go around telling all the other caterpillars that if they don't stop being caterpillars (*die, brother*) and don't try their best to be butterflies, then the great heavenly butterfly will be displeased with them. Any Christian trying to *"act like Christ"* outwardly in their Christ-as-me state is psychotic, just being stupid.

Christ as me means that I am just real as I am. I accept myself fully. When I do stupid things, I accept my own foolishness fully. When I react in frustration to a brother who is not thinking of me as I am not thinking of him, I accept my own foolishness fully. I laugh as I say, "Oh my, dear brother, forgive me, I was wrong." In the same way I laugh with all joy as I say, "And dear brother, I forgive you for being so thoughtless and so full of religious prickliness."

Christ, laughing together with Christ, friend with friend, one with one in the deepest of friendship, in overflowing and exuberant joy, over the bumbling silliness of being, so obviously caterpillars, that is, Christ as us.

By the way, there is a word in the Bible that also carries that definition, "overflowing and exuberant joy." Can you guess what it is? The answer is in the next chapter, "Father."

Let me give you a definition of Church at its core, in its very center. This is the only place where Church begins. If this definition is not the center of what anyone calls "church," it ain't Church. And here's the thing, this definition is NOT theology, but immediate and practical EXPERIENCE between two.

Notice that Father is in the center of this definition. Church IS:

– Christ, laughing together with Christ, friend with friend, one with one in the deepest of friendship, in overflowing and exuberant joy, over the bumbling silliness of being, so obviously caterpillars, that is, Christ as us. –

Frustration is normal; reacting out of frustration is normal, part of being human, part of being Christ as us.

But let's take this to the larger realm of all who belong to Jesus, the universal and catholic church. Jesus became all that is His church. All. And as all, He is perfect in His doings; Jesus does all things well.

To imagine, for one second, that another believer is "falling short of Christ" is to live in the presumption that Jesus is a stupid jerk who simply does not know what He is doing. That's why He needs someone to "fix" what He has so obviously fallen short in because Jesus, after all, is absent and derelict, but has assigned a "corrector" to be His vicar.

Let me define pope. *"I am responsible over other believers to make sure they 'get it right.'"* Christianity is filled with millions of popes.

Here's the deal. If Christ is as me, then Christ must also be as all who in some way call upon His name. If Christ carries me, He must also carry them. And if Christ is as me, and if they are "doing wrong," then the ONLY answer that could possibly be fully Christ as me would be as I now teach, drawing them into the Mercy Seat of love upon my heart, sprinkled always with Blood, and then I, laying down my life for them as the heavenly revelation of Jesus Christ regardless of earthly appearance.

Christ having become His church MEANS that Christ is doing all things well regardless of any outward appearance.

Church is Jesus Christ planted in the earth as many. Ministry in the church is Christ sharing Christ with one another. When there is sin, we do not engage in any outward atonement of sin – *"Get right with God, brother."* Rather, we draw all into love, laying down our lives for others. But if we must, we quietly walk away.

Ministry is showing Christ by being Christ.

What Is? — Blood, Was-Dead, Resurrection.

What is Church? – Christ Jesus, God revealed, living as us in all we find ourselves to be all the way into life.

When you shine the light of truth on your brother or sister, what do you cause them to see? — Christ who loves you IS your very and only life.

When the lights turn on, when all things are exposed, what do we see for the first time in the history of the universe? We see one thing only. — God.

Yet this God we see IS seen only out from very human humans, being together all that very human humans ARE. — Church!

11. Father

There is One God, the Father. 1 Timothy

The Hebrew word for father is *ab*, the first in its alphabet. "Father" occurs around 175 times in the book of Genesis, though none referring to God. Moses first called God "Father" in Deuteronomy, just before his death at 120 years old.

Do you thus deal with the LORD, O foolish and unwise people? Is He not your Father, who bought you? Has He not made you and established you? Deuteronomy 32:6

God was not called Father again until David. After David was established as king, just before he brought up the Ark of the Covenant into his tent pitched in his back yard, David said this:

A Father of the fatherless, a defender of widows, is God in His holy habitation. God sets the solitary in families; He brings out those who are bound into prosperity... Psalm 68:5-6

Then, as David grew old, approaching death, he asked God about building a temple for the permanent dwelling place of the Ark. God replied to David through Nathan the prophet.

Behold, a son shall be born to you, who shall be a man of rest; and I will give him rest from all his enemies all around. His name shall be Solomon, for I will give peace and quietness to Israel in his days. He shall build a house for My name, and he shall be My son, and I will be his Father; and I will establish the throne of his kingdom over Israel forever.' 1 Chronicles 22:9-10

Ethan the Ezrahite, speaking for Solomon at the height of his glory, spoke of David. It is apparent, though, that Ethan was looking forward to Jesus.

He (David) shall cry to Me, 'You are my Father, My God, and the rock of my salvation.' Also I will make him My firstborn, the highest of the kings of the earth. Psalm 89:26-27

Isaiah was the next who caught a glimpse of "Father."

For unto us a Child is born, unto us a Son is given; and the government will be upon His shoulder. And His name will be called Wonderful, Counselor, Mighty God, Everlasting Father, Prince of Peace. Of the increase of His government and peace there will be no end... Isaiah 9:6-7

This seeing of Isaiah was in his early thirties, not long after God visited him after King Uzziah's death. But in his older years, as Isaiah watched King Manasseh fill Jerusalem with wickedness and with blood, shortly before his own execution by Manasseh, Isaiah saw so much further into Father.

Look down from heaven, and see from Your habitation, holy and glorious. Where are Your zeal and Your strength, the yearning of Your heart and Your mercies toward me? Are they restrained? Doubtless You are our Father, though Abraham was ignorant of us, and Israel does not acknowledge us. You, O Lord, are our Father; our Redeemer from Everlasting is Your name. Isaiah 63:15-16

But we are all like an unclean thing, and all our righteousnesses are like filthy rags. . . And there is no one who calls on Your name, who stirs himself up to take hold of You. . . But now, O Lord, You are our Father; we are the clay, and You our potter; and all we are the work of Your hand. Isaiah 64:6-8

A generation later, Jeremiah warned a faithless Jerusalem.

Therefore the showers have been withheld, and there has been no latter rain. You have had a harlot's forehead; you refuse to be ashamed. Will you not from this time cry to Me, 'My Father, You are the guide of my youth? Will He remain angry forever? Jeremiah 3:3-5

Thirty years later, as Jeremiah knew that his words were not heeded, he looked to a future day in saying:

They shall come with weeping, and with supplications I will lead them. I will cause them to walk by the rivers of waters, in a straight way in which they shall not stumble; for I am a Father to Israel, and Ephraim is My firstborn. Jeremiah 31:9

Ten years later Jerusalem and the temple were destroyed. Father was not known again to Israel except by one sad parting note from Malachi.

Have we not all one Father? Has not one God created us? Why do we deal treacherously with one another by profaning the covenant of the fathers? Malachi 2:10

Jesus first said, "**My Father,**" at age twelve. Throughout the first year of His ministry, He was already stirring up the Pharisees by calling God His Father. But it wasn't until the latter part of His second year of ministry in the sermon on the mount, June, A.D. 27, that it is recorded, for the first time, the words, "**your Father**" and "**Our Father.**"

Suddenly, in a huge blast, God is called "Father" around 265 times in the New Testament. John used "Father" more than any other writer, placing "Father" into Jesus' mouth 53 times in His conversation and prayers in the upper room alone.

I have explored this layout because, I suspect, "Father" is the most important word in the Bible; I wanted to see for myself how it appears in the revelation of God. God fits into no one's box, especially not mine; though He fills our hearts full with all of Himself. In this letter, I hope to give an entirely different view of God than what I have given in prior recent letters, a view of God as Father.

I am in awe of His Glory, like the sheen of many colors flowing through untold multitudes of jewels and precious stones, light in all of its beauty and form. Dazzling. Iridescent. Luxurious. — Father.

It is impossible to say, "the God who fills me full with ALL of Himself," without being utterly overwhelmed.

When we speak of God in general, we say, "God," and we know that He is "good." But when we want to know Him as He really is, we say, "Father."

But the hour is coming, and now is, when the true worshipers will worship the Father in spirit and truth; for the Father is seeking such to worship Him. God is Spirit, and those who worship Him must worship in spirit and truth." John 4:23-24

And we know that the Son of God has come and has given us an understanding, that we may know Him who is true; and we are in Him who is true, in His Son Jesus Christ. This is the true God and eternal life. Little children, keep yourselves from idols. Amen. 1 John 5:19-21

Little children, keep yourselves from idols.

Those who worship God in heaven or God above do not know Him. God is not an idol; He is not an image we place before our eyes.

Those who, seated upon the Throne of heaven, worship the Father who fills them full and who flows out from them, being made visible by them, are the only ones who know Him, who worship Him in Spirit and in Truth.

Travail is that God might be known.

God known is Glory; Father revealed is overflowing Abundance.

Abraham, father of many, was the richest man in the near Middle East. David, a man after God's own heart, was the richest king of his day; half of Solomon's wealth came from David.

Brokenness before God, utter trust in Him, and overwhelming outward abundance go hand in hand.

The clearest picture of Father in the New Testament is the parable of the exuberant father. You haven't heard of that parable? How sad that it has been so badly mis-named. The parable of the exuberant father, found in Luke 15:11-31, is too long to insert here. You can read it in your Bible. Let me underline the central points of the parable.

> A certain FATHER had two sons. And the younger of them said to his FATHER, 'FATHER, give me the portion of goods that falls to me.' So FATHER divided to them his livelihood. – And he arose and came to his FATHER. But when he was still a great way off, his FATHER saw him and had compassion, and ran and fell on his neck and kissed him. – The FATHER said to his servants, 'Bring out the best robe and put it on him, and put a ring on his hand and sandals on his feet. And bring the fatted calf here and kill it, and let us eat and be merry. – And FATHER said to him, 'Son, you are always with me, and all that I have is yours. It was right that we should make merry and be glad.'

You see how reckless this father is in his exuberance. He spoils his sons rotten, pays no attention to their wastefulness or stinginess, but simply goes beside himself in the thrill of giving more and more and more in overflowing extravagance.

Father.

My parents gave and gave of themselves and all of their substance to us children. I always give to my children; it is the insistence of my heart. I cannot watch the TV judges when a parent is suing his or her child for a return of money. Such hardness of heart violates everything holy.

God is FAVOR, overflowing and abundant, love-poured-out, life-layed-down. To expect Father is to expect Favor; to expect not-favor is to expect not-God.

We expect Father; we expect Favor; God is always arising within us.

To treat God as a withholder is to dishonor Him; the problem is source. Is our source the God filling us full with all of Himself and always arising within us? Or is our source some Thing up there from whom we hope to get some thing. Everyone who does not know the first does live in the second, including those who hope to get a "thing" they call grace.

There is no such thing as "grace" from God; rather it is the gift of God. Father Himself is the gift.

The whole purpose of Christ is not to reveal Christ but to reveal Father. Jesus did not come to reveal Himself, but the Father. That's God's order. The Spirit comes first, but only to reveal Christ. But Christ comes only to reveal Father. Funny, but the Father basically says, "Do whatever you want to My Son and I will bear it, but don't mess with My Spirit."

Our hearts are Christ in us. The passion of our hearts, then, is to reveal Father. If we do not know that, we do not know ourselves. To know Father is to know yourself; to know yourself is to know Father, and He in Person. I am not speaking of the exaltation of self, but of Father.

Here is the whole purpose of the seemingly long-distance approach to God, we have found ourselves in, called the history of man and human lives on this earth. Christ belongs to us, but not Father. We possess Christ, but not Father. Father is not possessed by anyone, yet He would reveal Himself through us.

And that's just it. Father would reveal Himself through us. You and I can't do that. We can pretend Christness; we can pretend Holy Ghostness; but we cannot pretend Father.

This relationship between Father and us, Father through us, is known only by those who know it. Those who do not know it CANNOT know it. Only the full reality of John 14:20, that is, living entirely and only inside the consciousness of the Person of Christ Jesus, can take us to Father. No one can come near Father through them any other way.

Home is Father. Where Father reveals Himself through, that is Home. You and I are called to be Home to all creation. Heaven is not home. Father through us is Home to all, both heaven and earth.

John 14 is all about Home. John 14 is all about Father through us. Let's immerse ourselves in John 14, until every word of it has absorbed itself into the fabric of our consciousness.

In My Father's house are many dwelling places.

These words of Jesus are an understatement. "Many" means far more than one can count. The Father's house is the Body of Christ and nothing else.

If anyone loves Me, he will keep My word; and My Father will love him, and We will come to him and make Our home with him.

You and I ARE home to Father and Son.

"Many dwelling places" means two different things all the time. It means 100% one, and it means 100% the other, both at the same time. Home is the same. There is a "two-way street" in this chapter concerning home. Every two-way street goes both ways, both at the same time, never one without the other.

Here is the FIRST side of the street. — **That where I am, there you may be also.** — **In that day you will know that I am in the Father.**

You and I, every one of us, live inside of Father. Father alone is our Home. Inside of Father there are innumerable dwelling places, a perfect place for each one of us. My perfect place in Father is not yours, and yours is not mine. Yet we exult with all joy in the richness of Father through each one of us.

Let me reiterate. We cannot speak of Father without using all the synonyms of WEALTH and all the adjectives that apply to it. Every word you can produce that means wealth, every adjective you can think of that describes wealth, all are simply speaking of Father, all are speaking of Father through each one of us.

We see incomparable and overflowing value when looking at another believer in Jesus because we see Father.

Here is the other FIRST side of the street. **If anyone loves Me. . . We (Father and I) will come to him and make Our home with him.**

Every member of the body of Christ is the Home of Father. They may not know it yet; Father may not yet be free through them, no. But we call things as they are by substance, not as they appear at present. Those not simply awestruck at Father's dwelling place, another believer, are not awestruck with Father.

Our home is Father; Father's home is us.

He that has seen Me has seen Father. Jesus speaking as the first One of our kind. — **And whatever you ask in My name, that I will do, that Father may be glorified in the Son.**

Overwhelming abundance revealed, Father; that's what it's all about.

The next question is – how? Jesus gives a clear and complete answer.

I am the way, the truth, and the life. No one comes to Father except through Me. – Believe Me that I am in Father and Father in Me – At that day you will know that I am in My Father, and you in Me, and I in you.

Put on the Lord Jesus Christ; sink into Him as into a garment, or shall we say, as into the covers of your bed. The Person of the Lord Jesus Christ is not some THING from Jesus, it is Jesus Himself.

Grace is not some THING from God; it is Father Himself in Person. I say this over and over, because everywhere I look people talk about God as THING, getting some THING from this THING.

I just read someone speaking of "all fullness," not as the Person of God now, but as some "thing" we get from God at some point in the future after we have accomplished some sort of vague "dying." Speak Father! Speak "Father fills me full NOW!" Disregard absolutely what you see and how you judge. Speak Father!

We are inside the consciousness, inside the Spirit, inside the Mind, inside the Emotions, inside the Will, inside the Body of Another Person – Father. And we are inside of Father BECAUSE we live only inside of Jesus. That is, we continually see ourselves inside of Jesus regardless of any outward appearance, and we refuse to see ourselves anywhere else. More than that, we continually commune with this Person inside of whom we live BY continually thinking of what it means to be only inside of Him.

We are inside of Father because we are inside of Jesus and Jesus is inside of Father. Father is inside of us because Father is inside of Jesus who lives in our hearts. Jesus said, "If you don't believe that, then at least believe the miracles the Father does through me."

There is no other home for us or for creation, both heaven and earth, than Father through us.

But that the world may know that I love the Father, and as the Father gave Me commandment, so I do. Arise, let us go from here. John 14:31

Jesus is speaking of the Mercy Seat of God revealed now through us. I will speak more of that in an incredibly awesome upcoming letter, "Salvation." **Arise, let us go from here** is code for the Feast of Tabernacles.

In John 16, then, Jesus says this: **If you abide in Me, and My words abide in you, you will ask what you desire, and it shall be done for you. By this My Father is glorified, that you bear much fruit; so you will be My disciples.**

Let's work our way backwards. We are Jesus' disciples because we bear MUCH fruit. The reason that is so is that the whole point of everything is the glory of Father, and Father is glorified by the continual overwhelming abundance of fruit. Next, we bear fruit first by living entirely inside of John 14:20 and second by asking all that we desire. We don't say here, "according to the will of God," for we live only inside of the will of God. Those words were spoken in the context of people who were using God as the far-distant supplier of a gravy train.

Father is overwhelming outward abundance, but only He Himself. Abundance is not some golden-egg-goose we get from God. Father is known through broken hearts healed by Himself and filled with Himself; once known, then, Father does what Father is. And we know what Father is by reading the parable of the exuberant father and by seeing out through the eyes of a wildly exuberant Jesus.

All things that Father has are Mine. – Most assuredly, I say to you, whatever you ask Father in My name He will give you. Until now you have asked nothing in My name. Ask, and you will receive, that your joy may be full. John 16 — Father.

Finally Jesus said, **"Now I will tell you plainly about the Father."** Then He stopped speaking to the disciples and walked the Path of the Atonement.

John 17 is Jesus' prayer to Father. Oh my. Oh my! How these words grow and grow; every line is larger than the universe and never stops growing, not ever.

There is a rule in the grammars of most languages called pronoun-antecedent. A pronoun such as "you" serves only to take the place of its antecedent, a noun, because repeating the noun over and over becomes cumbersome; pronouns are shorter and simpler.

The first word Jesus speaks in John 17 is Father. In light of your knowledge of Father right now, read the entire prayer – EXCEPT, don't read "You" or "Your." Every time You and Your appear, they are simply a handy way to replace "Father." Let's not replace Father. Every time you see You and Your, simply say Father or Father's. Let me write it that way, also bringing these words into present tense, that is, speaking to us now. Finally, I eliminated another pronoun, replacing it with a blank. As you read, put your own full name in the blank. Remember as you read, this is Jesus speaking to Father about you.

> Father, the hour is come. Glorify Father's Son, that Father's Son also glorifies Father; as Father gives Him authority over ____'s flesh, the Son gives eternal life to ____ whom Father gives Him. And this is eternal life, that ____ may know Father, the only true God, and Jesus Christ whom Father sends. I glorify Father on the earth. I finish the work Father gives me to do. And now, O Father, glorify Me together with Father, with the glory I have with Father before the world is.
>
> I manifest Father's name to ____ whom Father gives Me out of the world. ____ is Father's, Father gives ____ to Me, and ____ keeps Father's word. Now ____ knows that all things which Father gives Me are from Father. For I give to ____ the words which Father gives Me; and ____ receives them (as a woman receives seed from her husband), and knows surely that I come forth from Father; and ____ believes that Father sends Me.
>
> I pray for ____. I do not pray for the world but for ____ whom Father gives Me, for ____ is Father's. And all Mine are Father's, and Father's are Mine, and I am glorified in ____. Now I am no longer in the world, but ____ is in the world, and I come to Father. Holy Father, keep through Father's name ____ whom Father gives Me, that ____ may be one as Father and I are one.
>
> While I was with them in the world, I kept them in Father's name. ____, whom Father gives Me, I keep in Father's name. . . But now I come to Father, and these things I speak in the world by which My joy is fulfilled in ____. I give ____ Father's word; and the world has hated ____. . . I do not pray that Father take ____ out of the world, but that Father keep ____ from the evil one. . . Sanctify ____ by Father's truth. Father's word is truth. As Father sent Me into the world, I also send ____ into the world. And for ____'s sake I sanctify Myself, by which ____ also is sanctified by Father's truth.
>
> I . . . pray . . . for ____ who believes in Me. . . that ____ (and all who are Mine) are one, as Father, Father, is in Me and I in Father; that ____ (and all Mine) also are one in Father and Me, that the world may believe that Father sent Me. And the glory which Father gives Me I give ____, that ____ may be one just as Father and I are one: I in ____ and Father in Me; that ____ (and all Mine) are perfect in one, and that the world know that Father sends Me, and loves ____ as Father loves Me.
>
> Father, I desire that ____ also whom Father gives me be with Me where I am (in Father), that ____ beholds My glory which Father gives Me; for Father loves Me before the foundation of the ages. O righteous Father! The world has not known Father, but I know Father; and ____ knows that Father sends Me. And I declare to ____ Father's name, and declare Father's name, that the love with which Father loves Me is in ____, and I in ____.

Father! – Know Him! God is all about experience, all about knowing. Read this over and over with your own full name in the blanks. This is what Jesus really prayed, praying directly into each one of us by name – **And I call them by name, and they follow Me.** Let the reality of Jesus speaking Father into you, personally and real, sink so fully into you that you cannot know anything else.

When we just use "Father," then Father appears 64 times in Jesus' prayer alone. Then, to really get the urgency and passion of Father's heart, look back through Father in the Old Testament and lay the poverty of Father as they knew Him for 4033 years against the Abundance of Father Jesus prayed into us.

How the church has not known Father either; though He has been right there on the page inside of Jesus all along. Father is glorified by the overwhelming abundance of fruit flowing out of you and me.

In the parable of the exuberant father, one son took all the abundance of the father and wasted it. The other son took all the abundance of the father and did not use it at all. The exuberant father paid no attention to either son, but continued towards them entirely out of his own abundance. Neither son speaks of us.

The Father is the One who reveals Himself through us.

The parable of the exuberant father is all about how Father looks upon our brethren through us. The parable of the exuberant Father is all about Church. To those who misuse Father's abundance, we say, "Joy of joys, they're back for more." To those who don't use Father's abundance, we say, "It's all yours, brother, enjoy." And look at this crazy father. When the wasteful son returns, he says, "Let's throw a party." When the poverty son complains, he says, "Hey, join the party."

Father.

Do you know that the Feast of Tabernacles was a COMMAND from God that the children of Israel were to take one third of the tithe accumulated for the year and throw a wild party, eating and drinking (wine – as in drunk) merrily before God as holiness unto the Lord? Yes, this party came after the Day of Atonement became known as life to all, but it was a party.

In my letters "God" and "The Sorrow of God," I presented for us to know a God who groans in travail, who reveals Himself through the travail of His creation. We know Jesus as a Man who bears our sorrows and carries our grief. Yet here we are talking about overwhelming abundance, of unending wealth, and joyous, out-of-control, hilarious laughter.

How can God be agonizing sorrow and exuberant hilarity, both at the same time? Well, first, God is weird, and He is always entirely too much. But Father through us is Church; Church is what Father is. And thus we are just like Him.

And if one member suffers, all the members suffer with it; or if one member is honored, all the members rejoice with it. 1 Corinthians 12

Think of how weird we are. Right now, many individual members of the body of Christ are suffering agonizing loss and heartache, their hearts filled with the intercession of the Spirit. We suffer, that is, we travail, with them. Right now, many individual members of the body of Christ are rejoicing as they dance through doors of favor and outpoured goodness, their hearts so full of the richness of Father. We rejoice, that is, we laugh hilariously, with them.

So, when you see a bunch of wild Christians laughing hilariously in church for no good reason, then you know Father has shown up. Stick around, Father might rub off on you! Some prefer to be the poverty son; why, I do not know.

Yet at the very same time and in the very same breath, the Spirit of God in us groans with groanings that cannot be uttered, in travail for the revelation of God through us to all. To know Father is to have one's heart stretched wide in all directions. To weep with those who weep and to laugh with those who laugh.

(I pray) **that you, being rooted and grounded in love, may be able to comprehend with all the saints what is the width and length and depth and height**— Ephesians 3:17-18

You see, Father is Heart, and Heart is stretched wide in every direction. Father's Heart stretched wide in every conceivable direction revealed now through us has a name: Church. Every single member of that Church, every member of one another enjoys a significant place inside this stretched-wide heart we share, each one of us, with Father. When I see heart extended over others, when it's fun and when it's agonizing, when it's easy and when it costs the heart-bearer everything, then I know I am seeing Church.

Then I know I am seeing Father.

As I look, now, across all the many verses in the New Testament that contain Father, I see there is just too much to write about. Abram, father, becoming Abraham, father of many, a critical part of knowing Father. We have hardly scratched the surface of all the avenues and realms of reality found in knowing Father.

Father in us is Church.

But there is a terrible thing we must face head-on before we can know Father as Church; we must understand scorn. We do not slay scorn; we cannot. The only thing that will ever remove scorn is the full presence of Father all and now. Scorn does not go so that Father can come. Blood comes by faith, then Father comes, and scorn is no more. Yet we cannot play games with scorn; rather, we must put it full in the headlights.

As we know, precious of all preciousness, Father, then we no longer desire scorn and the false exaltation of a religious self that it brings.

And as we know Father, we know Church.

— For the first time in our lives, we know one another.

12. People

I had thought to talk about people in general, both regenerate and unregenerate, people as we find them to be.

Let me explain a simple difference between "church" as most of our brethren experience it and cCchurch as I knew it for 18 years in 24/7 Christian community, cCchurch life. You may wonder at my spelling of cCchurch, I hope you see my meaning.

Here is a group of people meeting in an artificial, arm's-length capacity once a week for a couple of hours. They are all love and smiles. They are clueless. No Church is taking place. Church happens only inside of cCchurch.

Take a group of 100 people, every individual from a different family line. Let's leave out children so that we have a real range of personality types.

I have always been interested in human psychology; that is, what makes people tick. I draw my understanding of the human from the study of Adam, of Jesus as the express image of God's Person, of the full meaning and ramifications of Christ living as me, of humans as I have known them in the close social milieu of community, the school classroom, and my own personal relationships, and of what God says in the Word concerning the nature and construction of the human.

Any study of the human that does not move out from the fact that man is created to contain ALL of God in fullness and to release an invisible God out into visible manifestation, cannot be talking about man as he is.

At the same time, most of mankind, including most Christians, live out from a consciousness of God far-away and the weaving of a story of self that includes every form of pretending. Every time I observe people, I see all these things in full operation all the time.

The Bible is very much a handbook of the human; God wants us to know ourselves and humanity as we are constructed and as we operate. In fact, the knowledge and revelation of God through us can come no other way.

In this letter, however, I want to present a view of people as it applies to the breadth of human society. Differing ways of looking at people and what makes us tick, arranging the human experience into different patterns, can enhance our understanding of mankind. I consider this a critical task for us because man is the image and likeness of God, because Christ revealed through us requires a real Christ and a real us, and because our role in this world affects everyone everywhere.

Let's return to our group of 100 individual people; some may be married couples, but all are from different genetic lines. All are Christians, all meet together once a week in a Spirit-filled, union-with-Christ, present-grace environment. Their fellowship is rich and full; they express wonderful love and grace to each other during their two hours together each week.

This group of people has very little real knowledge of Church.

Now, take this same group of people to a piece of property together. Each person/couple will have his or her own little cottage, yes, but they will share the land, they will work together and eat more than half of their meals together. They will enjoy several worship services of differing kinds together through the week. Remember, these are people who believe in grace and the expression of love.

After six months, what will you see growing larger and larger in all?

Complaining, griping, complaining, gossiping, complaining, and scorn. And that's just for starters. The thing is not broken until after ten to twelve years together. Those who leave before it is broken in themselves will count their community experience the worst thing that ever happened to them, the biggest mistake of their lives. It was. Now scorn is embedded deep on their insides as the very thing they really WANT.

Unless. – Unless someone shows them how.

You see, people just treat one another with disrespect, thinking all the while it is "normal," never considering the other person. People don't know how to be wrong in relationships or to rightly value other people.

Notice that scorn shows up last, yet scorn is always first. Complaining, griping, and gossiping flow only out of scorn. But scorn has a religious manifestation as well, elitism and superiority. I know elitism; scorn is the father of elitism.

The scorner is the supreme pretender. Thus the scorner cannot truly know Christ as me, though He does carry them.

Christ as me is me as I really am, for real. Christ as me causes me to abandon all forms of pretending and allows me to be real, often wrong, often foolish, often nonsensical, often bull-headed, often thoughtless of others. Me. Christ as me.

No pretending I'm something that I am not. No pretending that I am a "man of God," or that I have some great "ministry" to the church. And only when I see me for real without any pretending do I look at you and see you for real with my heart filled with compassion and the delight of the Father.

Christ as me has one enemy, pretending, the true nature of Adam, useless and without reason. However, we in no way come to know Christ our only life by "getting rid of" pretending. Rather, we embrace Christ as us with all joy, coming to know that we are fully inside of God, fully accepted as Christ Himself, and bit by bit, the pretending just falls away simply because there is no more need for it.

A pretender pretends out of a false fear of God out of a false knowledge of God. Yet outwardly a pretender exhibits no fear of God at all. In contrast, I am NOT afraid of the God who fills me with all of Himself in Person; rather I walk in His utter delight. That means that outwardly, you see in me a true and very real fear of God. I will NOT mess around with His woman. Not for anything.

We must understand people. The moment you put two people together, those two people connect with each other spirit to spirit and mind to mind. Now, I wish to speak hypothetically. In other words, this "theory" of human society is simply a framework of understanding. Though generally true, it can never describe any exact gathering of 100 people.

Whenever two or more people come together, there is an immediate and continual jockeying for power. There are those who exude power-over, and there are those who draw power-over upon themselves for the sake of riding the coattails of those to whom power-over is just natural.

Power-over is the sickness that comes from Adam, it is the destroyer of all Church, it shows up in every gathering together, it is not part of Christ-as-us because it goes beyond "me" to manipulate others. Power-over is based on the deal made between the serpent and Adam, a deal continued all too readily by almost all Christians. It is the positioning of superiority over the "other"; it is the envy of the serpent against man, the image of God. Power-over expresses itself as *"thus saith the Lord,"* yet it's root is scorn of the other, of Christ as the other.

Every time there is a gathering together, two or more, the positioning of face against face runs as an electric undercurrent. People can be sweet for awhile, but the realities of life together in Christian community forces scorn front and center. Yet the faces of people are not all the same. Rather, there is a full spectrum of response to power that runs in a similar way across any group of people large or small. This spectrum contains two extremes with a range of differing responses to those extremes across the middle.

In the following chart, each small column at the top is 5 people or 5% of the population.

Relations to Power-Over

1	2	3	4	5	6	7	8	9	10	11	12	13	14	15	16	17	18	19	20
Independent but non-assertive. No desire to rule. Com- passionate, even to personal loss. 5% fully, the other 10%, the most giving, lean strongly their way.			Do respect others but in difficulty can pull back. Will at least know what is right.		These tend towards respect for others, but will go with the flow if needs be.			These always go with the flow, ready to move either way, jump on whichever bandwagon seems to be winning. Pleasant, neither grasping nor altruistic.				These tend towards selfishness. Manipulate others, but will go with the flow if needs be.			Not fierce enough to abuse freely but give rulers support. Quick to repeat disrespect.		Independent and assertive. Must rule over others. Hurt without care. 5% are for real, the other 10%, the most dangerous, lean strongly their way.		

Since we do not live in the tree of knowledge, we do not use a chart like this either for self-analysis or to analyse others. We use it, rather, to understand people and to understand Christ.

There is also a second division running all the way through these "groups" of people; we could call it a division of IQ, with a broad definition of IQ as all forms of natural ability. On the #20 side, we see that the low IQ people are those who commit crimes and go to jail. The high IQ people rise to the top and become the named rulers; they also commit crimes, but they don't go to jail. Conversely, on the #1 side you will find many diagnosed as Down Syndrome, but you will also find people like Isaac Newton, of brilliant mind, but incapable of hurting a bug.

I am very serious when I say that Down Syndrome individuals, when their bodies are transformed, will be seen to be those closest to Christ in heart and being. At the same time, God picked a man, Moses, from the very far left of this spectrum for the most terrible task in the history of His dealings with man, the speaking of the ministry of condemnation. Moses was incapable of commanding anyone; he was the meekest man in Israel.

That's why Paul said, in 1 Corinthians 6, that if there is a divisive issue in the church, always go to the bottom, the "lowest" people in the church, in order to find the wisdom of guidance from God. A true pastor of God's house will find it natural and normal to ask the janitor for advice in difficult matters.

We must also understand that, just as there are those in any group who tend to abuse others without conscience, so there are those who draw abuse to themselves. That is, there are those persons who need, almost, to be manipulated by power personalities. Look at the chart from #6 to #17, roughly 60% of the population. These people go from willing to be abused to needing to be abused.

Now, before going any further into this discussion, I must draw a line in the concrete. We do not use such a model to judge any individual person. People are people; you cannot put them in a box. Individuals have many differing expressions. No percentages could possibly be exact, no group would ever be quite the same. We use this kind of a model only to understand, never to analyse.

Everyone is different. God takes some from the bottom and places them in prominent positions. He takes some who would claw their way to the top if they could, and places them always bouncing along at the bottom of any group of people. In other words, just because someone is at the bottom does not mean they would not abuse others if they could. And just because someone is at the top does not mean they don't respect all others fully to their own hurt.

It all boils down to one word: respect. Christ our life brings everyone out of these "categories" and into love.

Respect means that I regard you above my own inclinations. Respect means that I never assume, but only ask. Respect means that I would find it more sensible to endure pain and loss myself than to see any element of abuse or hurt directed at you.

It is stated that 4-6% of any population are psychopathic, that is people who have no real conscience, no thought of any pain borne by others. Of this portion there are always one or two who simply need to inflict pain on others; their lives would be miserable if they were not making other people suffer. Typically, these are not the most dangerous unless all of society has been perverted. In a healthy society, the majority draw away from this two percent whose victims are found primarily in the low IQ portions of the #9 to #18 strata of the graph.

Joseph Stalin was a high IQ from the top #20 1/10 of 1 percent who weaseled his way into power and spent 26 years living off the death and suffering of millions. No "free" people can remain free if they do not know how such a wolf gained power.

Notice that both sides of the graph are "independent," that is, they never come under anyone else's control.

The most dangerous people in a group are the #18-19's on the chart, especially those with a higher IQ, and especially when they are anointed by God. These people, by nature, become the leaders because they will not be anything less.

I have discovered something amazing about this strata of human society in recent weeks. I have been astonished at how utterly religious the doctors of literary theory are. They are astonishingly religious. As I contemplate this religious cult I have stumbled into, a religious cult that fills all colleges across the world, primarily inside the arts/humanities/sociology/literature/psychology sections of human learning, I observe every single element of religious brainwashing and mind control in FULL operation.

When I say "religious," I mean they are powerful in the realms of spirit, and they use spirit to abuse and to control. The power people among them are in the high IQ #18-19 of the graph.

Amazingly, I see that running deeply through so many of these "literary experts" I am required to read is a deep loathing of a particular group of people through the centuries of the past. This hatred of this particular group of people is open and stated. They hate the scribes and Pharisees, the doctors of the law. They hate the doctors of theology in Roman Catholicism; they hate the doctors of theology in Puritan Protestantism. They hate all religious high IQ figures down through the centuries who have used "religion" to manipulate and abuse others for their own gain.

They hate themselves. – It's true; these are the exact same people. What astonishes me is their almost desperate NEED to speak scorn against others. You take these professors of literary theory I am required to read back in history when everyone was forced to be "Christian," and they would have been the very theologians condemning Galileo, the very Puritan "divines" condemning witches to be burned, the very doctors of the law who demanded the crucifixion of Jesus.

I have begun to thank God for modern secular society, for atheism and evolution. It has gotten these people out of the church. Much of the mucked up nonsense called "Christianity" was created by these very same people who now find themselves so wise to denounce all belief in a "fictitious" god! For the most part, they are no longer in the church. That's why the church of Jesus Christ today is much more able to hear the grace of God and the revelation of Christ our life.

Take 100 people and place them all together on the same property with the thought that they will work life out together as the church. Give them no structure and appoint no leaders. Someone says, "Okay, we're all equal here. Does everyone agree?" 100 people will raise their hands that, yes, they do agree that all are equal. Most of them are lying, even if they don't know it.

Within a few months, everything will have shifted.

Let me explain all human psychology again briefly. Adam and the serpent made a deal. Adam already was like God, like El, a judge. The serpent was all outward appearance and no inner substance. The trade was simple. The serpent got to call his outward appearance "what God looks like" – inside the human experience, and Adam got to be a serpent-kind of judge, that is, power-over.

The dynamics of all power-over – ALL power-over – RULES without question in ALL human interaction unless God takes a handful of people out of its horror and gives them CHURCH.

Power-over has two parts, domination and being dominated. Both are essential to 60 out of 100 people; of the other 40, 15 will think they must be abused, even though they aren't made for it and will be destroyed, and 10-15 will find a way to live with the abuse, even though they don't need it.

Within a few months, the dominators will dominate. Understand this, the person who says forcefully, "I don't believe in leadership," is a dominator and that person's domination is sabotaging the whole enterprise.

The dominators are the high ability #13-18's and all the #19's, about 15 of the 100. Low ability #18-19's have a name in society – bullies. They have a slight sense that they are not very bright or capable, and they just love pushing people around to make themselves feel superior. None of the #18-19's ever think of the other person. If there are any true psychopaths in the group, they will be mistrusted. Psychopaths rule only when they can manipulate (brainwash) enough #18-19's to grant them the power in the way Stalin and Lenin did.

This group of 100 are all Christians, all having had an experience with the Holy Spirit, all professing belief in the grace of God. Ideas change no one. Change comes only by the Person of Christ personal in us. No bully can ever change until he can stand in front of the whole group and say, "I am a bully. I am the worst sort of bully. I need your help. Please help me." In that moment he is real; in that moment Christ is as him.

Now, let me insert this. In my life experience – looking back, I see that God has graced me with an incredible range of experience with all types of people, male and female. I have had female bosses slightly more of my working life than male bosses. Females have the same range of power-types as males. I have known vicious female dictators, the very worst. The best bosses were male, but I have had wonderful female bosses as well. Male bosses tend more to being really good or really bad. Female bosses tend more to being middle of the road.

If you want to see what people really are, make them the boss, put them in charge, then strip them of everything. That's what all author's do to show the real center of their characters. It's also what God does.

Now, you might think, "This is all meaningless; I want to know Christ." Well, this is people, most certainly, and the Church is full of people, and the Church is the plant of Christ. So, you can't have one without facing the reality of the other. I have spent a lifetime trying to figure out people in the light of Christ; as I have come to know myself for real, so I know people.

All dominators in the church rule by religious psychology. And here is where we place scorn. Envy is the serpent looking at Adam, "I wish I could be God's image instead of that jerk." Scorn, on the other hand, is the serpent now in Adam, "I'm superior; you are all fleshy and inferior." Scorn is the expression of the serpent's envy. That's why Nicene "Christianity" hates the human.

Look at the graph, 99 out of 100 people are open to scorn. Only those who are fortunate enough to be Down Syndrome or something similar are free from scorn, thus gaining the most heart-shaping by God of all people in this life.

Some initiate scorn while others repeat what they hear in order to "belong."

You will know God has won your heart and is shaping it for Himself when you are thrust into horrendous awfulness and you discover there is no scorn in you. When you walk away from everything, losing everything, without blaming others and without blaming yourself, just holding onto Jesus, then you know that scorn is finally gone and now you belong wholly to Jesus. Such people can certainly make mistakes, all the time, but they cannot scorn.

And they cannot remain in the same room with scorn. Yet they will not "tell others" to stop scorning. They simply and quietly walk away.

Back to our group of 100. This is so important; no group will ever discover cCccCcCCChurch until they pass through the reality of what I am saying.

Without any need for "appointment," a natural leadership will arise. That natural leadership will come from across the whole span of the graph. Let's say that twenty-two people are in that natural leadership. And when I say "natural" leadership, I'm not speaking of those, necessarily, who "should be" leaders or who appear to be leaders. Leadership is by psychological power as well as by natural gifting. Just because someone does not have the appearance of power does not mean they are not a primary dominating force.

I have said that the 2% psychopath column does not produce leaders. That's not quite true. You see, the kind of psychopath who feeds off of hurting people does not usually show up in a church group, yet I have known such in community. This kind of person does not become a recognized leader, but you will see them underneath, biting at the weakest, seeking to maim and pull down. They know how to use psychological power-over better than anyone. If they obtain open power, then people start to die, even in "church" groups, aka Jim Jones.

Listen, I'm just talking about people. It's the reality of church. All this is 100% normal.

No one in the #1 column will be in the outward leadership, not even Isaac Newton or Moses. Moses "led" only because God did some big stuff all the time to make sure people noticed him.

The best natural leaders, wonderful people, come from the #2-5 columns. David was such a man. I have known many wonderful leaders from those columns, men and women who respect you fully, encourage you deeply, and always point everyone to Jesus. But the largest number of "leaders" will be from the #18-19's; Saul was such a man. The leaders we like the least are from the #13-17 columns. They can talk like the #2-5's, but they will always betray you. The #18-19's can be trusted to dominate; the #13-17's can be trusted to betray. The #13-17's gain their identity by serving the #18-19's; they are the obsequious ones, though they don't know that.

Don't think that you will gather together with your "group of people" and not find all of these types of relationships to power operating among them. Don't think that you (and I) will not abuse our brother or sister.

Let me point out this absolute of human life together. We will abuse our brethren, guaranteed. And we won't even notice it, not for years. But there does come a point, in the hearts of those who truly want the Lord, when the eyes open, and the horror of the endless, thoughtless disrespect comes front and center before the eyeballs and a person wants it no more. From my own experience, I would say a minimum of twelve years in Christian community, twelve years of treating others with disrespect and being treated by others with disrespect, is required to bust that thing out of my heart and yours.

God's leaders, the men and women He is preparing, are in the bottom 15%. That does not exclude anyone else. Anyone can follow those who are real; all they have to do is accept Christ alone as all that they are. That is, all they have to do is be real themselves. How do you identify the real leaders in the bottom 15%? That's easy; they will always make you feel like a winner, like you are as wonderful as Jesus. At no point will you notice in them any need to be "superior." Never do they wave their "ministry" before you.

Read *A Tale of Three Kings*. David had no idea why on earth all these men were following him. He never saw himself as any kind of boss.

Now, don't get me wrong. **To the froward** (to the pretenders), **God shows Himself froward** (pretends to be hostile), and so will His leaders. But they will be ready to drop into joyous laughter with any pretender the moment that pretender shows the slightest symptom of becoming real.

What is the first symptom of becoming real? You know someone is becoming real when you hear them say, "I am so wrong. Please forgive me; I don't know what I was thinking."

Let me pretend to be hostile. And sometimes its hard to remember that I am just pretending, even though lately I have been finding Gladness welling up in me, carrying me, just all the time.

I am hostile to all who will manipulate and abuse God's precious people out of the scorn of a false self. Typically, I will simply and quietly walk away, but that doesn't alter my hostility.

Scorn is rooted in "Christian theology" and draws its power from that theology. When you see me angry against certain elements in Christian theology, I am not angry because of the bad ideas, I am angry because of the use of those bad ideas masquerading as "deeper truth" to manipulate and abuse God's people.

My God, I know the devastation; I have walked among the ruined people. I have wept with the unhealed. I was most certainly one of them. As Christ rescued me, so I will withhold Him from no one.

We must never think that "our" sweet little group of precious saints would be different. It cannot be different.

I just watched a video someone had posted on Facebook of two young and healthy Christian fathers who agreed to be hooked up to a labor-pain simulator to demonstrate that women are just "making it up" when they say how awful travail is. When the pain had reached the half-way point, they were finished, utterly debilitated, desperately gasping for breath.

There is nothing in the human experience more difficult than Church. My wife, being a practical person with FULL experience of Christian community, tender and compassionate, who believes the best in everyone, wonders at me that I would even think about returning to community life.

There is nothing in the human experience more difficult than travail.

There is nothing in the experience of the universe more difficult than church. Conversely, there is nothing more glorious than discovering the reality of Church, found only inside of cCchurch.

Those who know Church also know unbearable pain.

What is the answer then? Is there an answer? Yes, there is an answer. That answer is part of the fulfillment of the Feast of Tabernacles in the life of the Church.

The answer is 1 John 3:16; that is, this is the foundation of the answer.

By this we know love, because He laid down His life for us. And we also ought to lay down our lives for the brethren.

You see, Jesus does not require us to "lay down our lives" in order to know Him in all fullness filling us with His glory. And His servants never ask their brethren to "lay down their lives" for the "leadership." Godly leadership is death always against me and my ideas, but life always towards you, lifted up and victorious. You know a godly leader, because that one is always laughing, that is, they are always laying down their life for you. You know a godly leader, because that one never asks you to lay down your life for their vision of "the kingdom."

But as the foundation of the answer, a core leadership that knows life-layed-down, that shies away from any form of manipulation, there is a further reality that causes Church to be the full revelation of Father.

You see, church has had the other for 1900 years, people "correcting" people and calling it ministry. I think it's time for something different.

I think it's time for the Song of the Lamb.

I think it's time for a ministry who will speak, not puff-up, but speak Christ into themselves and into one another.

I think it's time that all notice of outward appearance cease and with it all accusation of not-Christ coming out of the mouths in which Christ alone belongs.

I think it's time that we alter the substance and reality of the universe.

I think it's time for Father to be revealed.

I think it's time for Church.

13. Salvation

Then Moses called for all the elders of Israel and said to them, "Pick out and take lambs for yourselves according to your families, and kill the Passover lamb. And you shall take a bunch of hyssop, dip it in the blood that is in the basin, and strike the lintel and the two doorposts with the blood that is in the basin. And none of you shall go out of the door of his house until morning. For the LORD will pass through to strike the Egyptians; and when He sees the blood on the lintel and on the two doorposts, the LORD will pass over the door and not allow the destroyer to come into your houses to strike you. Exodus 12:21-23

Full salvation has three distinct parts in the New Testament. The first and second parts are portrayed in this storyline God gave at the beginning of Israel's journey, the third is foreshadowed by these Passover words, **"going out in the morning,"** pointing to that larger Salvation that covers the whole earth.

The first part of salvation is Redemption, the third Salvation-Revealed. In-between these two is the real joy of Salvation – **Put on the Lord Jesus Christ.** Redemption and salvation are closely connected, yet there are significant differences. Redemption is finished, but salvation is very much who and what we are.

Salvation hasn't changed, but my knowing of it sure has.

"The door is closed, children, and we are safe." — "But I don't see the blood, Dad." — "The blood is not for you to see, son, but for death to see. The door is closed, and we are safe."

The door is closed, children, and we are safe.

I and the children whom You have given me.

How the cross has been falsified through all the history of Christianity. My stomach is sick considering the long centuries of horror and the years of my own life through which the cross was falsified.

WHERE is the Cross? And where the Blood?

Those who do not know the first meaning of salvation, redemption, cannot even see the second, living only inside of Jesus, or the third, Salvation Revealed. Part of the horror comes when those who do not know redemption and who have falsified salvation into the Christian fantasy of "go to" heaven, take the verses that apply to the third meaning of salvation and twist those around to alter the entirety of the meaning of redemption, turning it into terror.

Consider an Israelite boy, firstborn in his house, fifteen years old, let's call him Jedidiah. Jedediah has watched the destruction of Egypt, and he is in awe of Moses. When Moses says that the angel of death will come into every home in Egypt to kill the firstborn son, he believes that Moses is telling the truth. Evening comes, the lamb has been slain and the blood applied to the doorposts in the shape of the cross. They all go inside and CLOSE the door. But Jedediah has an unmarried uncle in his mid-twenties, a younger son, a jealous man.

The uncle sidles up to Jedediah, anxiously waiting in the front room after the rest of the family has gone to bed. *"You don't see the blood, you don't see the cross,"* the uncle whispers. *"Here's what you need to do. You should be on your knees in front of the cross with your hands lifted up in supplication and hope that you might be saved. The only real place of safety is on your knees before the cross."*

Jedediah believes his uncle's words. The next morning, when the family opens the door, there is Jedediah sprawled dead before the blood and before the cross, with the terror of death etched across his twisted face.

Jedediah is 1900 years of the Christian church.

Before looking again at the first part of Salvation, let me state clearly the third part. The third part of Salvation is the Saved, going forth bearing Salvation, not "heaven someday," but real Salvation for all of creation. And when I say, "the Saved," I mean manifest sons of God in all the incorruptible glory of Jesus.

The second part of salvation is where we are, living entirely and only inside of John 14:20: **I am in the Father and you in Me and I in you.** In this place of safety, I hear the words, "The door is closed, children, and we are safe." I look over to the edge of the vast dwelling place in which I live, there, down low to the floor, I see a tiny door closed shut. I remember back to the moment, in a revelation of glory, that door, Galatians 2:20, opened wide for me and I entered into this safe, SAFE place, a place called Christ Jesus, the only place I know. But as I look at that door now, I see that it is closed tightly against the wild winds of death on the outside.

The door is closed and locked as a mighty barrier against all death.

"I don't see the cross," I say to Jesus. — "The cross isn't for you, My dear one," He says, "the cross is for Adam and for the world."

"I don't see the blood," I say to Jesus. — "The blood isn't for you, heart of My Heart," He says, "the blood is for death; it cannot enter here."

And I am content to turn away from the door, knowing that it is closed, knowing that I am safe, knowing that my everlasting joy is to know this glorious One in whom alone I live and who is all that I am.

Let's start at the beginning of redemption. Sin keeps no one away from God, not since the sacrifice of Christ. You look at a brother caught in the grossest act of filthy sin – that sin absolutely and in no way keeps that brother from knowing all the fullness of God right now. Those on the outside of Salvation imagine that it does, yes, but not those who live inside of Him who alone IS Salvation.

Quite the contrary, the absence of the knowledge of God Personal, Here, and Now is what is causing the sin. Union with Christ never "condones" sin, but it does not condemn it, either. Union with Christ eliminates the source of sin and then allows the knowledge of the immediate presence of God (the Guy who can't remember any sin), to cause the outer acts of sin to dissipate away – because they are no longer an issue.

Sin cannot cause the absence of God; the absence of God in present knowledge causes sin, big and small. In fact, everything done outside of knowing that all of God is present now in me (all fullness) is sin, even normal human activity. And as sin, it's simply no big deal (by the Blood); none of it keeps anyone away from God. The real sin is not knowing in intimate closeness this wonderful Person who has become our entire and only Self without regard to our actions and, in fact, only inside of our total inability.

When we KNOW this wonderful Person who fills us with all of Himself and has become all that we are, when we KNOW that sin and sinner are no longer in our consideration, when we KNOW that Jesus is our only Self and that pretending is unnecessary, when we KNOW the love filling our hearts and flowing out from us, then, guess what – the actions that God calls sin become less and less of meaning or value to us until they simply vanish away as utterly unimportant.

The fullness of God first and now, Personal in us, is the only thing that causes sin to vanish away. From heaven's point of view, that reality of all of God in us now is seen as fiery indignation, the sword of His mouth, from our point of view, a gentle word, a kind touch, high regard for us with zero sense of shame.

Let's look at the door again. You see, the door is open and closed, both at the same time. It is open to all those who would enter in, but closed to the accuser and death. Thus, God has His own ones, whom He has fashioned specifically to hold the door open to many and to invite them in. Those of us whom He has chosen to explore the full meaning of this same Salvation are never "superior" to the doorkeepers; we share all things together.

Now, I'm not speaking of what most Christians call "evangelism." Getting a "ticket" by which to escape "hell" and "go to" heaven after death is not in the Bible, thus it simply does not enter our thinking as we talk about God's path of Salvation. Christians are in as much need of evangelising as non-Christians. Christians live outside of Jesus in their knowledge almost as much as non-Christians. In fact, most Christians stand outside the door of Salvation, thinking they have found their rightful place.

The difference between Christians and non-Christians is that Christians are on the porch looking at the door and non-Christians aren't.

All who live outside of Jesus, though they spend their entire life on their knees before the cross, have never entered the door, nor lived inside the knowledge of Salvation, though He tenderly carries them. The door is Christ as us. The door is **"I am crucified with Christ, nevertheless I live, yet not I, but Christ."**

The door is closed, children, and we are safe.

We partake of communion to remember, as often as we wish, that the door is closed and we are safe, yes, but God gave us that practice, not to remind a bunch of forgetful sinners about the sacrifice of Jesus, but to help us remember the anchor of all the joy and wonder in which we find ourselves. – Because we are so busy exploring in awestruck delight this vast room in which we now live.

Salvation, this middle-realm in which we live and in which we will live forever, regardless of any manifestation of that same Salvation Revealed, is vast beyond measure and filled with an infinite number of glories, powers, and rooms of experience and knowledge. But none of that is its primary quality.

The most important thing we know about this realm, Salvation, is that Salvation is a PERSON, and that Person has a name, Jesus. – Jesus, this One I love, this One who lives in my heart, this One who fills me with all of His glory.

I put on this Person, Jesus, by my continual story-telling, the song I sing of myself. In my weakness, I see all of my weakness and inability as this Person, Jesus, sharing Himself with me. I see all of my difficulty as this Person, Jesus sharing His suffering and the intercession of His passion through me. I see this Jesus, this living Person, living AS me now in all things. I see this Jesus as my entire and only dwelling place now and forever. I visit with this Jesus whenever my thoughts tend His way, which is often. We are the best of friends. He is real, and I love Him. We walk together in sweet communion. All things are of His hand. All things are this Jesus sharing His unfolding, His revelation, with me and through me.

When I am depressed, I see only Jesus, in me, as me, with me, through me. When I am in distress, when everything goes wrong, when people I thought were my friends make a public mockery of me, when everything in this world goes haywire, when all things fall to pieces, when I am hurting and lonely and confused, ALL of it, I see only Jesus, sharing Himself with me, walking in sweet communion, all of it He living as me, all of it the Father, reconciling the world to Himself through my well-chosen path.

I give Him thanks and I know Him. — A reader of these letters sent me this note in the middle of God showing me again, in an ever deeper way, His perfect union with my own lack and distress.

> First, Daniel, let me say (again) how grateful I am for your letters and how much they help. Right now, particularly, the concept of substance versus appearance, in the face of weakness being held up accusingly to establish the strength of others around. Like the brothers throwing Joseph in

the pit. I understand it now. How they could not bear his way of thinking, which, by its very nature, showed them up. In the face of that accusation, the only thing is to cling to our weakness, to face it, to bear it, in and with Him. This, I realise, is what John means in his first letter, where he says that we do not need any man to teach us how to be one with our weakness and lay down our life for those in our lives. So, I have you to thank for bringing me here where I trust my own weakness, because of Jesus. Nothing anyone can say can be used to manipulate me into capitulating to whatever demand the other (whoever) has of me. My heart is clear. My heart is right. This is a big relief. This is the love of the Father. This is true power.

How much I know the depths of these thoughts this last several weeks! But I would not speak against anyone, thus I will hold this place of "laying down my life" for my brethren before God alone. It is all for the sake of Father, and not for anyone else. Whatever Father wishes to do with our lives, that's His business. We live and walk for Him; He does all His perfect pleasure with, as, and through us, for we belong utterly to Him.

Let us turn now, secure that the Door is closed against both sin and death, things we know nothing about ever again, and contemplate the full extent of this place in which alone we live, inside this person named Christ Jesus. We live now in the fullness of present salvation exactly as we find ourselves to be, just like Jesus, naked, bloody, bruised, and unashamed, saying **"Father, forgive them,"** to the worst pretenders the world knows.

Salvation IS a Person named Jesus, He who is the Christ of God. We live IN Salvation only as we live inside another Person – **Put on the Lord Jesus Christ.**

We know this Person by experience in four differing ways, all at the same time, yet there is a progression of knowing that is important always to keep in mind. Christ is first every Word God speaks. We receive Him as the speaking of God entering into us. But this Word, coming forth always from Father, becomes flesh, that is Christ is second the One who lives AS me. Third, we behold His glory. It is here that we see and experience and live in all that Christ as a Spirit of Power is and means. It is the Spirit who transforms us into the image of Christ. And fourth, full of grace and truth, Christ is a many-membered Body, rich with all the wealth of Father revealed.

Christ cannot be my only life except as the One coming into me as every Word God is continually speaking and being fulfilled though I see it not. All the realities of Christ as a Spirit of Power become twisted except they always come out of Christ living as me, as I find myself to be, a simple human without strength or ability or wisdom or any need for pretence. And finally, Church, Father revealed, Christ as a many-membered Body, cannot be real except it always flows out of that dual reality of Spirit and Flesh in full marriage union.

Spirit-power is not a part of Christ as me, though it is most definitely a part of Christ as His body. When we find any part of our identity in Spirit gifts, we turn those gifts into pretending. Let gifts and powers and anointings come and go; they never define us. The only thing that defines us is a Man on His knees to serve, a Man laying down His life for His friends.

I'm talking about living inside of Jesus – Salvation. This Jesus is our only Self, our only identity, ONLY by who He IS, in spite of what we do or don't do.

Let's zero in, now, on an "act of sin." Let's say I just got frustrated with my wife and hollered at her in an unjust and cruel way. I have hurt my wife; I have done badly. What does that mean, what do I do with that INSIDE of Salvation, inside of Jesus as the only Self I am?

Did Jesus just treat my wife in that terrible way? Of course not.

Moreover the law entered that the offense might abound. But where sin abounded, grace abounded much more, so that as sin reigned in death, even so grace might reign through righteousness to eternal life through Jesus Christ our Lord. What shall we say then? Shall we continue in sin that grace may abound? Certainly not! Romans 5:20-6:2

Here is the watershed between Salvation and another gospel. Another gospel never raises the question of sinning because we are "in grace." Only Paul's gospel allows that accusation. Jesus did not hurt my wife; I did. What I did was wrong.

There are THREE things I could do with my "sin." Three, not two.

First, I could enjoy the sin without concern because of "grace." Or, second, I could take the sin and place it between myself and God, claiming that God must be far away because *"look at me, look at what I just did,"* and then proceed to *"try very hard not to speak wrongfully at my wife,"* until the next time that I do. Both of these approaches are living in sin, the second more than the first. To use one's sin to drive God far away is a greater sin than simply to revel in it. The person who sins has committed one sin. The person who then takes that sin and places the sin between self and God as *"the cross,"* and, *"Oh me, oh my, Daniel has to die,"* is committing a second, far greater sin. In fact, placing sin between self and God is the very act that creates the false self.

Yet neither approach is found inside Salvation.

I do the third thing with my sin. I place it continually and only inside of Jesus-WAS-dead upon the cross on the outside of that closed door, outside of the only place I live. Then, with no consciousness of sin, I continue to behold the glory of the One in whom alone I live. I sorrow over the hurt I have caused my wife, but I do not regard or fix sin or sinner. Rather, I hold her inside of Love upon my heart. Anything that might come from me towards her is NEVER to "fix sin," but only as the river of life flowing out from the Love One who fills my heart full.

I do not live in the law of sin and death, but only in the law of the Spirit of Life, only in Christ Jesus.

I neither "enjoy" nor worry one moment over my "sin." And I never place it between me and Christ as all that I am. I see only His glory regardless. I see Jesus; I see through eyes of fire. And the "need" to react in frustration fades slowly away without any "trying" on my part. When I didn't get enough sleep, or am pressed by difficulty, and I react and speak badly again, I do the same thing again.

But inside of Jesus there is NEVER a voice of accusation. Accusation no longer even comes near my ears because I WILL NOT hear it.

You see, this is why it never works to try to "correct" someone who lives inside of Christ as their only Self using external words spoken at them. Your words won't even get close; they will strike those words to the ground and will never hear them. If you press, you will discover that they have simply vanished from your circle. The only thing that will ever cause darkness to cease is the full and continual acknowledgement of Christ. Those who continually cast down the accuser will never allow in external words. Those who will subject themselves to external correction do not know Christ as their only Self.

Recently I have been pressed hard by hurtful accusation. I woke up in the middle of the night with the horror of darkness and wailing accusations pressing all around. I did not regard nor hear their cries. Rather, I instantly reached up, as it were, took hold of Jesus' face with both hands, inches from mine – in my "seeing," looked straight in His eyes looking into mine, and repeated twice, "Jesus, You are my only life: You are all there is in me." After the second time, the press of darkness vanished and was no more. I had not heard it at all.

This is the crux of the present Salvation in which we live. Let me explain. In this three-part definition of Salvation, I am not speaking of being born again and being baptized in the Holy Spirit; that is, I am not referring to Passover and Pentecost, but only to Tabernacles. The Feast of Tabernacles has three parts, the Feast of Trumpets, the Day of Atonement, and then the Feast of Booths for eight days, culminating in the final Sabbath, the last day of the Feast.

I had always imagined that we "passed through" the Day of Atonement in order to arrive at the final part of Tabernacles. I was so wrong. You see, it's Trumpets (hearing) – Day of Atonement – Tabernacles. That is, entering Salvation, living in Salvation, revealing Salvation, or entering into Jesus, living inside of Jesus, revealing Jesus. The Day of Atonement is forever; it is the Day of Salvation. Regardless of any outward ministry or no outward ministry, we will forever be living inside of the Atonement, inside of Salvation, inside of Christ Jesus.

As individual persons, inside of Jesus is the only thing we know. What is true of Jesus must be true of us, because we live only inside of Jesus. What is true of us must be true of Jesus, because we live only inside of Jesus.

This is Salvation, and it is forever. Salvation Revealed, going forth bearing fruit, all the manifestation of Spirit and Body, all of it is just the out-workings of this most precious union and communion of Jesus and me – Jesus and you. The Day of Atonement is forever.

Trumpets is every Word God speaks coming into me as my very and only life. Tabernacles and its aftermath is Spirit and Body going forth revealing Christ to all. But Salvation, this most precious of dwelling places, this place where I live is Jesus having forever become me in what I find myself to be in all things in the present moment. Precious communion inside of forever union.

This communion that is Salvation takes place only inside of Union, thus the Door for us is always closed and sin and death are always far away, kept far away by both blood and cross on the outside of that Door. You see, in that moment of horror in the middle of the night, my Salvation was not the casting down of all accusation. My Salvation was Jesus; it was knowing Jesus alive and now and as my very and only life.

Yet God has placed the voice of accusation inside of our present knowing of Jesus, not for us to hear, but for us to cast down. It is in casting down all accusation, both within and without, that we KNOW this One in whom we live.

Our job is not "to set creation free." Our job is to know what living inside of Jesus, what **Put on the Lord Jesus Christ**, really is and means in its depths and reality. And then, our knowing of living in Jesus will by its very nature, set all creation free as that same Spirit flows out of us together as one Body.

With zero thought of "myself," my job is to enjoy this Place in whom I live, knowing Him in all that He is and as far as He goes. I'm not speaking, here, of anything outward. I cannot move out through One Spirit to connect with you as One Body except I know, ever more deeply, this Jesus in whom I live. And I do not know Him by His outward ministry, but only as He showed Himself to be, a Man laying down His life for me, and I also.

For, you see, you and I carry inside our chests the very Mercy Seat, the Throne of heaven, our own hearts.

You shall put the mercy seat on top of the ark, and in the ark you shall put the Testimony that I will give you. And there I will meet with you, and I will speak with you from above the mercy seat. . . Exodus 25

— I am the Ark of the Covenant, human flesh, with all of God on the inside of me and all of God on the outside of me. The New Covenant is not written "upon" my heart, rather my heart is all the Words of the New Covenant in its fabric and makeup. The Mercy Seat of heaven sits as the top part of my heart. And there, upon that Mercy Seat, between the cherubim, I meet with you and you with me. There, and there alone, we speak with one another and God through us to all. — (Please say this as yourself.)

This is the core and center of the Covenant.

This is My commandment that you love one another. — For we are members one of another. — He who loves God must love His brother also. — Love one another just as the Father loves you.

Greater love has no man than this, that a man lay down his life for his friend.

When friends hurt me so badly and without cause, what do I do with them? I draw them upon the Mercy Seat of God, my heart, here above the Blood, and I forgive them of all on my part, but on their part, I extend life and honor to them. You see, this Blood, though it is One with the Blood out on the outside of that closed door, yet this Blood is for a different purpose. By this Blood, sprinkled here upon my heart, I extend Mercy to you.

It is here and here alone that we KNOW this One, this Salvation, in whom we live. Whatever goes out from us, goes out from this place alone. The river of life flows out from the Mercy Seat. Spiritual gifts and ministries can operate freely inside of church. But Church comes only out from the Mercy Seat, only out from my laying down my life for you. You see, "laying down one's life" is just another way to say "Mercy, or "the highest regard," or "Love," or, as it turns out, "Father."

Let's go back up to the moment. – Friends who hurt me badly and without cause. – Every human emotion comes into play, this is normal. I am and will always be human, Christ as me. I am frightened, stunned, hurt, angry, and more frightened. Every part of this is Christ sharing His emotions with me. Don't think for one moment that Jesus did not feel this way as Judas betrayed Him to death, as Peter cursed and denied, and as all the others ran away.

In this place of frightful vulnerability and flagging weakness, what do I do?

I could create my own life either by striking back in some way or by withdrawing myself into bitterness and hurt. Or I could lay down my life, who is JESUS, for the sake of my brother or sister. I could, here inside of Jesus, in-between heaven and earth, here, inside of Jesus, above the Blood upon the earth, my heart, the Mercy Seat, I could continue as I have done, speak with the highest regard and the tenderest compassion.

If you want Church, this is the only place it is found. If you want Christ revealed to all, here is its only source. You gather together with other believers and they WILL offend you and you WILL offend them and both as awful as one can imagine, with each one arguing that he or she is "right." Church for real does not come out of Spiritual gifts or ministries. It is not known by place or order. Church comes only from one source, a man laying down his life for his friend.

And you know what? There is neither death nor dying to be found in my laying down my life for you. For here I know Father, and there is no death in God.

As the final days of this present age of human folly unfold, and we are most certainly in them, we will watch every form of pretend witness of Christ go forth across the earth. Do not be swayed by power or signs or gifts or anointings, even if they be from God. You will know the true second witness of Christ; they will lay down their lives for you. And you will know the true second witness of Christ as you also lay down your life for your friend. – You will know Father.

The second witness of Christ is the fullness of Mercy, the establishment of the Mercy Seat out from which alone the new heavens and the new earth come. Yes, we who walk inside of Jesus know gifts and power, anointing and ministry. Miracles are normal and incidental. But these things come and go as the wind; they are not our identity. They are not who we are; they are not the story we tell.

Those who receive power from power go out as power-mongers. Those who receive mercy from mercy go out as mercy-givers. Let us be Mercy; let us be Father. Then alone will we know real power, the power of life always springing up, love always poured out, joy anew every morning.

But God has given to us the greatest gift granted to anyone in the entire universe. God has granted us the gift of laying down our lives for one another. God has given us Himself; God has caused us to know Father.

I watched *Catching Fire* at the theater a second time recently. The *Hunger Games* movies speak truth all through me, a profound study of human integrity versus the abuse of power-over. In the first part of the movie, a primary background character spoke into the main character's hearing, Katniss Everdeen, as they waltzed slowly across the dance floor. When I watched *Catching Fire* the first time a few weeks ago, I had forgotten the real role of this ominous character from the books. Thus I saw him as the movie portrayed him, an evil character, a close ally of the dictator. Thus, as I heard his words the first time, I heard them entirely as ominous, as doom and destruction, as horror and loss and endless sorrow.

All of that changes at the end of the movie – that is, it all flips totally around. Then, when I watched that same scene a second time, hearing those same words from a totally opposite point of view, wow! Every word this character spoke was, "I am on your side; I am with you, Know that nothing will be as it appears." – But Katniss heard only what I heard the first time – horror and fear.

I live only inside of Jesus and Jesus inside of me, only inside of God and God inside of me. Thus everything in my life is found for me only here inside of God where I live. Every circumstance that comes my way, every incident, everything I do or am involved with is me inside of God and God inside of me. We walk together, God and I, in precious communion inside of perfect union. – I justify God in all things and give Him thanks for all.

My present ministry is to write, thus all things that come my way, inside of this Salvation in which I live, are for the purpose of flowing through my fingers onto this page, yet only in kindness and the highest regard for you. The difference of the sound of those words spoken by that character in *Catching Fire* was enlightening to me. The words were entirely the same. Yet the first time I heard them, I heard them as Katniss heard them, by appearance only. Then, the second time I heard the same words, I knew the substance behind them. And those same words spoke something totally the opposite as they did the first time I heard them.

The words did not change; my hearing did.

I am speaking of the Bible and of the Nicene Creed. The Nicene Creed has some words God spoke mixed up with the reasoning of man. Some of that reasoning is true ideas, yes, but God is not an idea; He is a Person filled with heart. The Bible itself can be heard in either of the two ways in which I heard the character speaking in *Catching Fire*. The Bible is a horror if you hear it by outward appearance. It is a glorious wonder if you hear it by the knowing of the substance of God. The writers of the Nicene Creed codified their knowledge of the Bible as a horror. They wrote down partly true words, yes, but they cemented their wrong hearing into the fabric of Christian theology and expression.

But when 1 John 3:16, known only by those living entirely inside of John 14:20, having entered by Galatians 2:20, has become the reality of the life of Jesus as us, this life we live in and love and know, then we read back through the entire Bible, and, oh my! Every word speaks totally different from what we ever thought.

Every word has become God with us inside of Salvation.

Hear Christ alone; hear nothing else. Speak Christ alone; speak nothing else.

Then, as we fling the door open to go forth across the universe, there, piled tightly against the cross and against the blood is a vast pile of corpses twisted in the agony of death. "What are these, Lord?" we ask aghast.

"These are they who listened to the preachers who told them that the cross stands between them and God, that they must 'die' first, before they will ever be allowed by God to enter His fullness. These are they who, looking up to the cross, saw ever their sinful nature. These are they who, looking at the blood from afar, saw ever their continual sin, their continual falling short."

And we say to one another, "Let's go among our brethren and judge them by the Mercy Seat upon our hearts so that they also may share this Life we love."

Only then will Salvation Revealed go forth upon this earth first, and after through all the heavens of God and throughout all realms created and yet uncreated, as a Body of Joy, as Life layed-down, as Love poured-out.

– As the laughing wealth of Father now seen and known and loved by all.

14. Face

You are free of me. You do not need me or anything that I write in order for Jesus to continue living you all the way into life. You belong to Him; He lives as you; He always leads you in triumph; and He most definitely does all things well.

Jesus lives us through seasons all through our lives. Wineskins must be changed regularly. It is destructive to anyone to cling to wineskins beyond their sell-by date. You belong to Jesus, and He does what He wants with His own, and He asks no man's pleasure, especially not mine. Jesus does all things well. The woman who is from above is free. She will lay down her life for you, but she will not be ruled by anyone but that which comes out with joy from her own heart; His name is Jesus.

Some may have picked up the idea that I am a man of God or that I am mature in "the things of God." Some may think that I am an outward expression of the things I speak. None of this is true, and if any of my words have ever led you to believe such a thing about me, please forgive me.

I once wanted to be a man of God for many years. I wanted a continual and certain anointing, the ability to speak with authority. I wanted the ability to pray and see great miracles so that everyone would know I am God's "sent one." All that has vanished away, and I find that all I can be is just me. I make big mistakes all the time in everything I put my hand to. I let people down. I get frustrated and the blinders come on, and I cannot see anything outside of the path right in front of me with the people around me on the outside of that path. I write, sometimes, out of that frustration.

You see, I always wanted to be with Jesus, but I couldn't make it. I couldn't produce or perform. I have great natural abilities, yes, but something has been cross-wired inside and in the crunch, I short-circuit, everything collapses, and I no longer have the strength of heart to continue.

But the most interesting thing has happened inside of me as well. I no longer need to be something I am not. I don't need to prove myself "mature" in Christian circles. I don't need people to leave interaction with me thinking, "Wow, Daniel sure is a man of God," or any such thought. I don't need to do anything except what I want to do in the present moment and what is necessary for my family. I don't need to be anything except what I find myself to be.

And what I find myself to be is a weak and vulnerable man – who still wants to be with Jesus and to know Him, even though I'm incapable of such a thing. Everything I write and speak, it's only because it's what I want, not because it's what I appear to be. I speak what I see written in the New Testament, at the core of the gospel. I don't know what else to write; writing other things goes nowhere.

You see, in this terrifying world we live in, a world that deceives everyone, and especially in the psychotic world of Christianity where everyone has an "in" with God and everyone will tell you the way it is, I don't know what else to do. Since I'm not a man of God, I have nowhere to stand. So many don't need Jesus; I do.

I write what I write only because I cannot imagine living without Jesus. And I can't have just part of Him in part of me. Such a way of thinking took me to the edge of mental illness and then kicked me over that edge. So in this place of insanity that I live in, I must see Jesus as all that I am, in all I find myself to be. And I must see me, especially my immature inability, as entirely and only and utterly inside of Him.

So if you find me to be immature and that I let you down, you are completely correct. And that's okay, for you see, I have lost my face; I have lost my self. I no longer need to appear in anyone's eyes.

I have made an arbitrary decision for myself. I have decided that the only real Substance or reality is the words of the gospel as they come to us through the Apostle Paul, that Jesus is our life, that He lives in our hearts, and that we live in and through Him. Thus I speak those words as if they are my only reality because, for me, they must be my reality; I don't know how to survive otherwise. If I'm wrong, if there is no living Lord Jesus, if the Bible is just a human book, if my reading of Paul's gospel is incorrect, if the role of anointed and mature individuals in the church is the correct leadership for me to come under, then having gambled all, I have lost.

But at this time of my life, all I have ever really wanted, I have found. I know Jesus in my heart and I know me only in Him, content with what I find myself to be, and I love Him as I always wanted to love Him, though I never thought I could. So if I am wrong, it's okay, because I have found all my heart's desire.

I have no need to save face, because I was never any good at putting on any kind of face that worked. There is the Face of a Man, bloody, bruised, and unashamed; His Face is sufficient for me.

I also want to apologize for not making myself clear on another point as well. I did try, with all my heart; let me try again. There is a practice, found almost only in Christianity, in which one person "sees" something "wrong" in another Christian and then "tells" them what's wrong with them with the idea that battering them will cause them to "fix" their "problem." This is an entrenched practice, very important to many people who read the Bible.

And I understand the feeling. I want so much to grab certain individuals and shake them hard. I want them to see how WRONG they are. I want them to feel the pain and embarrassment they have so thoughtlessly inflicted on me. I want to correct their "error." I want to fix their "problem" in a way that puts them beneath and me above. I want to correct people so badly that sometimes it's all I can think about for days and days. I work and work to come up with the perfect word that exposes their darkness and makes them KNOW how wrong they are and how right I am. And I do; I come up with incredible lines that just lays them low.

Except – that's one more thing I'm no good at. I'm too scared to say a word.

And in the end, I can't do anything else except justify God, find Him always right and true, and blame no one. You see, I can't live except inside of God's hand. I can't see anything as not from Him. I know some people argue a different doctrine, but I've never been able even to consider not-God in any part or time of my life. The whole idea of a not-God existence is an unfathomable horror to me, a chaos without mercy or care.

I think you can understand, in this vulnerable and frightful world in which we live, how I seized hold with all tenacity upon the glorious truth of Christ living as me in this world, from the very second I discovered myself, in a moment of revelation, entirely swallowed up inside of Jesus. Because I so very much need another self than this divided and incapable self I once thought was my burden, I was so determined to deny all thought of any such my self and make Jesus my only Self in my own mind and heart, that is, convince myself that Jesus was my real and only Self regardless of my continuing irresponsibility and foolishness, and all my embarrassing mistakes.

But alas, losing my self into Jesus as my only Self did not eliminate my reason. Thus it seems plain to me that if Jesus swallows up all of my darkness, then He swallows up yours as well. If Jesus is my only Self, in spite of my gross inability, then Jesus is also your only Self, in spite of your gross inability. If correct doctrine and correct outward performance have nothing to do with my knowing this One who fills my heart, then correct doctrine and correct outward performance have nothing to do with your knowing the One who fills your heart.

Then, something worse happened. In writing *The Covenant*, I discovered that my own heart of flesh filled with Jesus is the Mercy Seat of heaven. And in writing *Through Eyes of Fire*, I discovered that the sword of Jesus' mouth by which He slays all who oppose Him is the words, "**Father, forgive them**," and I discovered that "**And we also ought to lay down our lives for the brethren**," is the whole reality of Jesus going out from us.

Make note of those whom Jesus slew with the sword of His mouth. These were the ones who had devoted their lives to correcting Jesus. They followed Him around, urging Him to get right with God. They had the message that would fix Jesus' problem. Their whole ministry revolved around exposing people's darkness. And Jesus killed them dead with three little words, "**Father, forgive them**." Then He laid down His life for them and made them His dear and close friends.

You see, my reason tells me that **if God so loved us, then we also...**

But there is a wonderful side to these undeniable facts of common sense. I can feel hurt. I can feel frustrated and angry. I can feel very uncomfortable around certain people and in certain situations, and, oh, what a relief! All of it is just Jesus sharing His own feelings with me. Yet because it is He, and because it is me, I can, for the first time in my life, place my anger, which is our anger, entirely into His love, that He with me might carry those who I think are so "wrong."

And because I can place these brethren, whom I think are so wrong, entirely into Jesus, I no longer find any need inside to wear face, face I could never bear. My Face is bloody, my Face is bruised, and I am not ashamed.

I am not ashamed.

And here, in my utter lack of shame, I must cause you to understand something about me that I have tried to express, but have failed.

This practice of "exposing darkness" in a brother or sister, of saying words <u>at</u> some believer in Jesus that they are "wrong" in practice or in spirit or in doctrine, this practice of discovering fault and not Jesus and of failing to regard a brother or sister's heart – this practice I HATE and DESPISE out from years of experience. This practice I will rip to shreds in my writing. Though I do not and will never name names, those who practice this thing do not want to walk with me. Upon this practice I can show no mercy.

I am simply attempting here to be as honest and plain as I can.

First, I don't have to justify my hatred of this practice of "correcting" others, because I don't have to justify me. Those who offend me, I lay down my life for them, though they never know that I do. What I do, I do for my Father's sake alone.

Don't get me wrong; I am very much a "corrector." In fact, in all of my endless years of experience inside the demented psychosis that is produced by "correcting," I can boast that I have actually succeeded in more "correcting" than all that I have seen put together. A sister who has read my letter from the start mentioned in an email how her family, though they don't understand her knowledge of God, yet they love to be around her because of the freedom and joy and life in which she lives.

Now, all of that freedom and joy and life comes out of Jesus in her heart, entirely Jesus and her. Yet my words had something to do with it, because Jesus used the things I wrote to cause her to know Him as her only life. It may well have been only a small amount of bondage, sorrow, and death that my "correction" drove out of my sister, but regardless, freedom came from Jesus in her partly by my words and drove bondage out of her, life came from Jesus in her partly by my words and drove death out of her.

There are others who know life and Jesus and the loss of a useless and meaningless self as a result of what I have written. I got rid of their darkness BECAUSE I turned the light on. I got rid of my darkness by turning Christ on in me; I get rid of your darkness by speaking Christ into you. And it works because it's real. You see, I know how to bring down a city. The best way is to have an ally on the inside. A Friend of mine is on the inside of you; He really does share heart with you. All I have to do is expose Him to you and the walls come a' tumblin' down!

I never need to mention your "darkness" or your "bondage" or your "sin," because they died in Jesus 2000 years ago. God can't remember them, and if God can't remember them, He certainly can't "reveal" them to me.

Brethren, if a man is overtaken in any trespass, you who are spiritual restore such a one in a spirit of gentleness, considering yourself lest you also be tempted. Bear one another's burdens, and so fulfill the law of Christ. Galatians 6:2

Never once in my Church experience have I witnessed a heart restored by any correction of "fault" or exposing of "darkness." Those who practice such religiosity never fulfill the law of Christ; rather, that approach produces only pretending, the wearing of many faces. Yet I can remember fully those moments when someone showed me Christ in my own heart in honor and regard for me, and I can recount for you the volumes of darkness that disappeared from my life as a result.

I know the law of Christ. Here it is. Christ is always all first before anything not-Christ could ever vanish away. Again – Christ ALL, here, now, and me, causes all darkness to vanish without memory.

My sin doesn't matter because He already became all of it and took it into oblivion there in that grave where no dead body is found. I am free to know Christ alone in me. And I am free to know Christ alone in you.

And here is what I find. Common sense, REASON, seeing the joy of Christ as me, knowing that I am thus required to see all that you are as the Person of Jesus, my Friend, must grapple with a very difficult reality. The only thing that will alter the horrors of Adam's right and wrong universe and deliver all of our brethren still caught in such useless thinking is the same salvation of Jesus fulfilled a second time through us.

Jesus again lays down His life, this time by us.

Central to the other gospel wielded by the Nicene Christ, that is, by a Christ not in Person the ONLY life of the believer, is the terrible misuse of the cross typified for us by Constantine's using it as a symbol of conquest. This "cross" is the most effective psychological weapon in the manipulation of fellow believers.

A ministry, looking around at the obvious mess Christians are, sees the cross (not Christ as them) as the "answer." So they say, in one form or another, as if they have rediscovered the gospel and not because they are abusive manipulators of others, that dying must come to you before you will know life.

Anyone who places the cross in-between you and the knowledge of God in you in fullness is your enemy. The cross has already done its work; you are now entirely and only inside of Christ alive forevermore.

Now, this person who tells you that dying must come before you can know life will themselves never engage with this dying. If you "correct" them, they will show themselves to be very much alive, BUT they will use Bible verses and the catch-phrases of Christian psychotic control to subdue you back down under them. They do this to FEEL superior; they could care less about you.

But they tell you, with great argument, that you must die in some way first. Of course you can't do that and neither can they. But their power over you comes by your belief that they are speaking the "gospel" to you. The moment you "believe" that, you now see that one as ministry over you "in the Lord," and thus you grant them what they want, you "look up" to them.

Don't ever "look up" to me. You are as Jesus Himself, who happens to fill you with His glory. I am always looking up when I see you. Don't ask me for advice. If I make so many foolish mistakes myself, I cannot help you. I will share perspective with you, that is, I will seek to show you how Jesus is already victorious in you in all things and in every way, but I am incapable of giving you advice.

The best way for me to convey what I intend in this letter is to use the point-of-view of "I" and "you." So, for the next little bit, the "I" is the controlling I, that is, the judge just like God, but marred by the superiority/inferiority complex from the serpent. And "you" are my target, one whom "I" view as less than I, while "they" will be those "others" most necessary for controlling you, the "others" that all controllers use.

Now, I am speaking out of years of experience in human interaction in close-knit and continual relationships, in cCchurch community. I KNOW the words that denote Christian psychosis, and the words that reveal the existence of religious cult-building. I also know that these things are universal, prevalent in ALL, and few there be that escape them. I am writing this for those who would escape the cult-formation religious garbage so normal in Christianity and in the world. The only way to escape it is to escape one's false self, and the only way to escape one's false self is by casting one's self utterly into another Self as one's very own.

∽

As a judge, "I" judge by outward appearance. I see what I see and by God, it's real. I am a judge, after all, and I know what's real and what ain't, and I see that you do not measure up to my definition of Christ, who is so very much like me. But I am a powerful man (or woman – makes no difference), and I know that I am a man of God and that God has sent me as His emissary. I represent God.

Since it's obvious that you don't measure up to my definition of Christ (and I know what Christ is, because I am wise, my judgments are right and true and everyone else's are wrong), I tell you what's wrong with you; I expose the darkness in you. I tell you that dying comes first, before you will ever know God.

Now, I never think that "I" must die in this situation, that's a given; I'm the man of God. But you see, now that I have split you into two by the "cross," light and darkness, Christ and flesh, I have you divided against yourself. You look up to me quite naturally because we both know that I am a man of God. More than that, I have this thing called "discernment." The Catholics used confession to gain control over their flock, blackmail in its most powerful form. I don't need your "confession," because I have inside information on your sins given to me by God. I see your sin; I represent God; therefore, this inside info I have on you is the spiritual "gift of discernment."

This gift of seeing your darkness gives me blackmail power over you. Since I'm the man of God, you must now come under my covering in order to connect with God. But that's not enough. In order to exercise my rightful place, I need two other control objects. I need the "other," that is, the heretic, and I need those who "left," that is, the apostate. Joel Osteen makes a great "other." Look at him, he's wealthy and successful, he teaches God's favor; he is a deceiver. Let's all speak against Joel Osteen; he's a great "other." But there are more, let's find as many "others" as we can so that we KNOW that we are the in-group, the true "elect." With all these deceiving "others" out there, the only place of safety and protection is for you to stay close to me. I represent Christ to you.

And that's what makes that person who left our little in-group so immature. The fact that he or she left proves that I am right. That person's leaving the in-group means they didn't really ever have the "message." They left because they were so easily offended. You don't want to be like those apostates who are now following the heretics. Stay close to me so that you don't fall into their darkness.

I've heard these things said in so many different ways over the years, often from the pulpit, often under the anointing of the Spirit of God. I'm not easily swayed by "anointings." Someone who presents their "gifts" as their identity does not have my ear. The Word ALWAYS takes precedent over the Spirit.

But let me distinguish something very important. Part of our human foolishness is that we forget, and, moving out of frustration, we "correct" our brother or sister by throwing words at or about them. Early in my writing this letter, I did that to Bonnie Morris, using her private words to me in a public letter. I immediately received an icy-cold email from her, "You had no right to do that."

Now, my blundering was the normal foolishness of the human, just part of life. But the moment I read that reply from Bonnie, I saw the REAL issue. The real issue was this precious relationship with a sister in Christ and a friend. My being "right" was as meaningless as dog crap. The thought of losing her trust and her friendship was more than I could bear. I never looked again at my "argument." My being "right" in even a little bit was worth nothing to anyone; in fact, at that moment, any need in me to be "right" was the enemy of Christ.

I immediately replied to Bonnie. My first words were, "Oh Bonnie, I was so wrong, please forgive me. Your friendship is more important to me than anything." Then immediately I sent out a second *Christ Our Life* note explaining my fault and correcting what I had said. I also eliminated that section of my letter on the webpage. I could not do another thing until our friendship and trust was fully restored.

So, when someone else does the same foolish thing I can still too readily do, I have a very large heart that swallows all such stumbling up inside of love. I simply pay it no mind. But I cannot ignore the religious cult building that almost always comes out of this form of "correcting by exposing darkness."

Any group you may be a part of will enjoy the rich sharing of Christ with Christ, heart with heart, for awhile, depending entirely on a ratio of distance. The closer people live their lives together, the shorter the time of the enjoyment of Christ sharing with Christ. Then, a controller does his thing; he speaks thoughtless correction; she sets someone "in their place." Suddenly, everyone pauses and looks around carefully. "Am I next?" is the unspoken fear. At this moment, everything hinges on one thing.

You see, what the controller really needs is for the "corrected" person to leave the "in-group." There is nothing more important to religious control than heretics and apostates. Heretics are important, yes, those "others" out there who will condemn your soul to hell if you listen to them instead of to the "elect/elite" ministry (me). But far more important than a heretic is the apostate, those who were once "part of us," but who turned their backs on the true fellowship, the true light, the true message (me) and walked away.

Everything hinges on the next words spoken, words I have heard spoken openly and forcefully over many years in so many different ways and versions. I know those who have lived for decades by these words.

"The fact that the apostate left PROVES that I am right." – Speaking against those who leave our elite, I mean, "elect" group is the primary weapon of religious control. It's root is scorn.

I lived in Christian community for many years believing truly that "those who left" simply demonstrated that they were never really a part of God's elect. It was impossible for us ever to consider or think that God might have led them away from us. We are God's greatest thing in the earth; God would never speak to anyone to leave God, I mean, us. But when I moved with my family into Fort St.

John in the fall of 1998, having now become, myself, an "apostate," I saw over the next few months something I had never considered before. As one who had "left the move," I now fellowshipped with the Christians of Fort St. John. And in fellowshipping with them, I saw what they had seen for over 26 years, an unending, continual stream of broken, hurting, confused, and precious people fleeing those "elite" farms in the wilderness. A hemmorhage that just does not stop.

From the beginning of my writing, I have stated that any group I would walk closely with will bless the one who leaves, for WHATEVER reason, more in their leaving than in their coming, and that we will NOT assume one thing as to "why" they left. Jesus led them away in joy, and He does everything wonderfully well.

If you wish to practice what is reprehensible to me, that's okay. I do not hold it against you. I see you carried entirely by Jesus. I know that He will live you into ruin, of course, before He lives you back up into a willingness to live without pretence, but He knows what He is doing with you and I am content.

– I must draw two strong lines, here. First, there is a godly, Galatians 6:1 correction inside of Church. That correction is kindness only, spoken inside a prior relationship of trust and honor and coming with the only intention to see the hearer released into joy and the glory of Jesus. It is entirely private, heart with heart. It is spoken only by one who is also saying and willing to say, "I am and can be so easily wrong," as well. Second, we all act out of frustration, hurting one another, but we confess our fault and forgive one another. I'm not speaking of that, but of the thing that cares not for others and will not see the pain it causes nor bow itself in turn. –

But I am writing this to correct my poor communication. You don't want to associate with me if you wish to use psychological torture and manipulative abuse to impose yourself on God's people. Against that, like Jesus, I have no mercy. I have written my conviction on this matter from the start. There is no need for anyone to be ignorant of where I stand on this issue. If you believe it to be false doctrine, then, of course, you will find companionship elsewhere, hearts that agree with you. I walked for three years with what I did not agree; God used that time to teach me that's a really bad idea.

Here is what happens in any group that hears those sickest of all statements, *"The fact that he or she left proves that I am RIGHT."* By those words, everyone is split instantly into two, Christ and flesh. In a split second, everyone, just like Adam and Eve, puts on a mask, a face, a turning of the face towards the fear of power-over. Now, the person who has "corrected" has also established the "truth" that you cannot know God until you first die. Thus they now stand as the only door between a believing heart and this far-away God. The person speaking does not enter in, of course, they have little interest in knowing God. Knowing God would mean that they would have to lay down their life for others without saying a thing – not in their picture.

But the group also splits into two parts. There are those who willingly submit to "correction," thinking that by doing so they are somehow becoming more like Christ. They are not, of course, rather, they are learning to pretend for the "man of God." And there are those who would not submit to such, knowing it is not the Lord Jesus who lives in their hearts, but they are afraid of public exposure, and so they speak out from a different kind of face, but a face nonetheless.

And in one moment, the sharing of heart with heart morphs into the presenting of face against face. It's the way it works, and it happens every time.

Now, here's the thing. If you really want to know where someone's heart is at, what they really want, – right there, in that moment of supremacy, when the words are spoken against the "apostate" who already left, then do something quite daring. Without wearing any face at all, without any need to prove yourself "right" or "not right," correct the corrector.

Oh, my, that's when the proverbial stuff hits the fan. Then you will see whether this "man" or "woman of God" really loves Jesus and you or not.

Why did I respond the way I did when Bonnie sent me that very right "icy-cold" reply? The reason for my response has two sides to it, closely related.

On the one side was my hatred of this filthy, twisted, sick, perverted, satanic, serpentine, psychotic NEED in the pretending human soul to be "RIGHT," a hatred forged in me by the hand of my Father over years and years of heartache and abuse and treating others badly and being treated badly by others until I wanted something so different than all that psychotic hell forged by Adam and Nicene Christianity; I wanted something real.

BUT, counterbalanced perfectly with that is a completely opposite knowledge granted to me also by my Father, that so precious knowledge of the deepest of friendships, of the incredible fruit of walking together in full honor and respect, never assuming against your friend, but always assuming only the best. The knowledge that the relationship between two hearts is the only thing of value in the entire universe.

– The "issue" is never the issue. The only real issue is one heart with one heart holding one another in the highest regard. –

God lives in a house NOT built with hands. The Kingdom cannot be built; it arises only. The Church cannot be built; she is a free woman. Yet Church by Father is real, and it is what the entire creation is waiting for. Church by Father is real because Father is real and He really fills us with ALL of Himself.

The WORD itself, Christ Jesus, will fulfill the Bride entirely out from Spirit with no human hand put to her honor. As we flow together in that same Spirit, we will know the most glorious thing possible.

We will know Church by Father.

15. Church by Father

Where two or three of you are gathered together in My name, there I am in the midst of you. Jesus.

Laying down one's life for one's friends the way Jesus did has no apparent value. ALL human argument, emotion, and action cries the opposite. Every human story says FIGHT for your own. Those who will not fight for their own in time of danger are considered by all the worst of cowards.

Jesus was under attack; His own disciples were in danger of their lives. Everything He had taught and won for the kingdom was in mortal peril. If Jesus went down, everything He had tried to establish would go down with Him as well. ALL human counsel, all human emotion would say, "NOW is the time to fight."

I am convinced that a large part of Jesus' agony in Gethsemane was the very human question, "Father, what good is this? How will My silence and My yielding to My enemies' hatred and violence accomplish anything?"

Jesus did not fight for His own. He walked away from all those who counted on Him and allowed His enemies to win all victory against Him.

What good was that?

We cannot view this moment from hindsight. We cannot bring in all the doctrine of redemption. The only possible way we could understand the reality of Jesus in that moment is to see only out from His eyes.

Why did He do it? Why did He act, step by step, against all human reason, against all human emotion, against all outward appearance?

I know why. He did it because His Father asked Him to; He did it for Father's sake. As He walked the path of human cowardice, possessing all power to fight and to win, yet not touching that power for one moment, the only thing that kept His mind clear and His eye steady was one thought alone.

"Father, for Your sake, I lay down My life, for You, Father, because You asked Me to and because I love You."

You see, the blood, the cross, the resurrection, these things are in some sense symbolic, or inevitable, one might say. The real transaction, the real singularity was taking place inside Jesus' heart. As Jesus took each step, saying continually in His heart, "Father, for Your sake, because I love you," inside that very HUMAN love filled with God Himself in Person, something was birthed into the universe, something that had never been, something that could come no other way.

Church. — The Bride of Christ.

It was the joy of that Church that filled Jesus' heart as He rose to His feet in Gethsemane, but she herself was birthed out from "for Your sake, My Father."

But when they came to Jesus and saw that He was already dead, they did not break His legs. But one of the soldiers pierced His side with a spear, and immediately blood and water came out. And he who has seen has testified, and his testimony is true; and he knows that he is telling the truth, so that you may believe. John 20:33-35

That blood and water, coming out from Jesus' pierced heart, was the Church being drawn by Father out from the mightiest transaction of Heart with Heart in the universe. That relationship between two, heart with heart, is the only thing of value or meaning in Christianity.

When there are huge problems in the church, when you are the target of the ire and frustration of many, the craziest thing in the universe is to keep your mouth shut, turn to your Father, and say, "Father, for Your sake, I lay down my life. Here I am, lay upon me their wrong in their place. For Your sake, Father, because I love You."

The human heart wants vengeance; human reason cries out to fix the problems. Neither one will ever birth Church.

You see, Church is not some human thing; church is a Divine thing. It was the interaction between the Spirit of God and Mary that birthed Jesus, fully human and fully divine. It is the interaction between the Father and the Son living as us that births the Church.

The Church is not a bunch of people getting together once a week or so.

Where two or three of you are gathered together in My name, there I am in the midst of you.

Church is Jesus in the earth. Church is fully human and fully divine, but the human part exists for the purpose of revealing the divine part to the universe.

Church is to reveal Father.

Yet there is no Church except there be two or three (or more) gathered together as the Lord Jesus Christ. And there is one action alone that reveals Father – laying down one's life for one's friends.

No one is ever Church as an individual. One person, as an individual, cannot be Church. Jesus Christ walks the earth ONLY as two or three are gathered together. Inside that relationship of two, heart with heart, in mutual respect and honor, Christ Jesus lives.

You see, all those who are "building the kingdom" or "forging the vision" cannot be birthing the church. The only ones who are birthing the church are those who, in each moment, in each individual relationship, are laying down their lives for their brother or sister, refusing to "fix" the problem, taking upon themselves all fault and all blame, and who are doing so for Father's sake alone.

There is nothing more useless to the human mind, nothing. Every human inclination cries out to "fix" the problem. Yet the moment one reaches out to fix the problem, Father vanishes and Church is no more. Now you have a group of people meeting together as a church, yes, but without Church.

The most difficult thing about laying down one's life is that no one notices, including the one for whom you laid down your life. The only one who notices is Father, and Father is utterly invisible.

Now, I have shared that my condition of Asperger's meant that I could not comprehend other people. It was only in my late twenties, as I was finding my place in the school classroom as "the teacher," that I could consider what, exactly, these other entities all around me were, that they were humans just like myself. Since comprehending people did not come naturally to me, I have spent a lifetime trying to figure them out.

But now I'm beginning to realize something else. Most people never do. Most people seem content never to comprehend that other people are just like themselves. Now, I understand fully the zoning out when it comes to these entities all around us, the tendency to treat them as "others." It's something I do regularly. But being bothered by who and what these "others" are seems not a generally held condition, and trying to figure them out is not a generally considered practice.

When I hurt others, they are just others, what is that to me?

The ability to see the heart of one's brother or sister is a capacity few desire. If it doesn't exist, neither does Church. Yet Church is more than seeing the heart of one's brother or sister, though it must begin there, but Church comes out of the action of taking upon one's self all the pain of any difficulty, allowing the other to go free in joy without any sense of loss in spite of, even contrary to, "what they deserve." Of course, if such a thing is done in morbidity, it's completely worthless. What makes such an action Church by Father is when it is done for Father's sake, with one's eyes fixed on Father alone.

But I can assure you that such a course is God-only. The human may stumble along in sharing behind such a decision, but only One could ever do such a thing, only Christ. And the human can follow only as we call Christ our only Self and only after we have made His Gethsemane ours by knowing that it IS.

It is here, on this point, that the contrast between the real Christ and the Nicene Christ is made stark and complete. And when I say "the Nicene Christ," I mean all definition of the "power" Christ. I include that definition that was thrown at me by which I wrote "Christ Versus Superman," a definition of Christ that most deeper truth groups, including the move of God I was once a part of, share. I include that definition of a violence-wielding Christ coming someday to establish an outward kingdom by force. I include that definition of Christ as an all-pervasive spirit that awakens us to our "Christ-consciousness," a Christ separate from Jesus, a Christ separate from a Man laying down His life for His friends.

The power Christ wants to prove God outwardly to the world.

The real Christ wants to birth Church across the earth.

Thus all emissaries of the power Christ must fix the problems of all those "others" who are ruining his grand kingdom. But all ambassadors of the real Christ are laying down their lives in silence and ignominy for others, for Father's sake. They don't "represent" Christ; He represents them.

You will know who the power-Christ people are; they will make sure you know. You will hardly know those who lay down their life for you. What you will know is Father upwelling within you in joy, in tears, in an outpouring of wealth and goodness.

You will know Church.

No one wants to be like Christ; it's completely contrary to Adam's pretending to be silent, to take on one's self the hurt caused by the sins of others, that they may walk free without guilt or any shadow of loss, that they, the one's who deserve hurt and pain, can know only joy and life while you alone bear before Father your measure of the pain that they should have borne.

Surely He bears our griefs and carries our sorrows. – And we also... – Bear one another's burdens and so fulfill the law of Christ.

This is the well-spring, the only source of Church by Father. This is the only thing of any value upon this earth and in the universe.

I am speaking of two walking together, heart with heart, in the highest honor and regard for one another, each one taking on one's self the pain of all the thoughtless actions of the other, yet each one knowing it is so, and honoring the other for such Father love.

Where such a relationship exists, Jesus walks the earth. Those who possess such a relationship possess the wealth of the universe, those who do not are utterly poverty-stricken.

However, Church does not yet exist when I lay down my life for you any more than Church yet existed when Jesus walked the Path of the Atonement. Church exists only as one lays down his or her life for the other while the other is laying down his or her life for the first. Here, in this mutual relationship Jesus is made known.

We KNOW that it is God Himself in Person, the Father with us, because such a thing can only be Father revealed.

And here is the place for the mind, for the *dianoia*. Every inclination of the human cries, "NO! Fight for what is right." Only the pure knowing that this is Father, that this is for Father's sake can counteract the utter uselessness of such a course. Only the mind of Christ, only seeing out from Jesus' eyes, nothing else will ever take us there.

Now, I have laid out the only source of Church; if this is not the source, what we have is church, not Church, regardless of any manifestation of Spirit or any eloquence of Word. Next, I want to look, briefly, at the structure of Church before touching on the fruit of Church.

God has ONE order ONLY for His Church, the order of the wineskin. Yes, the wine is found in a wineskin, but it does not come from the wineskin. The tendency of the human to call the wineskin "God" is so prevalent, so universal, and so deep, that we really must be laughingly vicious as we cast out last year's wineskin. Every Christian group I know anything about takes last year's wineskin, places it on a pedestal, and calls it "God."

Throw it out.

No outward form ever produces wine. What drinker of wine will enamour himself with an empty wineskin, hoping that it will produce more wine? The wine comes from the vine. Any connoisseur of wine will show up at the wine vat where wine is produced (that is, laying down one's life for each other inside of Christ-as-us) knowing that here alone comes the new wine. However, many lovers of wine (that is, God revealed) come with their own comfortable wineskins from last season's wine. Inevitably, the old wineskins break and the wine seeps out, only the drinker of wine never notices, enamored as he is by his wineskin. In fact, most groups trade the wine for the wineskin and come to hold all new wine in suspicion as an enemy since it is so destructive of their old wineskin.

In complete contrast, the wise ones show up empty handed, receiving the new wine in a new wineskin provided by the giver of wine.

Church is a skin-changer. She takes on a new form every season of new wine. And every season of new wine, she throws away her prior form as presently and utterly useless.

I want to talk about what is called a "hive mentality." This is a misnomer; there is no such thing. In fact, the real "hive mentality," that is, real mindlessness, comes from what is considered to be the opposite of this supposed "hive mentality," and that is, command and control.

Whenever a bee hive or an ant colony is turned into a story or movie, such as the animated movie, *Antz*, the colony is shown as a top-down command and control class structure. The working "class" is entirely under the control of the Queen or her commanders. Yet this picture is entirely the opposite of an actual hive and indicative, rather, of violent human society, especially of socialist societies.

Every single individual ant in an ant colony, every single individual bee in a hive does ONLY what that ant or bee WANTS to do in that moment. The Queen bee or ant emanates NO authority whatsoever. There are no guard bees or ants waiting on the side to inflict pain on any ant that does what it "feels like doing." BECAUSE all the ants and all the bees are doing ONLY what they feel like doing and nothing else. However, it is a divine law of any society that like gathers with like. Thus those who want to pack food home to the colony, congregate with those who want to pack food home to the colony. Thus each individual ant also moves together with those particular ants on each side and before and behind who are also doing exactly what they want to do.

The amazing thing is that all those who want to pack food home to the hive would be unable to do so if there were no bees or ants who WANTED to go out by themselves looking for food. These solitary individuals spend their entire lives wandering around in dangerous arenas by themselves looking for food – entirely because they want to. Yet the moment they find food, they also WANT to rush back and tell others all about this new food they have found, where they also can find it. Thus all those who simply want to carry food back to the colony rush out with this new information to find this new food to carry.

Then, the line of ants carrying food is attacked by a vicious enemy. Guess what! There is another whole group of ants who, each one individually, simply WANT to rush out and fight the enemy. No one tells them to do so. No one appoints them to a place. They simply do only what they want to do. Others want only to take care of the newborns, and they do. Others want only to provide what the Queen needs, and they do. Every single ant, every single bee does ONLY what it wants to do all the days of its life, and it does those things in a quiet, but considered relationship with those others who are wanting to do the same thing.

So the children of Israel departed from there at that time, every man to his tribe and family; they went out from there, every man to his inheritance. In those days there was no king in Israel; everyone did what was right in his own eyes. Judges 21:24-25

Then all the elders of Israel gathered together and came to Samuel at Ramah, and said to him, "Look, you are old, and your sons do not walk in your ways. Now make us a king to judge us like all the nations." But the thing displeased Samuel when they said, "Give us a king to judge us." So Samuel prayed to the Lord. And the Lord said to Samuel, "Heed the voice of the people in all that they say to you; for they have not rejected you, but they have rejected Me, that I should not reign over them.
1 Samuel 8:4-7

A true "hive mentality" is the complete honoring of each individual person who, in complete freedom, does what is right in his own eyes. This is God's kingdom; this is God's order.

The serpent hates such freedom because it is the presence of Christ AS each individual member of His body and including all that individual's outward mess. Thus the serpent is always whispering "command and control" into those who would judge all things by outward appearance.

I was once taught that **"everyone did what was right in his own eyes"** was anti-Christ, the opposite of God's order. Thus a particular form of command and control was structured into the order of church. Like all wineskins, this form of command and control contained much that was purely of God, but like all lovers of wineskins, when the season of new wine came, the new wine was rejected and the form was honored as "God's order." This is utterly human and normal.

Look at the words, **"every man to his inheritance."** Every individual person was honored in his or her own individual inheritance. In fact, under Joshua, women were granted the same honor, and though that was only a partial granting of honor, yet it pre-figured the full inclusion of Christ.

Look at a flock of birds flying. Each individual bird does only what is right in its own eyes in conjunction with those individual birds close by. Yet the flock moves in beautiful formation, in an endlessly fluid order. More than that, the other individual birds close by each one change all the time, yet the same order prevails, each one does only what it wants in full conjunction with whichever other birds happen to be close by at the moment. There is no command and control, no orders flowing out of one bird's mind controlling all the others.

This is God's order and it works amazingly well. Yet in the Church, only utter faith in God would ever allow such an order to prevail. "Fixing people's problems" is a universal lust of envy; it is the endless cry of Marx we hear all around us in our world today.

Such an order for human life happened only twice in the human experience. The first time was under Moses, Joshua, and some of the judges. The second time was in the early years of the American experience. Yet in both experiments, the lust of envy weighed both down into oblivion. Such an order of human life, complete freedom, that is, complete honor and respect for each individual person with zero command and control, zero "governmental regulation" apart from those few laws of liberty, do not steal, do not kill, that is, the non-initiation of violence except to stop such initiation of violence, is attacked right from the start by those who cannot live without pushing their neighbors around.

In the American experience, the first major blow against such a way of living was the adoption of the Constitution, allowing the formation of the great Beast that rules America today. The second blow was Abraham Lincoln and his violent destruction of voluntary union. The third blow was the creation of the Federal Reserve Board and the implementation of the income tax in 1913, along with the triumph of Marxism over education around the same time.

The reaction of the American people and government to the events of September 11, 2001 was not the "final blow," rather, it was the unveiling of the complete loss of any concept of freedom in the American mind.

The free market ended in 1913. All economic problems we see in our world today are entirely the fruits of socialism, that is, of command and control. Yet we see "freedom" blamed as the cause of all present woes, and the answer presented is that all flee entirely into collective obedience to wicked and violent individuals masquerading behind the fiction of "human society."

Command and control is what causes mindlessness and ruin, poverty and war. The world is lying. When they say, *"Give to your neighbor by paying us taxes first,"* they are lying. It's called power, and most humans, wanting to participate in plundering their neighbors, give their power to the Marxist psychopaths who know exactly how to play the envy in non-thinking humans.

Complete freedom, that is, holding each individual person in the highest regard, is the only order that brings wealth and abundance for all.

And that is why CHURCH is the ONLY hope for mankind and the future of human history upon this earth.

Now, ALL command and control gains its power by using "the boogeyman." *"The boogeyman will get you if you don't do what I say. The Russians will get you, the terrorists will get you, the Muslims will get you; the only hope you have to survive is to do what you're told by your own 'government.' The heretics will get you, the demons will get you, if you don't stay 'under your covering,'* that is, if you don't keep yourself pliable to *"my control over you."* Some religionists turn even God into just another "boogeyman."

And that is why CHURCH is the ONLY hope for mankind and the future of human history upon this earth. The only ones who will break the endless cycle of Cain killing Abel are those who lay down their lives for their enemies, making their enemies their close and dear friends.

But one final thing concerning the structure of Church before we look at the fruit of Church by Father.

Here is a reality of church. You cannot gather together with others without regular governmental meetings to discuss the issues in a formal setting and to agree upon rules, which are then clearly presented to all. Then, for it to be a Godly church, the leadership must make sure NO one is enforcing those rules (leaving the parental role free). At the same time, the true leaders will be laying down their lives as the Lord leads whenever someone does break the rules. A laid-down life is a continual personal loss; it is never an imposition on others.

Rules, agreed upon together and clearly delineated, are essential to any kind of life together. Enforcing rules has destroyed more people than anything I know.

God is our only example. He gave a bunch of rules, then bore all rule-breaking and consequence inside Himself so that His friends could be forever free of the death of rules. Yet – as we live in Him, we find those same "rules" arising in our own hearts without condemnation, gently guiding our lives as we do entirely what we want to do in conjunction with those around us.

The "rules" of any gathering have to do, not with God's order, but with moving together in the present moment with those immediately in conjunction with us in that moment. Without simple rules, people WILL misunderstand each other.

You cannot have any Church except with regular governmental meetings. In a community, those meetings must be at least once a week; in a church where members live on differing properties, those meetings must be at least once a month. That governmental meeting must be conducted in a formal sense, with only governmental issues brought up, with time to speak kept short, with every adult being granted the opportunity to speak if they wish, and with every one's speaking listened to quietly and highly regarded by all.

Some issues can be decided by majority vote, other issues require a 100% consensus. Then the decisions arrived at by all, with everyone satisfied in their spirits with the outcomes must be written down so that they can be referenced and clearly understood. (It is possible to disagree with a minor decision while being fully able to flow with it in full unity of spirit.)

If this kind of governmental occurrence does not take place, then, invariably, the controllers will win control and the majority will either be subdued or driven away. It is only inside this place of formal respect that each voice will be heard.

Yet we never call any agreed upon rule, "God," but we are ready with joy to change the rules in a heartbeat, should it be convenient and agreeable to do so. You see, Christ having become His Church MEANS that Christ is doing all things well regardless of any outward appearance.

Let me dare, here, a completely different definition of "the return of the Lord" than any you may have heard. I dare this different definition only because the Father is whispering it right now in my heart. — Here it is.

Where two or three of you are gathered together in My name, there I am in the midst of you.

Let us take this word as literal. Let us take it as the actual fulfillment of the return of the Lord at this end of the age of human folly.

By this we know love, because He laid down His life for us. And we also ought to lay down our lives for the brethren.

"And we also" and "in My name" are the same thing.

By this we know God because God. And we also ought to God.

Church by Father.

And the glory which You gave Me I have given them, that they may be one just as We are one: I in them, and You in Me; that they may be made perfect in one, and that the world may know that You have sent Me, and have loved them as You have loved Me. John 17:22-23

In move community we tried one with "the group" in our desire to see God fulfill Jesus' prayer in our lives. God taught me two important things through being intimately acquainted with such a "oneness." First, being one with the group ALWAYS stood in-between any two people. One person could not relate with one other person except through the "group." Second, as I was leaving that fellowship, I learned that the friendship of one heart with one heart was the only thing real.

If one and one walk together heart with heart, then the whole Body is one. But if there are no one-with-one's, neither is there a Body.

As I consider my present relationships with many who read this letter, those relationships vary considerably from one to the next. Yet I consider each one individually. Each relationship is different; some I communicate with often, some seldom. Some relate with me in one manner, others in a different manner. Yet each individual relationship is special and unique, precious and particular in God. Thus, I desire not to write for a "group," but for many individual people who share heart with me.

In the communities I knew, the mentality revolved around what was good for the group and sometimes the individual was sacrificed for the sake of the group – I'm speaking of a group filled with the Spirit and moving in genuine love.

Church, on the other hand, is all about one-with-one relationships, allowing their addition and multiplication, subtraction and division, to take place entirely as the wind blows without anyone putting his or her hand out to control.

And now, for the first time, I understand how we can know Christian community without any hint of socialism. The foundation of Church is a leadership always laying down their lives for each individual person. Socialism is disrespecting the individual for the sake of the group.

Always, it is "greed" and "selfishness" that is attacked by those crying for socialism, whether in the church or in the world. But that's only a smoke screen. Rather, the target is each individual person, that each one would be viewed as a liability and thus subject to control or, if need be, elimination. There is no such thing as a group. Individual persons will ALWAYS be in control of the levers of power over any so-called group. I saw that working in benign ways in Christian community, truly good people moving in sincerely wrong ways. In the world, those individuals are simply wicked.

God's Church is the opposite.

In God's Church, Cain lays down his life for Abel AND Abel lays down his life for Cain. Some claim that's what happens on a battlefield, that fellow soldiers become such "brethren." Not even! I am speaking of the men on one side laying down their lives to preserve the life of the men on the other side.

But such kingdom-living cannot be legislated or even taught. It comes only by example, many examples, scattered across the earth, of Christians loving one another at that level.

> **– That they may be one just as We are one: I in them, and You in Me; that they may be made perfect in one, and that the world may know that You have sent Me. –**

I have always believed that this prayer of Jesus MUST BE fulfilled literally and completely here in the blood and sweat and tears of this life, among a simple people, little groups scattered across the whole earth, BEFORE the world will know that the Father has sent the Lord Jesus.

I look for no other kind of return.

And I know now that it is fulfilled by a people who live in John 14:20, having entered by Galatians 2:20, and who relate with one another through 1 John 3:16.

There is no other gospel; there is no other revelation of Jesus Christ.

16. Heart

To a sister: — You have used my words as part of your "confession," and they are stark words indeed. Emptiness hidden behind, in your case, mental argument and people/things. And this is the whole human race. It is the Lord Himself, in great tenderness and care, who has brought you to see this. This seeing of one's self as a lost cause is the only beginning, that is, the necessary door.

This knowledge of your own emptiness, your own lostness, is a vital and permanent part of your new Self, that is of Christ living as you, as your new and only Self. However, it must go into its proper place. In its proper place, our knowledge of our own lostness (somehow that word contains the largest part of what I am referring to, emptiness, vulnerability, inability, weakness) is a continual turning to the Lord. Outside of its proper place, it just as easily becomes part of the bluster and pretending.

I can explain only with myself. I have been very capable outwardly. I used to be fine inwardly. But over the years, God took me through circumstances that brought my outward capability to ruin and completely shattered all inward confidence.

But my problem is that I have always feared God. That is, I have always reckoned that there are only two options: **"Well done, My good and faithful son, enter into the joy of your Lord"** VS **"Depart from Me, I never knew you."** You see, I can't have the second. And I don't see that as anything to do with "heaven/hell."

I must know Him, how else could I live?

But I lived in a Christian view that said I had to get something right, no one knew exactly what or how much, but something right in order to hear the one and not the other. Because I always feared God and always sought Him, I don't know that my outward life was bluster and pretending so much as just doing the only thing I knew to do. Yet it all brought me to utter hopelessness.

I would not be "making it." I would not be "getting anything right." Yet how could I live?

This is a far bigger question than we comprehend.

Now that I know LIFE, and I do, the more my own sense of vulnerability remains. But it remains in its place. That is, it keeps me ever turned to Life and ever away from any need for my own face in this world. Yet it does not take the place of Life and become its own dead end.

There are many hopeless people. Their hopelessness does them no good. In fact their hopelessness is really just one more layer in the wall they hold against God. In complete contrast, we take our continual sense of lostness, of vulnerability, of inability, and use it to abandon ourselves every moment, with all joy and gladness, as a lost cause and hold to Jesus alone as our very and only Self.

I can see myself seated upon the throne of heaven with all boldness BECAUSE I continually know that I am a lost cause. I have nothing to lose and nothing to gain. I have failed. What a relief! I hold to Jesus as my only Self because I must, because I have no other "self" that will take me anywhere but into **"Depart from Me."** I speak all that Christ is as being my only Self because the alternative is continually unthinkable.

But you see, the fear of God is not really "fear"; it's just the first parts of Love. I speak Christ as my only Life because I love Him. I love Him. I would far rather be He than me. And if He allows me to be Him and not me (Galatians 2:20), I will always be He.

Because Jesus is real and alive and love, as I call Him my very and only Self, I become real and alive and love. But there is something else in the picture as well. I want to talk about your heart.

God is not whimsical. He offered us a Covenant, a full binding contract. We know He signed that contract by the Blood of His Son. We signed the contract when we first said, "Yes, Lord," and when we were baptized in water. The contract is binding and absolute. This is so very important. God is bound absolutely to us by Covenant. He has no choice in the matter; the Covenant is a done deal.

The first part of Covenant is a new heart, a good heart, a heart filled with Christ. Sister, your heart is GOOD. Pay ZERO attention to your emotions and desires, including frustration, anger, lust, and greed. Those things have nothing to do with your heart. Your heart is good and filled with Christ in all of His glory.

This is absolute. My heart is absolutely good. It is the first part of Covenant. God gave me a new heart the moment I was born again, for me, age seven. It was only when I could say, out loud with all zeal, "My heart is good," that God could begin to show Christ to me.

People throw around Bible terms and phrases without ever knowing what God actually says. God loves your flesh; it is His dwelling place forever. Empty of God, the flesh is all bluster and pretending, certainly, but the flesh is NOT the old man. Filled with God, the flesh is pure and holy. There can be no God-liness without flesh. God-liness is God manifest in the flesh.

But the old man is unredeemable. That's why God did away with it the moment you were born again. The old man is gone forever; just look at the cross and see him dead. No, that is not the full picture. We were buried with Christ as well. The old man was buried; no one digs up corpses to hold tightly to them, except

"Christians." More than that, look in the tomb for your "buried" corpse; you will find nothing there.

Now you are a human with your center, your heart, pure and good, filled with all the glory of Christ. You don't have to feel that, you don't have to see that, but you MUST know it to be true because God says. And you know it to be true by saying that it is true. "My heart is good and filled with Christ."

And so I take these two things together, side by side in perfect balance, my own human weakness, inability, vulnerability, right alongside my pure and good heart filled with Christ. These two things at the core of me are then the source of my growing knowledge of Christ my only life.

But we have a continual enemy, the accuser, and we must always refuse to hear him. He always attempts to turn those two things upside down and inside out. He wants to whisper "evil" upon your heart and "able" upon your weakness. He wants you to doubt your heart and trust your ability to "obey."

There is one way alone by which we cast the accuser down, and that is by speaking Christ our only life, anchored utterly in the Blood on the one hand and the Cross on the other. We cannot hear the accuser because we are speaking Christ our only life too much.

"Christ, You are my life; You are all there is in me. There is NOTHING in me that is not You in all of Your glory."

It's crazy I know, but we love Him.

To another sister: — Yes, Christianity is very confusing, every little group all ignoring one another, all seeing the others as totally "other." All claiming that their own minor distinction is the true truth. It is sad and silly both. We know that God is all in all and works all in all, that any problems any Christian or church group might face come only out of living with their backs turned to, ignorant of, the glory that already fills their hearts.

The church is one. Jesus carries all. Their problem is in their own minds as they construct their own definitions of God. And every definition of God they construct keeps God Himself far away from them. But understanding how they think is a big part of knowing how to walk with them in peace, for they are our brethren. They belong to Jesus as they belong to us, though they know it not.

Sister, you have put on the Lord Jesus Christ, fully and completely. You did so the very moment you gave Him your heart. Call it so regardless. "I am clothed entirely and only with Christ Jesus Himself." It's important to say this especially when you think the worst. Say it because it is true.

But I have realized that there is an ingredient God gave me before He began to reveal Christ my only life to me. I have not always brought this vital ingredient front and center. The Lord just reminded me of it. — Heart.

Sister, your heart, all of your heart, is good, pure, holy, and good.

The moment you gave your heart to Jesus you entered into a covenant with God. The first part of covenant is that God gave you a new heart. Your heart is good. There is no "old" heart at all. You know you have only a new and good heart because Jesus lives in your heart, making it entirely and always good, and He never leaves.

Now, here is the thing about the heart. The heart is the central organ of your body; it is the central organ of your soul; and it is the central organ of your spirit. Thus anything going from the realm of spirit through your spirit and into any other part of you, mind or body, must pass through your heart.

Your heart is good.

Your enemy's primary target is to make you imagine, even just a little bit, that your HEART is not good. If he can do that, he has gummed up your whole works. The problem is not the enemy; the problem is your thinking, even just a tiny bit, that your heart may not be good.

So say and sing, "My heart is good, my heart is good, my heart is filled with Jesus," over and over. But especially when you think and feel that it is not.

You see, just after you get frustrated with a family member and scream at them and they feel bad and you feel bad, but you're too frustrated to admit it. Right then, that is when you must say, "My heart is good, my heart is good, my heart is filled with Jesus." That is the moment you must "put on" the Lord Jesus Christ.

You are already fully clothed with Him, call it to be so.

We put on the Lord Jesus Christ by saying, "I am clothed with Christ and my heart is good, filled with Jesus," until we believe it, until we know that nothing else is real.

If Jesus is not real, then we are definitely becoming delusional. But Jesus is real and He really is our only Self. Thus when we call Him so, even when we appear to ourselves as being totally wretched, when we pay no attention to our own wretchedness, but say, "I am clothed with Christ and my heart is good, filled with Jesus" – until we know it is true – then we discover that He is real and that we are real and that He is our only life.

Call everything you are and everything you go through, Christ Jesus Himself. You are already clothed with Christ from the moment you gave your heart to Him and He made it good by making your heart His dwelling place. You "put on" the Lord Jesus Christ now by calling it to be so regardless.

"I am clothed with Christ; I am filled with Christ; there is nothing else in me or of me."

I KNOW your heart is good; it cannot be anything else.

And here is another secret we discover as we know we are, right now, fully and forever clothed with Jesus. We have always been so. Every moment you thought you were a sinner, you belonged utterly to Jesus. You didn't know it, but He did. And every moment of your life, every circumstance you've ever known, from conception until now, it was all He, clothing you with Himself, guiding your steps, carrying you, sharing things with you. Though you did not know it at the time, yet now you see that He was always revealing Himself to you.

When He led you into the church you were a part of, He did so that He might share His own sufferings, His own broken heart, His own understanding of the sorrow of His people, that He might share it with you. In every moment you spent in that part of your life, it was all Jesus with you, in you, as you, through you. You didn't need to know it for it to be utterly true.

Part of **"put on the Lord Jesus Christ"** is to accept Him as ALL that you are. You can't "make" Him to be so; He already is because He says. But you accept it as true and then cast down every voice that mutters otherwise. You cast down those other voices by saying, "I am clothed with Christ; I am filled with Christ; there is nothing else in me or of me" over and over.

Change the words around a bit, make them your own, make it your song and sing, sing, sing the Lord Jesus Christ, the only life you are.

I have found for Myself a man after My own heart.

I don't think it's possible to say anything deeper about God or to say anything deeper about man that this short line. I am convinced that any "idea" about God that leaves this line out of its center leaves God out as well.

Jesus' words, **"He that has seen Me has seen the Father,"** come entirely out from this original speaking of God through Samuel eight years before David was born (or vice versa, Samuel spoke out of Christ).

And thus we must ask the question – What is heart?

I don't think we can know – What is God? Or – What is man? Or – What is Christ? Without first knowing – What is heart?

If you write out every word in the Bible, from Genesis to Revelation, containing the word "heart," you would have a difficult time arriving at a specific definition. I have, on my website, every New Testament verse containing *kardia*, heart – *Nous, Dioanoia, Psuche,* and *Kardia* in the New Testament. One of the most peculiar references is in Acts 14 – **God fills our hearts with food and gladness.**

We will never arrive at a knowledge of – What is heart? – by any mental comparison of verse with verse. Thus I will be bold here and define "heart" as I understand it in the present moment so that I can explore out from that present knowledge into God's purpose for this thing called "heart."

In the first part of this letter I established the doorway into living in our present hearts. In the New Covenant, which is the only Covenant we know, a heart transplant WAS an essential part of the original deal. Thus we consider our hearts and every part of them as new, and especially, as GOOD. We cannot live in a shared heart with God unless we have entered fully by the door. That door is always Galatians 2:20, whatever was old is gone, crucified, buried, and no longer to be found. Whatever I am, as I find myself to be in the present moment, is Christ alone. Thus my heart IS His sacred heart.

I can never see my heart as Jesus' heart unless I have lived for some time in the knowledge that my heart IS good. Then, out from having lived in the knowledge that my heart, in its entirety, is both new and good, I can now proceed to comprehend what, exactly, this heart of mine really is.

Let me bring in two sets of verses that define my heart and yours, that define the heart of God.

You shall put the mercy seat on top of the ark, and in the ark you shall put the Testimony that I will give you. And there I will meet with you, and I will speak with you from above the mercy seat. . . Exodus 25

Immediately I was in the Spirit; and behold, a throne set in heaven, and One sat on the throne. And He who sat there was like a jasper and a sardius stone in appearance; and there was a rainbow around the throne, in appearance like an emerald. Around the throne were twenty-four thrones, and on the thrones I saw twenty-four elders sitting, clothed in white robes; and they had crowns of gold on their heads. And from the throne proceeded lightnings, thunderings, and voices. Seven lamps of fire were burning before the throne, which are the seven Spirits of God. Revelation 4:2-5

That mercy seat, that throne of heaven, IS the heart of God. That mercy seat, that throne of heaven, IS your heart and mine.

I know I am speaking very boldly. Such boldness, when entering into the Holiest and sitting down upon the Mercy Seat, is ESSENTIAL to the gospel, two of the ten most important verses in the Bible.

Let me describe heart for you, the heart of God.

– Heart always reveals Himself through weakness, swallowing up into Himself all that we are including our sin and rebellion, becoming us in our present state, limiting Himself by our weakness. Thus, carrying us inside Himself, stumbling and falling along the way, He arises out of death into life, ascending on high, and we in Him. –

You have seen this description before; I changed only one word, "God" to "Heart."

Now, you and I are definitely not equal with God in power and wisdom, reach and glory. But we ARE entirely equal with God at the level of heart. Our hearts and God's heart are equal; so equal, in fact, that they are the same.

Jesus lives in our hearts; Jesus lives in God's heart; we share heart with God.

Let me give one more verse that defines heart, that defines the Mercy Seat, that defines the throne of heaven.

By this we know love, because He laid down His life for us. And we also ought to lay down our lives for the brethren.

You see, those words, **And we also,** demonstrate a full equality of heart.

God's entire purpose for creation is to obtain for Himself one thing alone – a man after His own heart, that is, a many-membered Body, many sons to glory.

This Body exists, however, ONLY where 1 John 3:16 flows in a mutual relationship of respect and honor between one heart and one heart at all times and in every direction.

The flowing of 1 John 3:16 between one heart and one heart has a name.

We call Him Father.

I mentioned that we have received a heart transplant. God did not just give us a "new" heart; He gave us Jesus' heart. What other heart could we have received?

There are innumerable stories told by recipients of heart transplants, I read one just recently in *The Daily Mail.* Type into Google "young-mans-heart-craving-beer," in order to find it.

"Science" has a hard time with anything that does not fit into the hard boxes of present knowledge/ignorance. In other words, so-called scientists hate to admit their ignorance of many things. True science never bends the facts to fit the theory, but always allows the theory to flap in the breeze, ready to vanish away the moment any actual fact slays it. Today's "science," in its infancy, wants to claim that all of human consciousness is found in the brain. Reality agrees with the Bible that a large part of our human-ness resides in our actual hearts.

So, read the article (and I really do want you to read it) on the woman who was given a young man's heart and thus her first words after waking were, "I want a beer," when she previously had never liked beer – to the extent of her new heart actually speaking to her the name of it's former self, enabling her to find the family of the donor. After reading the article, consider your own heart. But, let's consider it in two ways.

The first way we understand our new heart is that our heart once belonged to someone else, namely, Jesus. Thus, it brings Jesus' own nature and personality into us with itself. It is easy to see, if this be true, why the serpent wants all believers to call their hearts *"deceitful above all things and desperately wicked."* It is a terrible thing for his game as we discover that our hearts are not only GOOD, but that they are, literally, Jesus' heart. His accusations cannot stand, and he is cast down.

But the second way we understand our new heart is that the shaping of our hearts to fit that particular expression of God each of us was made to reveal, and to fit that particular place in God we are appointed to fill, that shaping is the most important thing God is doing in our lives. I would never agree to a heart transplant, although any believer who has received one can walk in full confidence that Christ continues to live as them. However, I know my own heart, how it has been battered and shaped by God over many years. God has designed all of that for His place in me and my place in Him. I don't want someone else's shallow heart.

Both of these ways of knowing our own hearts must go hand-in-hand. While the revelation of the extent and meaning of our possessing Jesus' heart as our own is a glory that will increase forever, God does not do static clones. The sacred heart of God is very large and finds innumerable expressions.

Now, a reader asked a question concerning the soul of the young man who's heart was donated. Where is our soul? We have always thought that the soul goes with the spirit after both brain and heart dies. Yet it seems that aspects of the young man's soul remained in the heart, especially his name. My present understanding, with limited knowledge, would say that, no, the young man's soul went with his spirit, but the physical heart carries in it the memory of his person imprinted in the electrical frequency of the cells.

I was also thinking in the middle of the night that it might be a great thing to trade my tired heart for the heart of a young man filled with vigor. Tempting, eh? It's good that such an option is not readily available, else there would likely be a black market trade in young hearts!

I'm being silly for a purpose. My greatest strength and achievement was in my mid-thirties. We have been granted by our Father the heart of an eternally thirty-three-year-old man. All of His memories are written upon that heart. Is this not the Covenant?

You are our epistle written in our hearts, known and read by all men; clearly you are an epistle of Christ, ministered by us, written not with ink but by the Spirit of the living God, not on tablets of stone but on tablets of flesh, that is, of the heart. 2 Corinthians 3:2-3

Our new hearts are hearts of flesh, the heart of Christ. His nature is written all through His own heart, this heart we bear. Yet, to our highest delight, He did not just give us His "nature," how lonely that would be. Rather, He comes Himself inside His own heart, which is now ours. And the Father comes inside of Jesus.

Is this not the gospel?

This Heart of Substance, this Heart of ours, this Heart of Jesus, this Heart of God, this Mercy Seat, this throne of heaven, is formed and shaped inside of us by two things, by Voice and by Spirit.

Those who hear the Voice of the Son of God will live. – Transformed into the same image by the Spirit of the Lord.

I want to refer back to my opening point. A young man or woman does not know the difference between his or her own true heart, shaped by God, written with all the knowledge of Christ, and the outward face of Adam's pretending. It takes years of battering to come to know the difference. Thus we must recognize how bluster and facade can so easily trick us into thinking, "Well, this IS what I WANT." The truth is, it really is not.

I waited for many years for the wife God had gifted for me. Through those years I was attracted to other pretty faces over time, drawing a little bit close to a couple, imagining them to be the "delight" of my heart. When the first one proved not to be so, I felt that my very heart was being ripped right out of me. The second, God gave me a simple and clear choice. "If you want to go to her, then walk away from Me, but if you want Me, then forget about her." The problem was that "going to her" appeared to contain everything I truly wanted in this life.

God's holiness is the most comforting part of God; He keeps us wholly for Himself.

But now, every time I consider my precious wife, this one God chose for me, I am amazed and overwhelmed at how she is all the desire of my heart. Since this letter is "Heart," I will share the word the Lord spoke to me in September of 1981, nine years before we married. In one of those few landmark dreams in which I knew God was speaking a sovereign word to me, I was sitting outside on a bench, waiting to go into an "elders meeting," knowing that I was in trouble for something I had inadvertently done, though I did not know what, and feeling, what I know now to be, very autistic. In my dream, Maureen, eighteen years old at the time, came up to me and took my hand. She said to me that she wanted to share all my difficulty without condemnation.

I awoke immediately into the very vivid knowledge of His Presence. I had not considered Maureen before that moment. She was the youngest, and to my mind at the time, the "least" of three sisters. I raised the image of the other two before the Lord, one at a time, hearing nothing. Then, while I was fully awake, God spoke these words to me. **"Man looks on the outward appearance, but the Lord looks upon the heart."**

It takes a special kind of woman to love an Asperger's man through decades of marriage. Maureen is such a woman.

The reason for the chastisement of God is to cause us to know what really is our true heart and to escape all the pretending of Adam. But that is only one side of the equation. Chastisement by itself cannot ever lead us to our true heart, this new heart we have received by Covenant. Only one thing can do that: Voice in the context of Spirit.

One aspect of the young man's heart transplanted into the older woman's body, was that the young man hardly knew sickness. The woman had suffered from recurring colds; after receiving her new heart, she was not sick again.

This is a BIG deal. A cold comes from a virus, doesn't it? Yet with the right heart, no cold virus can prevail. Her old heart allowed the cold viruses, always present, to prevail all through her body. But her new heart had no time or thought for them, and thus they could not win against the strength of her white blood cells, now moving out from a new heart. This is something to think about – a lot.

This truth is absolute in both earth and heaven, in both the entirety of our physical body and in all the realms and dimensions of our spirit. The heart rules the body and it rules the soul. Jesus said that it also rules the mouth. Thus, if our hearts really are Jesus' heart, speaking as one voice with Him, that is, speaking Christ, must be the words of our mouth, and vice versa.

I just read a Google Ad that said *"Jesus promised death to those who follow Him."* Hello? Why do people who name His name lie? Jesus SAID that the one promising death is the devil. Jesus promises life to those who follow Him. Death does not bring life; Jesus, the One who LIVES in our hearts does.

To speak Christ is to speak life; it is to say, "I am." We do not "create" a new heart by the words that we speak; rather, we cause the heart of Jesus we already possess to be the only thing we know. Our speaking Christ gets rid of the false ideas of our imagination that limit this heart we bear.

How can we call ourselves by His heart if we do not speak what He speaks? How can we live by His heart if we do not know Him?

Think about this phrase: "The heart of a king."

This idea carries a definite connotation. I've often thought it would be interesting to assemble all the kings and queens of England into one room in present-day London, from Alfred the Great to Elisabeth II. Each one of them claimed sovereignty over all English people and all English land as the ruling monarch for a period of years. Most of them had a definite appreciation of their power and place. "I am king" or "I am queen" most certainly has governed their hearts all the years they have wandered in Hades.

By my present limited knowledge, Henry II would embody the human definition of "the heart of a king" the most, especially through his first decade as king. Some traits would be fearlessness, unstoppable energy, a wide and gripping vision, an inherent and complete sense of entitlement. Such men are easy to follow, for awhile at least.

In some ways the real King, the One whose heart we bear, carries these traits, except. Except they appear completely different coming through Him. The question is entirely, what is His kingdom, outward performance or the human heart? Human kingdoms are all about outward service. God's kingdom is all about heart: **the kingdom is within you.** The difference is night from day.

Those who define Jesus by His miracles see an entirely different sort of kingdom than those who define Jesus by His heart.

Those who are natural leaders among men, people like Henry II, see people as tools for the building of an outward work. Thus, they see themselves and are seen by others as "above" their less capable followers.

But the heart of our King sees people entirely differently. To Him, people from the inside out, that is, people's hearts are His kingdom. You can whip bodies, you can train minds, but hearts can only be won. A real king takes His own fearlessness, His own unstoppable energy, His own wide and gripping vision, His own sense of entitlement and uses it, not only to serve every heart in His kingdom, but He grants to each one who follows Him His same heart as their very own.

The best example of a king in world literature that I know of is Hazel the rabbit in *Watership Down* by Richard Adams. A King puts His own life on the line first whenever there is danger; He stays behind when one is weak. He finds ways for each of those who follow Him to contribute their particular gifts and to be honored by the others for doing so. He never commands, but only suggests. He leaves all free, never condemning anyone who chooses to go a different way. He forgives His enemies and makes then His allies. I'm speaking of Jesus, yes, but also of Hazel the rabbit; it's a great study in true leadership.

Put on the Lord Jesus Christ is utter nonsense if it is not true and real and literal. There is no way you or I or anyone could ever turn a human heart into the heart of Jesus. If He has not transplanted His own heart into us for real, than the entire Covenant is a hoax.

But He has. Our hearts ARE Jesus' own heart, the one He bore when He died at 33 years old, the heart that was transformed out from the atoms of Adam's universe into the atoms of the new creation. The heart of the King beats in our chests. We can know our own hearts only by knowing His.

16. Voice

Those who hear the voice of the Son of God will live. John 5

And God said, "Let there be light," and there was light.

Then He said, "Go out, and stand on the mountain before the Lord." And behold, the Lord passed by, and a great and strong wind tore into the mountains and broke the rocks in pieces before the Lord, but the Lord was not in the wind; and after the wind an earthquake, but the Lord was not in the earthquake; and after the earthquake a fire, but the Lord was not in the fire; and after the fire a still small voice. 1 Kings 19:11-12

Every description or picture of God in the Bible is figurative. God is not the thing people saw. The only picture of God that is truly the Father is Jesus walking the path of the atonement. Everything of the throne and the One sitting upon it found in Revelation 4 & 5 is figurative. Yet God is seen by most as some "other" thing, something measurable and definable, more of a separated human form than invisible and all-pervasive Spirit.

A significant part of my present knowledge of God comes from my having embraced as scientific fact the electrical theory of the universe. We were taught the gravity theory of the universe over many years; that theory rules people's knowledge of God more than you might realize. The gravity theory claims that the objects of the universe are isolated and separate from each other with only the weak bond of gravity slightly connecting them. So much of what is now seen out there, however, defies all laws of gravity, and thus the "scientific" fantasizers spin their ever more fantastic stories about black holes and dark matter and the warping of space/time, things that simply are not science in any sense of the concept. Real science deals only with presently observable fact.

The electrical theory of the universe, on the other hand, posits that the universe is a unified whole with vast electrical currents doing out there what those same electrical currents do in the laboratory. There is little in the electrical theory that cannot be demonstrated in the laboratory, including all of the fantastic things out there unexplainable by modern cosmology. You have devoted much time in your life to knowing the gravity theory of the universe, ideas that give you a false knowledge of physical reality; I propose that knowing the electrical theory is important to your present knowledge of God. I have studied this theory on a regular basis for almost ten years now. Here is the website I recommend. www.thunderbolts.info. Buy the books; watch the videos.

Electricity is invisible; when electricity becomes visible, we call it light on the one hand and heat/energy on the other. As the electrical currents flowing through our arm of the galaxy discharge upon the largest object in our vicinity, the sun, the result is both light and heat. All life on earth requires both.

Although electrical engineers know a whole lot about using electricity, they do not really know what it is. The same is true of light.

Everything is electrical. Atoms are simply a balance of charged particles circling in a powerful electrical bond. An atom looks just like a solar system. A galaxy looks just like a hurricane. A human cell moments after conception looks exactly like vast stellar objects seen now in outer space. Seen from a different angle, a galaxy also looks just like the human eye. Everything is formed by the laws governing electricity.

The human body is electrical. In fact, there are whole arenas of electricity not yet studied by science, including the science of electrical frequency. Principles of natural health come out from the operation of electrical frequency in the human body. Modern medicine disregards and fights against that reality of the human body; it is primarily a religion of death, not science.

God is omnipresent Spirit who fills all in all and WORKS all in all. Yet He is a Person. My present knowledge of the electrical universe informs (not rules) my present knowledge of God as Spirit. Yet here is a law of electricity: electrical events are scalable. That's why the newly formed one-celled fetus looks identical to objects out there as large as galaxies. The same electrical laws are operating in very similar ways in both.

God is not electricity, but electricity most certainly comes out of God. The people at The Thunderbolts Project attempt to steer clear of anything religious, wanting to establish the science of their understanding. That is what scientists should do. However, consider that the human mind is electrical. If electrical events are scalable, then, just as there is a small-sized human mind, so there must also be a cosmic Mind. Just as there are human persons, so there is a cosmic Person. Actually, it's entirely the other way around. We are persons because He is a Person.

As I sat in the college Poetry class last semester, listening to the present-day understanding of poetry, what it is and how it works, I was listening to a description of Christ and of God. Because they relate to, and thus reject, a Nicene God, they could not have understood what I was hearing. We listened to a webcast on "Word." Fantastically inspiring! We watched a video on light. Wow! These things speak the nature and reality of God and Christ all the way through. Yet few Christians could hear Him in those things because they know only a God and a universe divided as differing and unrelated objects.

I thought to attempt a study on how poetry shows us Christ, but lost interest. Yet such a study would be wonderful. The same with modern takes on light and word. Both reveal Christ as we are coming to know Him. Yet we are the ones who know Him, and thus this Christ, personal in us and revealed through us, will be the very thing informing all other knowledge, what it is and how it works.

The effort to remove personhood from God is everywhere. I fell in love with a Person; His name is Jesus. I am filled full with a Person; His name is Father.

At the center of Person is Heart. The absence of heart, the absence of desire, is the absence of God. But the expression of Person is Voice. It is Voice that makes God Personal to us.

Heart and Voice equals Person.

Writing teachers place voice at the center of good writing and the single most important element of good writing, yet voice is so very hard to teach. Voice is the person coming through the words.

Wind, earthquake, fire, all these things come out of God, but God is not those things. God is a still small voice, speaking on the inside of us. As I shared in "Life," this Voice is not giving us commands to obey. Commands to obey are part of Adam's separated creation, part of the Old Covenant; they correspond to the limited "gravity" theory of the universe. God commanded Adam not to eat of such a relationship with Him.

In "Life," I was speaking of seed bringing forth life, but that is not the only aspect of Voice. Voice is also creation: God spoke and light came to be. Tolkein, in *The Silmarillion*, posited that all things come out from singing, from the voice of Song. Voice is also Communion, Person inside of person.

Voice is the expression, the singing, of the Heart.

Three primary things make a person a person: a heart, a name, and a voice. The Lord Jesus Christ is all three; we wrap ourselves with Him. The Lord of the Universe is Heart; Jesus, the man, is His Name; Christ is all the speaking of God sustaining all, Voice. He calls each one of us by our name, by a name known only by Him and us. We live by His Voice.

We have not known Voice as God wants us to know it. I have no idea what I'm reaching for, but I write so that Voice might come into view.

Here is the definition of "voice" in writing as given by Education Northwest in their "Six Traits of Writing."

> "Voice is the writer coming through the words, the sense that a real person is speaking to us and cares about the message. It is the heart and soul of the writing, the magic, the wit, the feeling, the life and breath. When the writer is engaged personally with the topic, he/she imparts a personal tone and flavor to the piece that is unmistakably his/hers alone. And it is that individual something – different from the mark of all other writers – that we call Voice."

He who enters by the door is the shepherd of the sheep. To him the doorkeeper opens, and the sheep hear his voice; and he calls his own sheep by name and leads them out. And when he brings out his own sheep, he goes before them; and the sheep follow him, for they know his voice. John 10:2-4

When we hear His voice, what do we hear? **"He calls his own sheep by name."** We hear our own name, the name that is known between Him and us alone. His Voice is that which calls us forth, calls us to Him, calls us into His glory, calls us into our place.

When I am in public and I hear the cry, "Daddy, daddy," coming from some little child, I instinctively turn, thinking it is the voice of my own, though they are now grown. I was leaving a movie theater awhile back. A little boy, barely two, was standing at the top of the dark stairs, alone, not knowing where to go or what to do. I saw what was likely his mother most of the way down, yakking on her cell phone, oblivious to this little one who held an overpowering claim upon her. Such a thing is beyond me. The bond that held my wife's and my own heart to our little ones was so strong; they were never apart from our immediate thoughts, especially when we were in public.

A child knows his mother's voice before he is ever born.

Heart – Name – Voice, these things are so personally and intrinsically related. **He calls his own sheep by name.** The Old Covenant says, "Obey the voice," over and over. The New says "know His voice."

Paul said we are not like Moses. We ARE NOT LIKE Moses!!!

Moses covered the glory upon his face, a glory that was passing away. Paul said that, out from this new heart, the very heart of Christ which we bear, **"we use great boldness of speech."** Then he says, **"And since we have the same spirit of faith, according to what is written, 'I believed and therefore I spoke,' we also believe and therefore speak."** 2 Corinthians 4:13

What do we speak?

But what does it say? "The word is near you, in your mouth and in your heart" (that is, the word of faith which we preach): **that if you confess with your mouth the Lord Jesus...** Romans 10:8-9

Voice = Christ made personal in me.

The word "confess" is the Greek *homologeo*, which is the action form of the noun, *homologo*, which is, literally, "same word," that is, "to speak the same as."

In previous letters I saw that the Word, Christ Jesus, is in our mouth. We speak the same as He with great boldness of speech. This is the Word that comes continually out of the mouth of God.

I am meek and lowly of heart. – I am among you as the One who serves.

I am the bread of life. – I am the living bread. – I am from Him and He sent Me.

I am the light of the world. – I am not alone, but I am with the Father who sent Me. – I am from above.

I am the door of the sheep. – I am the good shepherd. The good shepherd gives His life for the sheep. – I am the good shepherd; and I know My sheep, and am known by My own.

I am the resurrection and the life. – I am the way, the truth, and the life. No one comes to the Father except through Me.

I am in My Father, and you in Me, and I in you.

I am the true vine, and My Father is the vinedresser. – I am the vine, you are the branches. He who abides in Me, and I in him, bears much fruit; for without Me you can do nothing.

And all Mine are Yours, and Yours are Mine, and I am glorified in them. – Father, I desire that they also whom You gave Me may be with Me where I am.

Those who believe, speak; those who do not believe place these words upon a Christ far away from themselves. But notice what Jesus says: "**No one comes to the Father except through Me.**" We have learned that these words are, in every conceivable way, literal.

We know that our heart is Christ, because God says. Thus we speak out from our heart, because we know that God speaks only the truth.

We do not look at the things which are seen, but at the things which are not seen. For the things which are seen are temporary, but the things which are not seen are eternal. 2 Corinthians 4:18

This is not speaking of separate geographical places as in heaven over there and earth over here. Heaven is seen and temporary. It is God who is not seen, just as electricity is not seen. Electricity is made visible ONLY when it discharges upon an object and in becoming visible, electricity becomes light and heat. God becomes Son and Spirit.

In the Old Testament, thunder was considered to be the voice of God. Thunder is caused by electrical discharge. In fact, consider the vibrations of the voice-box that cause voice. The splitting apart of air by electrical discharge and it's slamming back together is much the same. In our day, electricity is common and ordinary, even though no one knows what it is. Yet all things are made and sustained by it.

Who being the brightness of His glory and the express image of His person, and upholding all things by the word of His power, when He had by

Himself purged our sins, sat down at the right hand of the Majesty on high. Hebrews 1:3

The Word God speaks is everything to Him, yet that word is quiet and never pushes itself onto anyone. We ourselves must draw it off the page and make it live again in us.

That the genuineness of your faith, being much more precious than gold that perishes, though it is tested by fire, may be found to praise, honor, and glory at the revelation of Jesus Christ, whom having not seen you love. Though now you do not see Him, yet believing, you rejoice with joy inexpressible and full of glory, 1 Peter 1:7-8

The Father spoke the Word; the Word revealed the Father by purging our sins. The Spirit reveals Him to us: Voice. Voice, heat, *energia,* is the manifestation of God that births God made visible, God manifest in the flesh.

What does God hear when we speak Christ? He hears the only thing that matters to Him arising, for the first time, out from creation.

Speaking Christ with great boldness of speech against the sight of our eyes and against the judgment of our self, just BECAUSE God says is the whole point God is after in this entire exercise called creation.

His Voice in our mouth.

"Correcting" other believers when you "discern" darkness in them is not the sin. The sin is failing to speak Christ, failing to turn on the light.

A reader recently shared with me that, as she spoke Christ her only life and as she contemplated my letter, "The Altar of Incense," by the travail of the Spirit she experienced passing through a portal such that now everything looks entirely different to her. "Christian" things she used to be comfortable with now seem empty and far away.

I have found in recent days that the words of Jesus in red in the gospels now sing in unison with my very DNA. That doesn't make us anything special. It's just that we know His voice and are known by Him as His voice. We vibrate in harmony with His Voice.

Thus, when others speak out from their own voice, we cannot hear Him in those words. We are filled with momentary sorrow, but we keep speaking Christ.

If any man hear His voice!

⸺

I have passed through a few days of great emptiness of soul. I know God has spoken His vision for me, yet He does not provide. Did Jesus not say, **"Ask whatever you want and the Father delights in doing it"**? I quoted that in my letter, "Father." It seems to us that God just does not respond.

Then, to finish the college credits I need, I am immersed in atheism. Don't be deceived about "sending your child to college." The primary purpose of secular college is to convert all to atheism. But this atheism is not neutral. It's progenitor is Karl Marx, and they follow him. They do not understand that the exaltation of the "group" over the individual always results in murder. Yet, when I look at the Christianity of history, I see more violence and murder. God's people have so twisted who and what Christ is, making all of it a mockery and a horror.

God doesn't help, either. He is neither seen nor known.

By faith (Moses) forsook Egypt, not fearing the wrath of the king; for he endured as seeing Him who is invisible. – (Christ) is the image of the invisible God, the firstborn over all creation.

Belief in a future "heaven" is a faithless excuse for the obvious reality of the present "absence" of this invisible, unseen, unknown God. "Someday?" No, Today. – **Today, if you will hear His voice.**

Elijah saw all the ways we want to see God, but God was not in any of them.

People who break fully with Augustine and the Nicene Creed in order to contend with God through what He actually says in the New Testament, often go mad. Entire groups who make that attempt go full circle, coming all the way back around to their own version of the Nicene Creed in the attempt to deal with an invisible God who just does not do what He says. Those who blame God for not doing what He says often become atheists. Those who want to remain "Christians" create Nicene Christianity all over again, and in doing so, place the blame upon man – *sinner, your flesh is the problem.*

Inevitably, "heaven" always takes the place of God in us now, and some form of the rapture, "*Someday, God will do something, if we just keep saying things that aren't real,*" becomes people's hope.

So when I am angry and discouraged, embarrassed and hurting, when I doubt that God even exists, something I've never done until I've had to wrestle with entrenched atheism versus a bankrupt and violent Christianity, and contending with an INVISIBLE God, why do I sing His praises and give Him thanks in the middle of the night? — Covenant. I gave my heart to Jesus fifty years ago. I have no inclination to take it back again.

A God who is INVISIBLE. The word "invisible" is very large. It doesn't just mean that He can't be seen with natural light. He is as invisible to heavenly beings as He is to earthly. It means that He is simply undetectable by any created form of detection, whether heavenly or earthly.

We say that we know God, but there is no outward proof of that. We speak Christ, yet nothing seems changed, not really.

I am writing in this way, sharing these things, for a definite purpose.

Electrical engineers cannot explain what electricity is, nor do they ever see it. Yet they know exactly how to channel this invisible power that sustains all things in order to do all kinds of fantastic work for human beings. Electricity is our slave and makes our modern comfortable lives possible. Most of the abundance we enjoy in modern life comes from the service of electricity.

It's been more than a year since I made the bold proclamation concerning Blair Valley as Lazarus coming out of the tomb, in "My Vision." I got all excited several days ago that God would provide at least several of the millions it would take to make that happen. Then nothing but discouragement.

God says that He shows Himself mighty on behalf of those who wait upon Him. But it doesn't seem so. He remains, in every possible way, invisible.

Every way, that is, except one. Voice.

I received another email this morning and understood why the God of travail causes me to pass through His own agony. Here is part of it.

– Daniel, the past few days you have been heavy on my heart. So I am wondering if you are all right? Also I wanted to let you know about your book you sent me months ago, *The Unveiling: When the Day Star Arises in Our Hearts*. You know I devoured *The Jesus Secret*. But for some reason every time I tried to read *The Unveiling* I just couldn't. I desperately wanted to. I didn't understand it. I have kept the book close by me knowing I would be led to pick it up again to read but at the Lord's choosing.

Well the past week that is exactly what happened. I have only read the first two chapters so far but THEY WERE LIFE CHANGING FOR ME!! You know that it is not enough for me to receive revelation or knowledge. But that revelation MUST become my reality. For some time there were some things I was pondering, feeling like I was missing something. Then your letter "Heart" came, a real turning point. After that I was led to pick up *The Unveiling*. There is so much in the first two chapters alone that has changed something inside of me forever! The part of the old man being gone but we go on the memories really helped to FREE me from my past.

I realized now that the reason I was not able to read the book until now is there were other things I needed to receive first and your letter "Heart" was a big part of that. I am so thankful for you and for your faithfulness to the Lord. Every time I go through this I know the Lord in ways I never knew Him before. I see Him like I never saw Him before. Oh how can we ever think we KNOW HIM ? How can we ever think WE KNOW ANY-THING AT ALL? I realize now for the first time EXACTLY what you mean when you say WE ARE BLIND. We do not know who we are or who we will be. AND I LOVE IT!!!

The Voice of the Spirit, what we sometimes call "revelation," comes, and in a moment, we see and know things that are true and real that we could not know before. – Voice.

The real beginnings of the story of God in the earth begins with these words: **Now the Lord had said to Abram: "Get out of your country."**

God always comes first as Voice. He always comes second with **"Follow Me."** It's not a matter of "getting out." It's a matter of Christ alone. **My sheep hear My voice and they follow Me.**

The definition of "madness" in human thinking is to follow an invisible voice, a voice no one else hears.

> **"Now My soul is troubled, and what shall I say? 'Father, save Me from this hour'? But for this purpose I came to this hour. Father, glorify Your name." Then a voice came from heaven, saying, "I have both glorified it and will glorify it again." Therefore the people who stood by and heard it said that it had thundered.** John 12:27-29

The Old Covenant imposes itself in "Christianity" with the idea that this "Voice" comes to test us, to prove whether we will obey God or not. Paul said that the law was given to prove that we would not.

> **So it was, when you heard the voice from the midst of the darkness, while the mountain was burning with fire, that you... said: 'Surely... we have heard His voice from the midst of the fire. ...This great fire will consume us; if we hear the voice of the Lord our God any more, then we shall die... You go near and hear all that the Lord our God may say, and tell us... and we will hear and do it.'** Deuteronomy 5:23-27

They did not share heart with God.

In the New Covenant, entirely because of the Blood and the Cross, God's real intention comes through. God is invisible and unknowable. He enters into His creation, both heaven and earth, as Voice. Reading through the accounts in Exodus and Deuteronomy, where voice and fire figure so much, it is clear that God demands no visible form of Himself in the human imagination. Man wants a visible "power" God; God is not visible.

Yet the greatest longing in the heart of God is to be seen and known and touched, to take little children into His arms and to bless them.

There is one transition only from an invisible God to **"Christ, the image of the invisible God."** We must understand that transition. David understood God in a way that few did. Here is most of Psalm 42

> **As the deer pants for the water brooks, so pants my soul for You, O God. My soul thirsts for God, for the living God. When shall I come and appear before God? My tears have been my food day and night, while they**

continually say to me, "Where is your God?"

When I remember these things, I pour out my soul within me. For I used to go with the multitude; I went with them to the house of God, with the voice of joy and praise, with a multitude that kept a pilgrim feast. Why are you cast down, O my soul? And why are you disquieted within me? Hope in God, for I shall yet praise Him For the help of His countenance...

Deep calls unto deep at the noise of Your waterspouts; all Your waves and billows have gone over me...

I will say to God my Rock, "Why have You forgotten me? Why do I go mourning because of the oppression of the enemy?" As with a breaking of my bones, my enemies reproach me, while they say to me all day long, "Where is your God?" Why are you cast down, O my soul? And why are you disquieted within me? Hope in God; for I shall yet praise Him, the help of my countenance and my God.

Wow, David sounds like me. David wrestled with the difficulty of an invisible God as well, but inside his tears, He said two things that point us to the day of the revelation of God in which we now live.

My soul thirsts for You, O God. – Deep calls unto deep.

Picture the center of the Sistine Chapel ceiling, the place in Michaelangelo's painting where the finger of God reaches out to touch the finger of man. That is exactly what is taking place right now with us and God, only it's not finger to finger, but voice to Voice, Deep calling to deep.

What God is about to do has never been done. You see, not only is creation created, but it is marred by sin and ruled by darkness. The sacrifice of Jesus has broken that darkness by faith, but the reality is not yet seen.

Look at the promise and reality of the gospel apart from the unbelief of Nicene Christianity. All of God in us now! Victory over sin and death! Rivers of living water flowing out from us setting creation free! God manifest in the flesh! Being JUST LIKE Jesus! Then compare what God says in the gospel with the experience and practice of Christians for 2000 years. **My enemies... say to me all day long, "Where is your God?"**

God has placed His own voice in our mouths. Our engagement with Christ, with our backs turned utterly against any thought of sin or self or the separated human, but seeing Christ alone, this deep thirst we speak calls unto that very thing inside of God, that Holy Essence that He is bringing forth out from Himself to plant inside of us that God would now be seen and known.

Likewise you also, reckon yourselves to be dead indeed to sin, but alive to God in Christ Jesus our Lord. Romans 6:11

A Christianity that includes sin and a separated human nature in its picture cannot call forth that inside of God that will transform the universe. As we face God eye to Eye inside of having put on the Lord Jesus Christ, Christ in our mouth calls the deepest parts of God into visible reality through us.

Voice comes through Spirit. Voice is God coming through into the thing He has always desired, to be seen and known – though us.

The Source of Voice is Heart, the deepest center of God. Voice makes that Personal Heart known. Voice births that same Song, Christ, in our hearts; we sing with Him the Song of the Lamb. God sings Himself into visible manifestation through the singing of our mouths.

Voice makes a Personal Heart known by name; Voice calls each one of us by name. Voice sings in each one of our mouths.

And I heard, as it were, the voice of a great multitude, and as the voice of many waters, and as the voice of mighty thunderings. Revelation 19:6 — **And His voice as the sound of many waters.** Revelation 1:15

Voice is not about "what Jesus did for me." Voice is God Himself singing through our voicebox, making an invisible God visible, through us, His image, the visible expression of a forever invisible Being.

"Voice is the writer coming through the words."

Voice is God coming through us, though our mouths, the only way He will ever be known and seen.

When God becomes visible, when people see God for the first time, what will they see?

They will be looking at us.

What will they see?

They will see ordinary people who are utterly real with no need for any pretence or bluster, laying down their lives for one another in love.

They will see God.

17. Spirit

God is Spirit, and those who worship Him must worship Him in Spirit and in truth. John 4

What is the Holy Spirit?

The Holy Spirit never speaks of Himself, but always speaks of Christ. In following God's order in placing the Spirit last, we discover that we cannot know anything of God except by Spirit, and thus the Spirit of God brooding over the face of the waters was really the beginning of all creation. We also discover that this whole endeavor to treat the Spirit last, has served only to re-shift the order of importance.

In some ways we have built upwards in importance to the most important.

– Spirit.

In a recent posting on Facebook, a reader linked to a typical explanation of the fulfillment of the "prophetic word" in the earth, that is, a discussion of nations, events, and an individual Antichrist. He then made the following comment.

> "The *Through Eyes of Fire* Series is important, because it turns our eyes to the spirit realities. The prophecies were born in the Spirit... and it is true... if we pursue the wrong spirit to the nth degree we will see everything in outward form... but Daniel describes very clearly how just about everything is already true and happening right in front of us, but we haven't mostly the eyes and eye salve to see it."

Sometimes one doesn't really know what one is doing or saying until you can see it through the eyes and words of another. – Think of that, **"Buy from Me eye salve so that you might see."** No one pays any attention; we just rush right on by imagining that we sure can see and have no need of eye salve. Thus all the non-seeing of John's vision.

Everything exists in Spirit. Everything is bathed by Spirit. Everything is energized by Spirit. When we say everything, we mean all things and all beings in both earth AND heaven. Heaven substance bears the same relationship to Spirit as earthly substance, yet earthly substance is continually coming out of, is being always acted upon, by heavenly substance as well as Spirit.

When Jesus said that God is Spirit, and when Hebrews says that angels are spirits, the two words denote some similarity, yes, but not entirely. The Spirit that is God and the spirits that are angels are of differing substance or quality.

What is the Holy Spirit?

I do not believe that God is a "Trinity," though He is always revealing Himself in three different ways. Here is how I would say it, in conjunction with what God actually says.

— There is one God, the Father, who reveals Himself in the heavens as His Spirit and in the earth as His Son. — Yet this same God reveals Himself through many persons.

Is the Holy Spirit a distinct Person?

The Bible says, **"the Holy Spirit," "the Spirit of God,"** and **"the Spirit of Christ."** Are these three different things? John saw seven Spirits of God. Where does that fit? Is the Holy Spirit seven Persons? There is no definitive answer to these questions because God doesn't want His Spirit analyzed. Yet this same Spirit upholds and sustains all things.

I am convinced, though, that God is very big on "personhood."

Researchers now know that dolphins are much more advanced than we had imagined. They speak to each other with a grammatical language and call each one by his or her own individual name all their lives. They clearly demonstrate heart in their dealings with other creatures and with one another. There is no reason for us not to call dolphins "persons." God's universe does not fit into our tight prejudicial boxes, nor is there any reason for it to do so.

There is only one Spirit, and yes, He/She must be personal. There are many spirits, billions and billions of them, including ourselves, and each one is uniquely personal.

There is one God, the Father, forever invisible, yet He reveals Himself through many persons.

I can say with all truth that the Father reveals Himself through me in precisely the same manner as He revealed Himself through Jesus. Certainly, Jesus is forever pre-eminent, the Atonement was His alone, He is our Beloved, our King, but we are of His same kind. I am as much a part of God as Jesus is, in fact, I am Christ Jesus revealed uniquely through my person.

I have always been inside of God; there is no other place to be.

— **Pray without ceasing.** Paul

I have never been a pray-er, though I have certainly tried. Since reading Norman Grubb's *Rees Howells* at age nineteen, I have been drawn to intercession, but never capable of doing it. Prayer lists make me very uncomfortable. It's not that I can't pray for people; it's that I can never sustain prayer. I have spent hours walking the woods in prayer, hours on my knees with others in the early morning, praying some, certainly, but most of the time thinking about something else.

When I do pray aloud, I can't pray for long. Eloquent, meaningful prayers out loud are not in my capacity.

One of the most wonderful realities about Christ living as me is that when I forget, when I think of other things, I don't worry a bit. I accept all my forgetfulness as Christ Himself living as me. The result? Since I spend zero time condemning myself when I think of Him, I actually think of and commune with Christ more often. The result? The time I spend communing with Him increases. And I never worry one second when I forget.

That doesn't make me a prayer warrior, however. Last night, in the middle of the night, prayer became something entirely different for me.

Let me explain the primary difference between an Augustinian God and the God I have come to know. The difference is simple. But the knowing of all things out from that difference is giganormous!

The Nicene God is up there, out there, far above, and far away. He is superior to me. Prayer, then, is me down here, imploring this Entity up there somewhere in the divine Haze, to do something He is not typically doing. Most prayer to that image of God is rooted in a type of unbelief.

The Father of the Lord Jesus Christ fills me with all of His fullness. He is as much a part of me as I am. We share heart together. We walk together moment by moment as two Ppersons in one. I know God filling ME full.

Last night God and I prayed together. Who does God pray to? He doesn't. "Pray to" is not and never has been prayer.

I've never prayed before, not once. Last night, for the first time in my life, I prayed; God and I prayed together.

Now, I am a forgetful man, but as I shared, I worry about none of that. Our minds so easily treat God as the Nicene God, far away. We forget that He is not, that He fills us full with ALL of Himself. If God fills me full, then I cannot pray "to" Him, I can only pray with Him.

God and I pray together. – That's pretty cool.

But God has revealed them to us through His Spirit. For the Spirit searches all things, yes, the deep things of God. For what man knows the things of a man except the spirit of the man which is in him? Even so no one knows the things of God except the Spirit of God. Now we have received, not the spirit of the world, but the Spirit who is from God, that we might know the things that have been freely given to us by God.
1 Corinthians 2:10-12

You who read my letters KNOW that nothing can be known of God except by an immediate, miraculous experience with the Holy Spirit. The "portal" that a reader mentioned passing through is that experience. We know that until God opens our eyes by His Spirit, we cannot see even when we are looking straight at something. A sister on Facebook was laboring over what I was sharing concerning 1 John 3:16. She could not "see" any of it because she was parsing the verse with her intellect, unable even to see the words as Christ.

The Baptism of the Holy Spirit is not an incidental and irrelevant practice of certain Christian groups. Those who do not know full immersion into the Holy Spirit CANNOT see Christ in His own Word, though they look straight at the words on the page. We already know that; but we also want to know this Spirit in whom we live and move and have our being more deeply and more experientially than we have known. I write that I might know Him.

In Him you also trusted, after you heard the word of truth, the gospel of your salvation; in whom also, having believed, you were sealed with the Holy Spirit of promise, who is the guarantee of our inheritance until the redemption of the purchased possession, to the praise of His glory. Ephesians 1:13-14

Guarantee – an installment; a deposit ("down-payment") which guarantees the balance (the full inheritance).

Christ comes into me by the Holy Spirit. The Father comes into me inside of Christ. All of God is in me now, in all fullness. Yet there is far more to come in my experience. The Holy Spirit is the down payment, a very LARGE down payment. The Holy Spirit teaches us Christ. Christ teaches us the Father.

Again, I am reaching to know – "What is the Holy Spirit?" So I will wait upon Him that I might know Him.

The Holy Spirit is that sending forth of God out from God and me praying together. (When I say "me" or "I," you say it as yourself.) As God and I pray together, the Holy Spirit goes forth to accomplish what we have purposed.

As God and I pray together, it is I, as the body of Christ, as God revealed in the earth, who goes forth to touch things in the earth. But it is also I, as one Spirit with God's Spirit, who goes forth to touch things in the heavens.

All things God and I do together are accomplished by faith, speaking our prayer into darkness, calling all things good, and waiting with expectation for the full measurement of our faith to come back to us by love. Isn't that how it works?

Praying "to" God is unbelief. Praying with God, and then, with God expecting all that we have spoken to come back to us by love is faith. Faith works by love.

How this understanding changes everything. The first part is always the Mercy Seat. As I draw that which offends and is offensive to me into my heart upon the Mercy Seat, above the Blood, and there set all things free to arise into life, I am dealing with the negative. (And let me tell you, this practice WORKS.) But prayer is the positive side of that same reality.

Prayer is the going forth of God (Spirit). But this God is never alone, for I am always inside of Him.

Our marriage union with Christ changes all things in the universe and all things in God in our perspective. Our marriage union with Christ places us as the actor upon all the works of God's hands. We can never speak or think of ourselves except that we are in God and God is in us. We are never thought of or seen or known as separate from Him; we never act or speak separately from Him.

The Father and I are one. — I am God revealed. That's not blasphemy; that's the normal human life, exactly what God created us to be.

Now, I used the word "negative," just above. I was not speaking of the Mercy Seat, but of the elimination of the negative by the Mercy Seat. The sixth most important verse in the Bible states that our hearts are sprinkled with Blood. The Blood is absolute. The Blood is a Rock. There is nothing more substantial than Blood in God or in creation.

John saw the river of life, that it flows out from the throne of God. That throne is the Mercy Seat, sprinkled with Blood; that throne is our hearts. Yet that river of life is the sending forth of the Holy Spirit out from God in us. When we send forth the Holy Spirit in prayer together with the God who fills us full, that Holy Spirit proceeds forth from Blood, the Blood sprinkled upon our hearts.

This is a big deal. — **Pray without ceasing.** The Holy Spirit is continually flowing out from the Blood upon our hearts.

Both Son and Spirit are "Sent." That is, both are the going forth of the Father.

For as the rain comes down, and the snow from heaven, and do not return there, but water the earth, and make it bring forth and bud, that it may give seed to the sower and bread to the eater, so shall My word be that goes forth from My mouth; it shall not return to Me void, but it shall accomplish what I please, and it shall prosper in the thing for which I sent it. Isaiah 55:10-11

This reality is true for both Son into the earth and Spirit into the heavens.

"**It shall accomplish what I please, and it shall prosper in the thing for which I sent it**" IS God's faith in action, the expectation of God.

Faith is the mechanism by which God accomplishes all things. **Faith works by love. Faith works by love** means God sets all things free of Himself. Then, by His expectation ALONE, all things, responding to that love, come back to Him.

Prayer. – Spirit. – Word.

God is in us as much as we are in God. There is no place inside of God that one could go without finding us there as well. The Holy Spirit is the down payment; all of God is our inheritance. Yet this same God fills us with ALL that He is.

If prayer is us with God, then prayer is also God with us.

God places His supreme confidence in His Spirit sent forth into the heavens to accomplish all He has purposed in the heavenly realms. God places His supreme confidence in His Son sent forth into the earth as the Body of Christ to accomplish all He has purposed in the physical realms.

The expectation of God is pure rest; the expectation of God is ceaseless activity. – **Faith WORKS by Love.**

You and I are God's Son in the earth, the Body of Christ. We are one Spirit with the Spirit of God in the heavens. Upon our hearts the Blood is sprinkled, making our hearts God's authority in the universe. You see, all these things are clearly stated in the New Testament and we know the words. We just have never considered what they meant, blinded by the Nicene definitions of God and man.

We never pray "to" God, for God fills us full. We pray with God.

Thus the Holy Spirit is that part of God that goes out from our hearts to accomplish God and our purposes in the heavens. As God and we pray together, we place our supreme confidence in the Holy Spirit to accomplish in the heavenly realms all that we speak. Yet we and God never push anyone around. The only reality we accept coming back to us is that which comes by love out from hearts moved by love.

God never expects an instantaneous response to His faith. His supreme confidence that love would come back to Him from the earth has taken the Spirit of God 6,000 years to work its way through the tangled world of the human heart, wooing, breathing, calling, inspiring, until our hearts, sprinkled with Blood, now engage fully with this God who fills us full. Rooted and grounded in love.

Unbelief is treating the Holy Spirit very badly. That is, though He is sent out, unbelief is "confident" that He will fail.

As I've shared before, Romans 8:28 is poorly translated. It should read: **God and we together make all things good – those who are called according to His purpose.** This is His purpose, to make all things new, to make all things good, to draw all creation into love.

God created the proto-universe by speaking His Word into His Spirit (prayer). The serpent and Adam together marred that universe, both heaven and earth, by unbelief, by expecting both Word and Spirit to fail. They are totally wrong.

God is not just creating a "new" universe. Rather, by that same Word, this time in our mouths, by that same Spirit, this time flowing out from us, God and us together draw every single element in the old creation across the Blood upon our hearts, across the Mercy Seat, and by love, raise it up into the new creation.

God and we together make all things good. – We are the proof that Adam and the serpent are wrong.

Yet here's the thing. Since neither God nor us ever pushes anyone around, we must give the Spirit time. We must give Him our vote of confidence with patience. He is working as God and we speak together. But He is working upon hearts, and hearts can be won only by love.

We have all the time in the universe; we have forever. Because we know there is no such thing as the "next life," we never fall into the evil reaction of thinking, "Well, it will all work out in the sweet by and by." We are in life and life is forever. I plan on living forever; I see no interruption or distinction from my present life in God to a "next" life as if I am not entirely in God right now.

I see only the defeat of death; I am not planning to die. Living forever without dying is the promise of the gospel.

Now, even though Spirit is infinite and all-pervasive, it is not "ethereal." Spirit is specific and definite.

So let's bring the Spirit into something definite, the vision of my heart that God and I are believing for together. Now, I am not tied to that vision being fulfilled at Blair Valley, an isolated valley in north-eastern British Columbia. I would be just as happy if God and I together brought forth its fulfilment in warmer climes, where there is plenty of water. Yet both Word and Spirit inside of me continue to hover over that unique place, wintry and isolated though it might be.

The vision of my heart is a school, a particular kind of school, centered in a Christian community in a rural setting. One distinctive nature of this school/community is that many can come from across the earth to gain from it a knowledge of Christ, and thus carry that knowledge in their hearts back to their own country. I see only a river in and a river out, a place of refuge and a sending forth.

That is, I see God.

Prayer is the sending forth of the Spirit in the expectation of faith. So what, exactly, is the Holy Spirit doing right now concerning the prayer of God and me together continually sending Him forth?

EVERYTHING that is needed to cause the vision I carry to be fulfilled at that location is right now in the hands of other people. More than that, there is no way, at this present time, that I could "earn" any of it.

What, precisely, is needed to fulfill our vision? Three things: word, anointing, and money.

There is no community without people, the right people. And people are made "the right people" by the hearing of the same word. At this point in time I am sufficiently settled in the word presently flowing through me, that it is a word worth giving one's life for, and that others are recognizing and embracing that same word.

But in every instance, people + word = legalism. No thanks. Thus there must also be the anointing, that unction, that enablement coming out from Spirit that causes the Word to be alive, that abounds in hearts with love, that convicts of wrong, that joins all together in worship.

But, I tell you what, you can preach up a storm in the power of the Holy Ghost, and without MONEY, ain't nothing gonna' happen.

And that's where Father comes in. Father's the One with the dough. He's the wealthy Guy. The problem, of course, is that all of His earthly money is already out on credit, in the hands of people.

About thirty families came together in 1972 and 1973 to build Graham River Farm, the first Christian community I knew at the age of twenty (1977 – five years later). Most of them had sold everything they owned and put their moneys together to buy the property, build the buildings, and purchase all the needed equipment for a late 1800's style of rural agricultural life, with just a bit of modern, such as tractor, truck, welding shop, etc.

In the first two years, they burned through a couple of million dollars. Everything had to be bought until the farming was sufficient to provide the needs of a simple life. Two million in 1972 is more than ten million today. And when the money was gone, their life together was simple and limited, great fun for a twenty-year-old boy, but very difficult for mothers with little children especially, and with no ability to be a "river in and a river out."

More than that, the nature of poverty works against the gospel of Christ for the simple reason that people tend to replace money with ego and elitism. In other words, "We're the true people of God, and we are poor. You people out there in the world with all your fleshy wealth are not as close to God as we are."

I will not take my family back into poverty and the inability to be a blessing to others that comes with it. Such is not Father.

So how, then, does prayer work, this sending forth of Spirit out from Father and me in our full confidence in the Spirit's ability to perform all things well?

First, this same Spirit must be upon me before any Word coming through me will attract the right people. Different word attracts different kinds of people. The word that I write comes out from the Holy Spirit. You know, this is so neat. I can say that with all confidence and with no ego. The simple reason why is that I trust the Holy Spirit utterly to be upon all that I write. Yet at no time am I bound to any particular words, but am ready to edit them for any good reason, whether mine or others. Yet my desire for that which alone is REAL causes me to rest utterly in the Holy Spirit through me.

At the same time, the people who hear the Holy Spirit speaking to them by the words that I write are the only ones who continue to read. But my present readers may or may not be the ones who will arrive at Blair Valley, sent by God to give their lives to the vision I carry in my heart. Wow. That's a big deal; I dare never take such a thing lightly. Yet there are individual people right now, across this earth, who will give their hearts and strength to the fulfillment of that vision. And there are individual people right now, across this earth, who will give their money to the fulfillment of that vision.

How does that happen? – Spirit.

All things and all people exist inside the same Holy Spirit going out from Father and me to fulfill our expectations. This same Holy Spirit is all the *energia* of their lives.

Faith works by love. The Holy Spirit's job is to win the heart of each individual person who has some role to play, large or small, in the fulfillment of this dream of mine. Okay. That sobers things up a bit.

Do you see how it is that great visionaries in the church who will "use" God's people to fulfill their vision as they see it, have done so much damage to so many for 2000 years?

The love of God HAS BEEN shed abroad IN our hearts BY the Holy Spirit who is given to us.

ANYTHING that comes by any other means from anyone is not God, though He bears with all.

So when we force spirit, we win by fair means and foul together. You know, that does describe Sam Fife and the Christian communities I lived in for eighteen years. The Holy Spirit was most definitely upon us, but at times "forced," and most certainly fair means and foul together. So much goodness; so much ruin. God most definitely works inside of such a mess (otherwise there would be no hope for anyone), but only to teach us to flee the false and wait upon Him for the real.

We must wait upon the Spirit to do His work BECAUSE He wins hearts only by the wooing of love. And since everything I need to fulfill the vision in my heart is right now in the hands of other people across the earth, the only way it will ever happen is for the Holy Spirit to win.

You know, I've never cared much for "patience." I always imagined some bold sort of faith that "makes things happen NOW!" There is no such thing. Oh sure, forceful human spirits can cause a spirit reaction of WOW and submission in other human spirits. It happens all the time, even with that which is "miraculous." But if it's not the winning of the heart by the Holy Spirit up from within the person's own heart in full respect and honor of each individual one, it may be of use to some, but not to me.

I want only that which comes out of the full freedom and honor of love. And thus prayer, praying without ceasing, and the expectation that the Holy Spirit is doing His task well, and possessing all things with patience are all three the same thing. – Spirit.

But the trigger is in my hands, the power switch, my own confidence that the Holy Spirit is indeed doing well right now all that the Father and I have sent Him out to do. As I am confident with the Father in the Holy Spirit, that He will come back, His work fulfilled, then He is free to do what He does best, win hearts by love. But when I doubt that the Father and I are together, when I expect that the Holy Spirit will likely fail (because people are too much for Him), when I am impatient and in my impatience seek to ram my vision through people's minds, emotions, and wills rather than that which comes up out from their hearts and from Christ living as them, then all I am doing is binding the hands of that same Holy Spirit so that He simply weeps and cannot win.

The Holy Spirit NEVER pushes anyone around. The moment there is any commotion, any striving, any manipulation of others, like a dove, He vanishes from the immediate. Yet the only thing eternal, the only thing of value, the only thing I want, comes out of that very gentle wooing of a welcome Holy Spirit.

Faith works only by Love.

You know, for myself, for my own understanding and walk, I think this is one of the most important bits I have ever written.

Everything we do and say we wrap in our hearts (the Mercy Seat) with the expectation of Spirit, that is, in conscious conjunction with that very personal part of God that woos all hearts with tenderness and concern. Every interaction we engage in with people, we expect the Holy Spirit to bathe with His wooing. You see, it has to be "wooing," there is no other word for it, the winning of a heart to love. The Holy Spirit forces NO ONE. Thus, all work He does must come out from the tender willing consent of the person. And there is no "work" of the Holy Spirit on our behalf that is not on persons.

If we are led with joy to share a Galatians 6:1 word with a dear brother or sister in private, we speak bathed in the conscious awareness of the Holy Spirit's tender wooing both upon ourself and upon the other.

Jesus did not immerse me into the Holy Spirit until I had said "Yes, Lord" in response to His word, "Will you give all of yourself to me." Up until now, I had imagined that my surrender was the removal of a barrier keeping me from God. When we are far away from God in our imagination, it can't be anything else. But that's not what it was at all.

My surrender was simply the Holy Spirit honoring me with utmost respect, unwilling to force Himself upon me in any way, but waiting until I knew that I truly wanted Him flowing all through me.

Respect – Honor – Love.

Thus, having been treated with such utmost respect by this same Holy Spirit (who is so merged with my spirit that we are one, as Paul said), I/He continues to regard all others with that same respect.

All of Father's money is in other people's hands, on loan, yes, but nevertheless theirs. And I use the word "money" as a clear and practical term for all the provision of God. Thus no provision can come my way except from a person whose heart has been romanced and won by the Holy Spirit for that purpose.

The key to the power of the Spirit is to regard who and what He is and how He works. When Jesus said, **"I am meek and lowly of heart,"** He was speaking of all the fullness of God. God never moves in any other way in any part or expression of Himself. Even when He displays His wrath, and He does, it's just a face, angered by the rejecter of love for his or her own self-infliction of pain.

When Paul said that the love of God has been shed abroad in our hearts by the Holy Spirit given to us, he was speaking of the base of the Spirit's operations, heart calling to heart, heart wooing heart by name.

When we hear His voice, we hear our name.

When I look at the means by which so many imagine the "truth" must be spread, speaking endless words at people, I've never seen the Lord Jesus in that. The Lord Jesus is the One who romances one heart by name, wooing that person into Love. His Spirit works no other way.

That which has not been won by love has not been won by God.

Those who "persuade" people to support them and follow their ministry do not have God with them, though God uses anything and everything to work Himself in the lives of all.

Only a heart won by name, and that between that person and the Lord Jesus alone, with me just standing unseen in the shadows, only such a one would I have to walk with me and I with them. And I would have many such ones in a community of honor and respect as the revelation of Jesus Christ.

The Holy Spirit flows forth from me, yet I always with Him, for we are one spirit and I am found in all places that same Spirit is found. By Spirit, Jesus and I call each one by name who has some part with me, wooing each one by love, honoring each one with utmost respect.

The Father and I pray together, and then wait in the full rest of expectation, knowing that our Spirit wins every heart in the universe, His elect ones first, and then, through them, all, each in his or her season of favor.

19. Body

There is so much confusion in Christian thinking concerning both the body and the flesh. And there is good reason for that confusion: God contradicts Himself big time. It's not just that Paul says something different than James and Jesus seem to say; it's that Paul also contradicts himself.

Most people assume that flesh is "evil," that it has nothing to do with God or God with it. Thus, they emphasize those verses that seem to cast the flesh as bad, they darken the majority of verses that present the flesh as neutral, and they adamantly IGNORE those verses that tie the flesh into marriage union with Christ. Most are also confused about the difference or sameness between the "flesh," *sarx*, and the "body," *soma*. This confusion is entirely God's fault, for He says so many differing things on the topic.

God created Adam as both God's likeness and God's image. That means two things. First, likeness means that Adam was fabricated to be just like God in so many, many ways, but beginning with just like God in heart. Second, image means that Adam's purpose was to be the revelation of God, so that God Himself might dwell in all fullness in Adam and show Himself to His creation through Adam. Adam was God's likeness and image in all of his makeup: spirit, soul, and body.

Yet God does nothing apart from human consent, thus He gave Adam a choice. If Adam had eaten of the tree of life, he would have been sealed forever into full union with Christ as God-revealed in all the realms of the heavenlies and in all physical realms forever. Adam would have been God-revealed through his spirit; he would have been God-revealed through his soul; and he would have been God-revealed through his body.

More than that, Paul pointed out in 1 Corinthians 12 that we bestow more honor on our weakest parts. Thus God held a special place in His heart for Adam's body. Adam's body, as God designed it, was most incredibly the likeness and image of God.

We have seen that the lie of the serpent is not immediately visible in the serpent's words, as nonsensical as they were. The lie, rather, is found in the assumptions beneath the serpent's words, the reasoning out of which they came. Because most Christians assume that the serpent was speaking the truth, they then also assume that the assumptions out from which he spoke were also true. Those assumptions, that is, the lie, are then woven all through Nicene Christianity, all through Christian theology.

Adam's physical body, his flesh, was the primary target of the serpent's assault; Adam's body was the weakest element in his construction, the doorway into Adam's heart. As I shared earlier in this series, when the serpent said, *"You shall be like God,"* those words were the battering ram that shattered everything to pieces, opening the entrance into Adam's heart and mind for both lie and curse.

It is easy for us to believe that our spirits could be "like God" since God is a Spirit, and spirit is "heavenly." It is not hard for Christian thinking to postulate that the soul could even be "like God"; Thomas Aquinas stated that we are "like God" in our reason, that is our mind. But the body? No. The body just does not look like God in any way you cut it.

The body is weak; the body gets tired; the body stinks; the body wants things it doesn't have; the body hungers and thirsts; the body "weighs us down." The body looks absolutely ridiculous. Eve may have been beautiful and Adam a hunk, but most of us fall woefully short of either.

Adam knew he was just like God, spirit, soul, and body. But the moment he saw the glorious outward appearance of the serpent, he doubted himself. What the serpent really said in his words, *"You shall be like God,"* was this. *"Adam, your body, your outward earthly appearance CANNOT be God-revealed. No way!"*

And Adam believed the serpent. Believing the serpent, that he was not already 100%, spirit, soul, and body, just like God, was the fall of Adam. Adam believed that Jesus, hanging bloody and naked upon the cross could not possibly be the express image of God's Person. Adam believed that if God showed up in the earth, God would look like the glorious serpent, He would not be Adam himself.

Thus Adam's first actions in his unbelief were to work on his body, to make it look better than it did. Covering his body with fig leaves was Adam's declaration of hatred for the image of God in the earth.

Here is my present understanding of the difference between *sarx*, flesh, and *soma*, body, in the New Testament. *Soma*, the body, refers primarily to the organ of the physical body, though it is often used to mean the human limitation and weakness found in that body. *Sarx*, the flesh, refers primarily to the human limitation and weakness found in the physical body, though it is often used to mean simply the organ of the physical body. The two are often interchanged by the writers of the New Testament, with little or no affect on the meaning.

Both *sarx* and *soma*, flesh and body, are 100% neutral in themselves. There is nothing good in the flesh; there is nothing evil in the flesh. The flesh, the human body, is simply a vessel. What the vessel contains is what is good or evil. Flesh breathed upon by demons is evil. Flesh filled with God is pure and holy and good. The difference is the source, not the actions or the weakness of the body.

People who do not believe that God fills their flesh now with all of His fullness, join with Adam in seeing the flesh as their "problem." They believe, with Adam, that it is their job to make the flesh look like Christ ought to look like, that is, the glorious outward appearance of the serpent, BEFORE God will ever deign to come and live in them. Those who teach "obedience first," live according to the flesh in the rebellion of Adam.

The reason Jesus was hated and murdered was that He looked entirely like a man, that is, like God in the earth. If He had looked like the serpent, everyone would have worshipped Him. No one wants the flesh to be the image of God; it's just too humiliating. Being "like God" ought to look better than that.

There is a trigger in the human mind, a trigger that does not come from Christian theology, rather it comes from Adam's rebellion THROUGH Christian theology, that automatically reads EVIL when seeing the word "flesh," in the New Testament. Thus those verses that place God in the flesh are studiously ignored, or relegated to a deified (outwardly superman) "Jesus" that is not a Man, God-revealed, at all.

Let's bring in the most important verses that must rule our knowledge of the flesh. All other verses must come in under these verses to serve them and to expand their meaning. All other statements in the New Testament concerning the "flesh," must be read and understood by and through these absolutes.

The Word became flesh and dwelt among us. John 1

And without controversy great is the mystery of godliness: God manifest in the flesh... 1 Timothy 3

But we have this treasure in earthen vessels, that the excellence of the power may be of God and not of us. – that the life of Jesus also may be manifested in our mortal flesh. 2 Corinthians 4:7 & 11

And He said to me, "My grace is sufficient for you, for My strength is made perfect in weakness." 2 Corinthians 12:9

Now the body is... for the Lord, and the Lord for the body. And God both raised up the Lord and will also raise us up by His power. Do you not know that your bodies are members of Christ? — But he who is joined to the Lord is one spirit with Him. — Or do you not know that your body is the temple of the Holy Spirit who is in you, whom you have from God, and you are not your own? 1 Corinthians 6:13-19

For we are members of His body, of His flesh and of His bones. Ephesians 5:30

The single most telling statement concerning God's purpose for our flesh is 2 Corinthians 4:7, **– that the life of Jesus also may be manifested in our mortal flesh.** It is here we must begin. If this purpose of God is not the ruling definition for our flesh, then we cannot know what to do with anything else God says in the Bible concerning our physical bodies.

God created our flesh specifically to reveal the life of Jesus to others, and it does so even in its present dying state. Everything else God says in the New Testament about either "the flesh" or "the body" teaches us how 2 Corinthians 4:7 is fulfilled in our lives. But if we believe that our flesh is "evil," that it cannot be found inside of Jesus, that it cannot be filled with God, that it can never reveal the life of Jesus or be transformed from the inside out into His very Body, then nothing else God says will ever teach us the truth concerning our flesh.

Life swallowing up our mortal bodies I will leave for the chapter on "Victory." Here I want to look at our flesh as it is presently dying.

A caterpillar is a skin-changer. Consider the phrase I have used previously to denote the popular view of judging all things by outward appearance. *"The old skin must be shed before the new one can come."* That view is entirely from the outside, seeing by how something seems to appear in the present moment, without considering for one moment what actually happened.

Here is what happened. "The old skin is not shed until the new one is fully formed and ready for full exposure." Moments before the new skin bursts onto the scene fully formed, the old skin looks its worst to all who see by outward appearance. Yet that new skin was forming all along underneath the old, and no one could see it, except those who can see by reality and not by outward appearance.

But if the Spirit of Him who raised Jesus from the dead dwells in you, He who raised Christ from the dead will also give life to your mortal bodies through His Spirit who dwells in you. Romans 8:11

Someone objected to my calling our present state of "Christ as us" the caterpillar state. This person believed that no, "Christ as us" is the butterfly state, having come forth fully from the chrysalis. That's the problem with using the things God created to understand God's truth, we like to put strait-jackets on them.

Here is my understanding. Right now, we are in the womb of the Church, in-between being conceived of God and the birthing into the full light of day. That birthing, that butterfly coming out of its chrysalis, IS the redemption of our physical bodies, the resurrection, the moment in time, in the twinkling of an eye, when we know the full experience of incorruptibility and are just like Jesus in all ways as He is right now in all outward experience.

But right now, when I read Romans 8:11, I can only shake my head in wonder. I "feel" and "see" NOTHING of what Paul claims the Holy Spirit is doing right now in my body.

Of truth, I see our present state as both the caterpillar and the chrysalis. In fact, there's hardly any difference between what both picture to us. The caterpillar doesn't worry about a thing, he just eats and eats and eats Christ. The goo in the chrysalis doesn't worry about a thing, it just speaks and speaks out from the Christ that is its DNA, knowing the DNA of Christ Himself is transforming all that goo into a butterfly. At the same time, I see us now as the fully formed butterfly, beginning to press against the chrysalis in order to cast if off.

We do not think highly of ourselves. We are more than happy to be the caterpillar in all joy, eating of Christ. We are more than happy to be sticky goo right now, confident that Christ in us will make something good out of that goo. And we are quite happy to press against the restraints, but only as Christ through us, never in some "burden" of our own.

The flesh is NOT evil; and our time of transformation inside this present flesh is the most glorious honor ever granted to any created being.

The butterfly is what we speak – Christ. We call that which "is not" as though it is. But we don't imagine that our present outward appearance is the full inheritance. Yet we rejoice in our present weakness, knowing that it is here alone that all the power of Christ is perfect.

We have this treasure in earthen vessels, that the excellence of the power may be of God and not of us.

It's a very simple equation, really, but one that we so easily forget when we find ourselves in the press of what other people think we ought to be and do, that is, in the face of Eve.

I want to include here a question asked of me and my response. The question I consider to be of vital importance, because it must be asked and then fully answered inside each one of our hearts.

– What of the statement Paul made **"In my flesh dwells no good thing"**? Did he mean the residue of sin in his members? He called that evil. Just what is he talking about? –

We cannot take Romans 7:7-25 out of its context. It does not mean what people take it to mean when they separate it from Paul's gospel before and after. Paul says very clearly in 7:4-6 that we have NO relationship to the law. Then, in verse 7, Paul brings the law back in. Then, in Romans 8:2, he states again, so clearly, that we have no relationship with the law of sin and death. Romans 7:7-24 is all about a "Christian" trying to have a relationship with the law, a "what-if" scenario. It's either Christ or the law, we can't have both. If we engage with the law, then there is no good thing in our flesh and we are under bondage. But if Christ is our only life, then the Holy Spirit lives in our body, and, as Paul says in 1 Corinthians 6, there is NO sin in our bodies.

It's either all Christ or all the law; there is no mixture, no going back and forth. Those verses in Romans 7 are all about the agony of a Christian trying to live in both at the same time. If you are filled with all of God, then God dwells in your flesh, and He is good. More than that, Jesus, when He walked the earth, said, **"Don't call Me good, only God is good."**

What makes us good is God. What makes evil is trying to have both God and not-God. John said that those who try to mix the two, He will vomit out of His mouth. Paul said that those who try to mix the two, that is, those who try to live inside of Romans 7:7-24 are **"fallen from grace."**

The only reason we read Romans 7:7-24 is to rejoice in verse 25, thank God for Jesus - our only life. Those who contemplate living inside of Romans 7:7-24 are dancing with death, circling around the tree of the knowledge of good and evil, trying to find life in the law, the very thing that always kills all. Those who try to live in Romans 7:7-24 divide themselves, split themselves into two, creating the false self. That's what the law does; it's awful. That's why God commanded Adam not to live there.

Galatians 2:20 sets us free from all that. We are dead. There is no evil in us, nor any claim of the law. The life we live right now in the flesh is only Jesus.

This letter is not on the corporate body of Christ, but rather the place of God's working, this furnace of affliction God has given us called "the flesh," our present physical bodies in all of their weakness and lack.

I am a cabinet-maker and some of my happiest memories are working in a wood shop, well-equipped with high quality tools, with a nice selection of raw materials to choose from, forming and fashioning wood into something beautiful and useful. If I had the money, I would most certainly build a really nice shop in my backyard and equip it with the finest of tools. I would also fill another such building with a wonderful selection of the finest woods – preferably in a relatively rough state. (Prior indiscriminate machining can eliminate the most beautiful elements in a log.)

Think of **"the life we live in the flesh"** as that shop, the place in all the universe where God is doing His finest work. The Nicene Creed is written on the assumption that this present flesh-time is evil only and that God's "salvation" is to *"get us out of here."* I am convinced we will know forever that our present life in this flesh is the MOST IMPORTANT time and place in both heaven and earth.

But before exploring this "cabinet shop" of the flesh where God is doing His finest work, I want to address a question, already asked in this series, but asked again recently. "Will we know Jesus in outward form, that individual body that came out of the grave and ascended into the clouds?"

Although my bottom line answer remains the same, "I don't know," I have thought more clearly on this idea. Let's make it practical and real. An idea floated in the Nicene interpretation of the end if the age is that **"every eye will see Him"** by means of television. This placing of Jesus into the image of the beast comes out of the very real understanding that Jesus' physical body, the one that ascended into the sky, was finite and limited. That body could be in only one place at a time.

When Jesus breakfasted with His disciples on the shore of the sea, He was not, at that same moment, appearing to Lazarus, say, in Bethany.

If that is true, than you and I will never see Jesus. There are too many pushers and shovers who will get in line far ahead of us.

But if Jesus duplicates that same body, so that He appears in physical form in a hundred million places at the same time, what is that? Why would Jesus clone that same body many times over? And what would it be if one of Jesus' body clones came into the same room with another? That would be weird.

If Jesus is to walk this earth in that same finite and limited body that the disciples saw after the resurrection, then either of these two scenarios would be the only way it would work. But if Jesus is to appear in many different physical bodies at the same time, why would it be so wrong to know that He does appear, in full literal reality, in your body and mine?

Put on the Lord Jesus Christ, spirit, soul, and body.

I say, "I don't know," because I don't, yes, but I do now think that Jesus' full return is, literally and actually, in your body and mine, as us. **"Christ lives in our hearts"** is real and actual; the **"by faith"** part is only how we presently KNOW that absolute and literal reality.

I am the container of another Person; I am NEVER alone.

I am the Ark of the Covenant.

The work God is doing in this workshop He has made, our present life in the flesh, is the MOST IMPORTANT thing going on in time and in eternity.

Of truth, the metaphor of a wood shop and the crafting of a piece of fine woodworking is identical all the way through to the metaphor of a caterpillar being transformed into a butterfly.

The butterfly that will be, the cabinet (ark) that contains Himself God is crafting, takes on its eternal form and shape entirely by what happens inside the shop, inside the eating, the goo-ifying, and the transformation.

This body of flesh. — The life of Jesus revealed.

God's task is to so merge Himself with us that He might always be the One seen and known through us.

This merging of God and Jesus was complete, two Persons in One. Jesus is not just our pattern, but also our life, Christ as us. Thus Christ as us is already programmed to complete this full merger with the Person of the Father inside of us.

Now, there are certain elements or difficulties in this merger. First, both God's consciousness must be in my full awareness inside of me and my consciousness in my awareness must be inside of God. Jesus said, **"The Father has never left Me alone."** We are always two persons together. But the tricky thing for God is that

He will never violate our person.

Coming into full union, communion, and expression with us, His consciousness inside of ours and ours inside of His in continual ongoing experience is hindered by this propensity in God NEVER to violate another person nor push anyone around. And at the center of this conundrum is the human heart, a heart as bold and daring as God's.

You see, the human heart, created to contain Almighty God, and thus crafted to be like God's heart in all daring confidence and extravagant recklessness, has imagined itself to be empty of God. Thus God begins this task in His workshop, our life in the flesh, by a complete merger of His heart and ours, the Mercy Seat.

Jesus did not "set aside His divinity" when He walked the earth; there is no such thing. That whole way of thinking comes out of Nicene definitions. When God shows up in the physical realms He IS a Man. Man is God's appearance in the physical. Since we are one with the Spirit of God, man is also God's appearance in the heavens; we just can't see that yet.

Yet man, as the express image of God's Person, is never alone. Man is always two persons together, the person of the human AND the Person of the Father, walking together as one.

The Father has NEVER left Me alone. – I and the Father are One.

Now we can place a difficult verse. It is here alone that this verse must fit, inside this perfect union of two persons in one, revealed into the earth through the same body and into the heavens through the same spirit.

Who, Jesus, in the days of His flesh, when He had offered up prayers and supplications with strong crying and tears unto Him who was able to save Him from death, and was heard because of His godly fear, though He was a Son, yet He learned obedience by the things which He suffered, and having been perfected, He became the author of eternal salvation to all who obey Him. Hebrews 5:7-9

This verse in Hebrews MUST always flow together with Jesus' assertion that He and the Father are One. We cannot see this as separated entities, the first pleading with the second, the second demanding "obedience" and making the first suffer until he has it right.

New Covenant obedience MUST carry a totally different definition than the obedience of the Old Covenant. Yet when I see people teaching "obedience," it is evident to me that they are teaching the law and not marriage union with Christ. There is no curse in New Testament obedience; thus, the "suffering" in this verse is not curse, but workmanship – the fellowship of His sufferings.

God perfected His perfect union with Jesus before Jesus went forth as the Christ of God. The two walked in full consciousness together, inside of one body, every step of the way. The "obedience" of the New Covenant is a perfect synergy together, God with us and we with God in one body. We can walk with God as His revelation through us because we are Christ as us.

The life that I now live in the flesh I live by the faith of the Son of God who loves me and gives Himself for me.

There is one place alone where God can accomplish His great work, this merging of Himself with another – that place is inside of the weakness of flesh.

I can of Myself do nothing. – My strength is made perfect in weakness.

Inside of a dying body.

You see God's recklessness? He has set Himself to pull off this most difficult of tasks even for God in this short space of time while a dying body is dying, but before it is dead, to come into a perfect union, communion, and expression through another person, you and me, without ever once violating our persons.

Every tool in a wood shop that applies to wood is a chisel, in one shape or another. A saw blade is simply a large number of small chisels in a row or in a circle. A planer is a wide chisel; a router is a shaped chisel. A screw is a spiral chisel, a nail a pointed chisel that drives through and remains.

That I might know Him in the fellowship of His sufferings. – Whom He loves He chastens and scourges every son whom He receives.

Never do we see this work of God upon us in terms of any law carrying any curse. What curse is there in being shaped into the Ark that contains and reveals Almighty God?

That the genuineness of your faith being much more precious than gold than gold that perishes, though it be tried in the fire, may be found unto praise, honor, and glory at the revelation, at the unveiling, at the removal of the outer covering **of Jesus Christ.** 1 Peter 1:7

Jesus, the express image of God's Person, hanging bloody, bruised, naked, and unashamed, saying, **"Father, forgive them,"** to the most offensive people on the planet. — God-revealed.

Would we be like Him?

You can tell a son of God. Poke him with a chisel and see what comes out. Any piece of wood that strikes back against the chisel is ruined and tossed into the bin for the wood stove. I've had a piece of wood striking back against the chisel take me in the gut and knock me to the floor.

To abide in Him is to abide in Him in the midst of His sufferings.

Jesus hurt upon the cross, not just from the physical wounds, but far more from the jibes and mockery of these offensive men. Why did He not strike back?

Because He was not ashamed of being the image of God in weakness.

Those who strike back do so because they are ashamed of themselves. In other words, they believe that they got a bum deal from God, that their weakness is not what they should be, that they deserve far more.

Shame is the cloak of arrogant pride. The only way to defeat it is the full acceptance by faith that this body of the likeness of sinful flesh IS God's flesh, the place of His revelation – in weakness.

A son of God, when he or she is cut by the chisel in the hand of God (and no chisel ever touches us that is not in His hand), hurts, yes, and in that hurt and confusion, may take a bit to come around, yes, but in the end, a son of God first, in all ways, justifies God. And second, gives thanks. And third, speaks only kindness and blessing, "Father, forgive them."

You see, to the wood, the hand is invisible. All the wood sees is the chisel coming at him. Faith alone will share the fellowship of His suffering. Faith alone sees God in the midst of the pain.

As I look at my list of the ten commandments of the New Covenant, I see that only one thing is entirely in our hand, a thing we can do or not do, that God Himself does not, by outward appearance anyway, fulfill in our lives.

Speak Christ — Ask — Give thanks. All are the words of our mouth.

You see, in this great task God has set for Himself, to become seen and known and touched through us, His body, all of everything is God's doings, in His hand and wisdom to accomplish His expression through us. And in all of everything, our place is to rest utterly in our present and perfect full union with Him.

Everything except one.

In the midst of the endless assault of chisels, when people hurt us badly, when we lose everything we hold dear, when our way ends in ruin, when we are humiliated and put down, we give thanks.

Give thanks, give thanks, give thanks, give thanks, in all things, for all things, through all things. And speak Christ and blessing to others.

We can do that because of the Mercy Seat, our hearts, and because of the Blood sprinkled there. We take all that hurt, those chisels in all their offensiveness to us, and we draw that offence into love, here within our hearts, here above the Blood, where God meets with us and we with God.

And here, inside this Communion between God and us, between the cherubim, we give thanks.

Those who give thanks inside the pain, justifying God and blaming no one, know Him in the fellowship of His sufferings. Those who strike back against the chisels have no idea whatsoever what we are talking about.

The marriage union between God and us is found entirely inside the marriage union between our giving thanks and our dying flesh. It is here alone that the great work of God's revelation is crafted. People in heaven only can worship God in all joy, but they cannot be crafted into His image at present because they have no place of God's workmanship, they have no dying flesh.

No man ever hated his own flesh, but nourishes and cherishes it just as Christ does the Church.

Paul's words are true, that is, until that man becomes a Nicene Christian. Then this marriage between God and flesh goes right out the window.

God-revealed is known only through those who, hanging exposed for all to see, bloody and bruised, having lost everything, having been denied and betrayed, yet knowing nothing of shame before either the face of Eve or of his mother, those who are content to be the flesh of God. And inside the Joy set in their hearts, without blaming anyone, they draw all that is offensive into Life. – The express image of God's Person.

20. The Two Gospels

In 1996, I came across a little booklet titled "The Two Gospels," written by a brother in the Lord. This brother attempted to argue his version of what is "another gospel" and "another Jesus." The brother mentioned a teaching he had recently come across about present union with Christ and attempted his best, in great Biblical argument, to show the wrong view in that teaching. In doing so, he presented his version of "the gospel."

The problem was I believed what this brother wrote in his booklet. And in doing so, I entered the time of deepest despair in my life. The author of the booklet? You may have heard of him. His name was Daniel Yordy.

Here, I intend to refute this guy's sincere, but sadly wrong thinking, to discover the core of it's hostility to God. But first, I place before you the joy I now know.

There are two premises underneath this entire series claiming that the Nicene/Augustinian definitions of God, of man, of Christ Jesus, and of salvation, are the "other gospel" that Paul warned us against and that the gospel of the New Testament is something quite different.

This is eternal life, that they may know You, the only true God, and Jesus Christ whom You have sent.

We know that we shall be like Him for we shall see Him as He is.

When the brother contended with me that I cannot be like Jesus because Jesus is "God" and I am not, he was speaking out of the knowledge about God and about man derived from Nicene/Augustinian Christianity. **We shall be like Him** is the core of the Covenant. If it is not true, nothing else can be true.

In "The Altar of Incense," Chapter Four of *The Covenant*, I presented this declaration of faith as the doorway into our actual full Covenant with God. Put your own full name in the blank.

"I, _____ _____, will be just like Jesus. I will walk just as He walked, right here on this earth, in this age, and in this life. I will walk without sin, just as Jesus walked. I will walk revealing the Father just as Jesus walked. I will walk in open ministry as a manifest son of God, just as Jesus walked. The Spirit will move through me without measure, just as the Spirit moved through Jesus without measure. I will know and reveal God, just as Jesus knew and revealed God, right here on this earth, right now in this life, me, as a human BEFORE the resurrection, just as Jesus walked in all these things before His resurrection."

Only those who believe enter into Covenant with God.

Now, some have believed this and not seen it in their time – so what! Read Hebrews 11: These all died in faith, not having seen the promise. Faith places us in God regardless of the seasons appointed by Him. But this confession of faith is referring partly to Jesus as He was when He walked this earth. The full Covenant is that we are just like Jesus as He IS right now, the ascended Christ of God, the King of the universe.

Eternal life is nothing other than one thing: to know God and to know Jesus-Sent. Knowing God and Jesus-Sent AND being just like Jesus, conformed to His image ARE the same thing. Since writing the letters on "Spirit" and "Body," I have been pondering a statement of Jesus.

> **I tell you the truth. It is to your advantage that I go away; for if I do not go away, the Helper will not come to you; but if I depart, I will send Him to you. Then Jesus said this: . . . the Spirit of truth . . . will guide you into all truth. . . He will glorify Me, for He will take of what is Mine and declare it to you. All things that the Father has are Mine. Therefore I said that He will take of Mine and declare it to you.** John 16:7 & 13-15

Jesus was saying that so long as He was outside of the disciples, He could not be inside of them, He could not be their life. More than that, when He said that the Holy Spirit will "declare" to us ALL THINGS of the Father and of the Son, He did not mean that the Holy Spirit will give us informational knowledge about God. Jesus meant that we would know God and Jesus-Sent in intimate and perfect Union, Communion, AND Expression.

So – our human spirits are merged entirely into the infinite and omnipresent Spirit of God; where He is we are. That same Holy Spirit DWELLS in our bodies, where He is busy, busy, busy, applying the resurrection life of Jesus to our dying flesh. That same Holy Spirit flows out from us as rivers of living water. Christ Jesus LIVES IN our hearts, and inside of Jesus comes all the fullness of the Father. We HAVE the mind of Christ; we have a mind to know God; eternal life fills our hearts and souls. And Christ Jesus Himself lives as us, our very and only Self.

What else is there? What else would we want? We are humans, that is, God-revealed. The problem, of course, is just who and what this Fellow is that fills us full. He recklessly and continuously, without any visible hope of success, lays down His life for His friends – all while they are still His enemies, attacking Him in all ferocity!!!

And the worst of the matter is that, if we are just like Him, then **we also** – lay down our lives for the brethren.

And here is where too many revert back to the safety of a Nicene God, far above, far away, or worse yet, divert "Christ-as-us" to mean God's support for their desire to manipulate and control God's people.

God has chiselled away at me all of my life. I would guess that about a quarter of all the letters I have written were either written in the agony of great difficulty or written in the joy just after the pain has vanished. Sometimes the letters I have written in the deepest of His sufferings have brought the greatest help to my readers. At other times, the letters that came in the joy of release just after such a time have been the most inspiring. That includes my recent letter, "Spirit."

But the most difficult year of my life was 1996. Through that year, God did not just bear with me the assault of many chisels all at once, but on top of them was a great sledge hammer that, by December of that year, had left me all smashed to pieces, having lost everything I had devoted my life to win, numb and confused, but holding utterly to His hand holding mine.

I have shared of that time and how God spoke to me a few months later, "Son, you passed the test." He spoke it in that way because that's how I thought at the time. Last night, God gave me an entirely different view of what took place through that most difficult of years. He showed me what He did deep inside of me underneath the blows and in the midst of all my confusion.

God reached deep into my innermost parts and removed from my heart that voice that would speak the words of Satan, that voice that would accuse others, that voice that would strike back against others when God uses them as the chisel in His hand. That I had "passed the test," meant outwardly that I justified God in all my confusion and blamed no one, inwardly it meant that God had given me that greatest of gifts, a heart that could lay down its life for my brother.

I had no knowledge of such a heart then, but such a heart has shown itself just a little bit in recent years. I know that it will only grow as I see Him as He is and am just like Him.

There is nothing sadder than a fellow believer who speaks accusation against another in anger against God. This is the true test of any eunuch in God's ministry. When God chisels you through your brother, will you justify God and speak blessing and Christ, or will accusation flow through your lips?

God orders my steps; He is responsible for all things that come my way. His ways concerning me are perfect, and I justify Him in all things. No chisel ever chisels me, no hammer ever delivers its blows except entirely IN the Hand of my Father, this One who fills me full. Every moment of the fellowship of His suffering is of more value to me than the universe, for by it, God is giving me Himself.

Yet this God who fills me full is joy and gladness as well, always laughing hilariously, especially when I take myself too seriously. And thus I must never make a fetish out of my difficulties, but dance for joy with you in the celebration of His love.

What does this have to do with "The Two Gospels"?

We cannot know the false except we have our hearts filled full with the true. And we do.

We know Him and we love Him. And in knowing and loving Him, in believing all things that He speaks in the Covenant He signed with us, in making all that is Christ personal in us, we come to understand that the "Jesus" and the "gospel" we once knew in our mental definitions bears no relationship to this Jesus and this Salvation we now know and love.

We see Him as He is, and in seeing Him as He is, we discover that we are, right now, just like Him. And in discovering that we are, right now, just like Him, we realize that we must now be hated for the same reasons they hated Jesus, as Jesus said we would be. We have dirtied their "God" in exactly the same way that Jesus dirtied their "God."

The God of the Nicene Creed is God as known out from the tree of the knowledge of good and evil, a God far away. The substance of the Christ of the Nicene Creed is a Christ we could never be of His same kind. God's desire to be seen and known and touched through His image, man, is removed entirely from the Nicene Creed, and thus God's heart is ripped right out of their whole picture.

Nicene thinking reduces God to mental definitions, ideas of the mind. It places "God" in the control of man.

Okay, I have finally pulled this booklet titled "The Two Gospels" written by this Yordy fellow in 1996, but not completed and printed until early 1998.

I am speechless. I had no idea. – There is almost no difference between that little booklet and the gist of what I write now. Same verses, same truths, same view of most everything.

All except one thing. One thing that brought me to the loss of everything.

Here's the thing. I did not realize until I was looking at this letter, back and forth at parts written on different days that the writing of that book in 1996 and losing everything I had hoped to be for twenty years came at the same time. I then printed it as a polished booklet in 1998, during the winter of my deepest hopelessness.

Oh my, now I look back up at the last thing written here before I opened that booklet to begin reading it.

"It places 'God' in the control of man."

I have not looked back at this booklet since I left move community in late summer 1998 numb and frozen inside. Please bear with me, this is very difficult. I can share now only out from a "stream-of-consciousness" sharing of my present very real search to understand how a man could speak the same things from the same verses with a view to the same end and one speaking be darkness and death and hopeless loss and the other be light and life and unending joy.

I cannot convey to you the highest importance and greatest value of one thing alone in all the truths I have ever heard or shared.

This one thing, that Jesus, my Lord and my God, drank His Father's cup, drank me, all of me, into Himself and then allowed the Father to send Him back to walk this earth again, planted now as me in all I find myself to be. Oh, oh, oh – how utterly I can cast myself into Him.

In 1996 it was all about me making it somehow into a God so far away. In 2014 it's all about Jesus carrying me all the way to the full knowledge of the Father. To know that my own gross inability to fulfill any requirements, even of the gospel, cannot remove me from Salvation nor prevent me from walking right now in full union with Christ.

Again, I am feeling pulverized right now, this is not easy. There is almost nothing in this booklet to refute. Yet it brought me into utter despair.

Let me quote one bit.

Eternal life is a gift from God. We neither earn it, or deserve it. God gives it to us freely out of His great love for us.

What is eternal life?

Your answer governs how you view your walk with God.

There is a traditional understanding of eternal life not supported by Scripture. I read a gospel tract that said, "The gift of God is eternal life (going to heaven)." Wait a minute! Where does the Bible say that? It does not!

What is eternal life? What is it not? Eternal life is not where you live or how long you live.

Eternal life is not going to heaven when you die . . . (I then say exactly the same as you have read me now.)

What is eternal life?

John 17:3 "And this is eternal life, that they may know You, the only true God, and Jesus Christ whom You have sent."

Eternal life is knowing God.

Eternal life is not knowing about God. It is more even than knowing Him really well. "That they may know You" is an intimate marriage union with God enabling us to bear His life. Eternal life is coming into union with Him who is eternal, whereby He plants His life in us and enables us to bring forth out of our beings that very same life.

Can we walk in full union with God here in the earth? Certainly.

I rest my case. Yet as I typed these words now onto this page, the dark hopelessness appeared to me in one little phrase. Can you find it? You see, I started my rendition of the "true gospel" back then with Galatians 2:20 as the only doorway into salvation. Can you believe that?

Here's the deal. I had thought all through this series that in this letter I would pull out that booklet and address it. However, when I finally "had to" write this letter, I wimped out. I chose just to start with my opening and then give a present rendition of "the two gospels."

The Lord did not let me escape. (He has a way about such things.) I'm saying this because I realize, inside this present feeling of utter astonishment mingled with feeling pulverized and numb, that the Lord wants me to strip aside all other knowing, all other teaching, all other glory and wonder and power, and look right now at the one thing that is important, the only thing that counts.

Did you find the hinge in the above quote from "The Two Gospels" by Daniel Yordy © 1998, the sling shot that casts all this wondrous truth coming through my mind and fingers back then into darkness and despair? And if I could take you back to those dark months of December, January, February when and where I finalized what I had written in 1996 so that you could see me in that setting, you would likely go quiet. You would understand and be astonished.

Here are the awful words: – *"Coming into union with Him."*

I can't do that. I tried; God knows I tried. I cried out to Him for years in the wrenching despair of my heart, in the deep places of God taking a man all to pieces inside the depths of desire, and I could not. I could not. I didn't know how. I didn't know why I could not do what everyone else must be able to do, as I thought.

I could not "come into union with Him." And I did not know why.

You can understand, I think, the deep sobs wrenching my breast right now as I tell you that there is only one thing of any meaning and value to me in this life or any other:

Jesus came into union with me.

Jesus came into union with me.

"Father, I will drink Your cup." And in that moment my grief turned entirely into Joy inside His heart.

– Okay, I had to go out for a bit. I am calm again; I can breathe.

I want to take you now back to the letter "Christ Versus Superman" and the email I received that sparked such turmoil and desperate longing to know God as He really is out of which I wrote *The Kingdom Rising*. I truly believe that the Lord Jesus squeezes me in His grip right now for your sake, for your understanding. The difference between the two gospels is not a difference of ideas or verses. Yet the difference is night versus day, hopeless despair versus all overflowing joy.

It is a difference of heart.

The email I included in that prior letter attempted to force back upon me the horrifying, awful darkness of a Christ far away from me. You see, there was a very simple problem in the booklet I wrote called "The Two Gospels," from the front page of that booklet to the back. – I was all alone.

But while striking back against the horrific image of a far-away Christ by writing *The Kingdom Rising*, my definition of God changed into a description of Him. God caused me to see that He is utterly different than I had ever known or heard of Him.

– God always reveals Himself through weakness, swallowing up into Himself all that we are including our sin and rebellion, becoming us in our present state, limiting Himself by our weakness. Thus, carrying us inside Himself, stumbling and falling along the way, He arises out of death into life, ascending on high, and we in Him. –

The Father has never left me alone.

Christ became us long before we ever thought about becoming Him.

I have returned to this letter, now, in a new morning, fresh from sleep. Before continuing here, I began to work on editing the first two letters of this series for the book. As I did so, I understood clearly what this exercise is about, what God wants me to see clearly and to convey to you.

Here are two things I wrote, one near the beginning, the other near the end of the first letter of this series, "Another Gospel, Another Jesus."

– We face an almost insurmountable difficulty. Both Paul's Jesus and another Jesus share the same name, both promote a gospel using similar words, and both use Bible verses to promote their claims. –

– So few seem to be speaking out from God's interests and intentions. Almost all repeat what they hear from others. But why can't they stop and think? I do not know. Part of it is the power of the Nicene Christ image. –

How could I be speaking the same truth I speak now, using the same verses I use now, and yet be myself in utter hopelessness, seeing, as I realize now, the very opposite of what I know now by those very same words? How could it be?

Tiptoeing back into the horror of those years of hopelessness and seeing there the same words I teach now was shocking to me. Yet it is the whole point of this series.

The POWER that sat upon me preventing me from seeing the wondrous reality of Christ my only life though I spoke almost the same words I speak now was the POWER of the Nicene Creed, of the Nicolaitan Christ.

I now understand God's incredible purpose for the most difficult three years of my life. I worship before Him and give Him thanks.

God wanted me to hate, with all the passionate fervency and eloquence He crafted as Himself in me, the Nicene Christ, the far-away Christ, the some-day Christ, the "get out of my way, loser" Christ, for your sakes as well as mine, so that you, by seeing my testimony and the truth of the Christ who is your only life, of the God who fills you full, can lose forever the lie of that wicked image, a separate-from-you Christ, a Jesus far-away.

At the core of my blindness as I wrote "The Two Gospels" was a specific theology expressed by these words:

– If I am not walking with God this moment, I am not in eternal life, even though eternal life is in me. I can have eternal life in me and not be in it. There are two lives in me. One is called death and the other life. One is my own way and the other His. I can be in one or the other, but I cannot be in both at the same time. –

That's the key darkness: *"There are two lives in me."* That statement is the creation of the false self.

Now, there are multitudes of powerful and anointed preachers who push that line in every word they preach and never know hopelessness. In fact, I received that understanding from the press of those to whom I had subjected my own life. Why did writing "The Two Gospels" bring me to such hopelessness?

This is so neat. I KNEW I was speaking truth AND I KNEW I was lying.

What I did not know was the difference.

I knew I was twisting certain Scriptures, particularly this line, **"We shall be saved by His life,"** when I said, *"By His life, not by ours."* In other words, *"Get out of your life, loser, and into His,"* something I could never do. I did not know how.

And neither do those who teach the Nicene Christ. They don't know how to escape their own life either.

When I left move community, I made a covenant with God. I took everything I had written, everything I thought was "truth," everything except the Jesus I did know and trust, put it on the shelf, and walked away from it. I said to God, "God, You will bring back off that shelf ONLY what is You. That way, everything not of You will remain there."

God is a Keeper of covenant.

As I said, so much of what I wrote in that booklet then, I write the same thing today. EXCEPT. – Except my unbelief.

You see, I never believed that what I taught was true. *"There are two lives in me"* causes blindness of the eyes, hardness of the heart, and all the rebellion of Adam.

"There are two lives in me" is the horror of all things evil.

"There are two lives in me" is another gospel, another Jesus.

You see, the email that sparked "Christ Versus Superman," spoke of the dark Christ I had known so very well, that high-above-you Christ that brought me to such hopelessness and ruin. The brother insisted that "Christ" cannot be my autistic difficulty, that Jesus does not conform Himself to me, that the only way I could ever know this "power Christ" was to escape my human frame.

Jesus came into union with me first.

I will never know Him in His power until I know Him as my weakness.

My strength is made perfect in weakness.

Okay, here is something God left entirely back on that shelf. He had to bring me to complete hopelessness before He could. This is what I said then. – *"To exalt the weakness of man is to reject the power of God."* –

I KNEW I was saying things contrary to the words of the gospel, I just did not know what or how. The thing is, a large part of my reasoning in making that statement is truth I speak today. Yet, I did not see or know.

Here's another: – *"I cannot walk in my own way, do my own thing, or think my own thoughts, without using my body."* You see my blindness? I (not Christ), I (not Christ), I (not Christ). That's the problem through the entire booklet. Me, me, me, and Jesus far away.

I made this statement: *"What many in the Church call faith is really self-reliance,"* yet it was I teaching self-reliance, though I sincerely believed the opposite. I was hopelessly alone, and in my hopeless inability, I believed that I had to prove something, to perform obedience, in order to be found in this Jesus whom I did know and love. What a pickle. What a contradiction.

Speaking Christ and not Christ, both at the same time.

You see, even as I wrote those words, even as I sent out that booklet, I KNEW there was something missing, something I was not seeing, something critical I did not know. I just did not know what it was. But I did know that something would be found in the words of Paul's gospel alone, nowhere else.

Thus in leaving everything on the shelf, I held to one thing alone. "I will take into myself only what God Himself says about me in Paul's gospel as God makes it real to me, everything else waits in the distance until the center, my heart, is true and Christ."

The first thing God brought back to me? "Daniel, I love you." Do you see that period after "you."? Most precious period. For years I was taught to say, *"God loves me, but. . ."* It was impossible for me to speak, "God loves me," and nothing more without feeling that I was in open rebellion against God.

Do you know what God says about me in Paul's gospel? God says, "Daniel, you are in the Spirit, you are NOT in the flesh. Daniel, you have the mind of Christ. – Daniel, you are complete in Christ. – Daniel, you are already dead; it's not you, it's Christ. – Daniel, Christ is your life."

Show me one place in the gospel where God says that we are in the flesh or that we possess a carnal mind or that we have a life not Christ. It's not there.

God talks about those things, yes, but He never places us in them or them in us. – God sees Christ alone.

I said at the beginning of this letter that I intended to uncover the core of hostility against God found in the writing of this sincere but hopeless Daniel Yordy.

I have done so. Here is that core. – **I, not Christ.**

Here is the core of all the joy in which I live today. – **Christ, not I.**

The first is hell, the second heaven. The first is darkness, the second all light and joy. The first is rebellion and hardness of heart; the second is all submission and repentance.

The Father has never left me alone.

⁓

The two "gospels" are not one set of ideas versus another set of ideas. Rather the distinction is built entirely on the human definition of "God" versus a God who is known only up from within ourselves, carrying us inside Himself.

I have postulated that Jesus in no way "set aside divinity," that God showing up in the earth is exactly what was seen by those who saw Jesus, a Man, God-revealed. That same God showing up in the heavens is seen and known as Spirit. Neither One, in and of themselves, are "the Father." Both are the Father revealing Himself through Another.

This same Father desires, now, to reveal Himself through many, through you and me. Christ is His forerunner in our earth; Spirit is His forerunner in our heavens. Father-revealed is our full inheritance.

There is no "God" of violence, other than the serpent. The law of the Old Covenant and all the imagery in it was entirely for one purpose alone. Man chose to live by knowledge about God, empty of God. God gave man the full experience of what that means. God is "terrible" only apart from Christ.

There has been much discussion in this series concerning "politics," that is, the nature of power-over. The Nicene God is entirely a God of power-over, ruling from the top down, giving commands and expecting immediate and explicit obedience, a God who inflicts pain to get His way.

You may gather that I am 100% libertarian when it comes to violence against others. Small l libertarian means one thing only – the non-aggression principle, best stated by Jesus, **"Do unto others what you would have them do unto you."** All initiation of violence for any other purpose then immediate and minimal self-defence, is immoral; that is, God is not involved. The same morality applies to all, including all individuals acting by "government."

Thus we have a God who reveals Himself only as a Man laying down His life for His friends, protecting them from the assault of death, a Man who possess all power, yet uses none of it because He will not hurt anyone. A Man who forgives out from His pain those who most deserve punishment of all created beings.

The Nicene Christ was forced all throughout Christianity at the point of the sword. Out from that image comes the most reprehensible doctrine in human thinking. — Hurting other people and calling it "God"

You must understand that the Dominican priest, inflicting pain upon the heretic in the torture chambers of the Inquisition, was moving in sincere and heartfelt love. I have no doubt some were anointed of God. He truly believed that this person was heading for unending awfulness and that his present infliction of pain was the very MERCY that would save. He truly believed, out from Christian principles, that this heretic would thank him one day for saving him, that the pain he was inflicting would bring forth Christ made visible. - A Nicene Christ.

The only Christ that is true is that which comes up from within each individual person by Spirit, who, when seen in outward form, is a Dove, one who never strives, never pushes, never violates anyone's person.

What I shared about the fellowship of His suffering in the last letter, "Body," is NEVER to be taken to justify any infliction of suffering on another. Jesus did not just say, **"Offences must come."** He also said, **"But woe to him through whom they come."** In the move communities where I lived it was often heard this way, "Suffer, brother, it's good for you." Here is another way it is said, **"Let us do evil, that good may come."**

I left the move because I will not treat others with disrespect. The fellowship of His sufferings is known only inside of God; it is God sharing with us the chisels attacking Him, or shall I say, God takes the brunt of the assault against God, allowing only a little to come through to us, thus allowing us to know His heart.

God just spoke to me as I read the following paragraph this morning.

- The real question here is a very personal one. Do the ends justify the means? If you bend on a bunch of principles along the way to get your message across, is it worth it in the long run? I don't know if there's a definitive answer, but for me, it was "no". - Vedran Vuk

Though the Father never leaves me alone, I am never certain of myself outwardly. Yet of one thing I am certain; I will stand before Jesus and He will ask me what I have done with what He has placed in my heart.

I fear God; that's why I'm not afraid of Him. Those who do not fear God will be terrified when He reveals Himself. And of course, there will be no condemnation in Jesus' question. But what eternal sorrow I will know if I am forced to say, "I kept it safe, Jesus, here it is. I did not share it with anyone because of what everyone else says."

"Get your message across" is the greatest trap sent against the sons of God. Most everyone, it seems, wants me to compromise what I share in order to join with them. When I will not, I am sometimes attacked. I am neither wise nor strong. I have no ability to "get my message across."

And neither did God as He walked the earth. When push came to shove, He just went silent. Then He laid down His life for His enemies.

Only the Spirit will ever get His message across, and only coming up from inside each individual person, a Spirit always sent, but never forced.

This is God. Can you see Him? Do you want to know Him?

– God always reveals Himself through weakness, swallowing up into Himself all that we are including our sin and rebellion, becoming us in our present state, limiting Himself by our weakness. Thus, carrying us inside Himself, stumbling and falling along the way, He arises out of death into life, ascending on high, and we in Him. –

The Father has never left me alone.

Christ became us long before we ever thought about becoming Him.

21. Victory

Thanks be to God who gives us the victory in Christ Jesus our Lord.
1 Corinthians 15:57

What is Victory? When we are standing in full and complete victory, when all that speaks against God concerning us is vanished, what will we be, what will we know in that moment?

Victory must be an individual experience before it could ever be a corporate experience. A "group" whose individuals do not each know victory cannot itself know victory. Yet the moment each individual knows victory personally and completely, then all relate with all in perfect order as the full many-membered body of Christ.

What is Victory?

In 1 Corinthians 15, Paul defines exactly what Victory is, that Life which swallows up death in the physical body and eliminates it, and he makes it clear that Victory is known as a specific and definite experience in a moment of time. He also says that God has already given us this same Victory. Victory over death right now is our personal possession.

Adam was alive, yes, and fully without sin. Yet Adam possessed neither death nor life. Rather, God placed both death and life before Adam, outside of his own person, and allowed him to chose. Once Adam chose death, there was nothing in his humanity capable of eliminating death or any part of it. Thus those who "try to obey" out of their humanity are just playing games with Adam's sorry death.

Adam did not have Life nor any access to it once God drove him out.

Life alone eliminates death. That life is IN Christ Jesus our Lord. That word "IN" goes both ways. We IN Him and He IN us. Since Jesus won that Life for us, He receives all the honor of it, and not some nameless "christ."

Every one of us desires many things as humans. What we must understand is that we desire only one thing, and all other desire flows out from winning that one thing.

We desire an immortal body, which, in conjunction with our already perfected spirits, causes us to be an incorruptible soul. We **must PUT ON immortality**; we **must PUT ON incorruptibility**. We PUT ON the Lord Jesus Christ. *Enduo*, sink into as into a garment or into the covers of one's bed. Cast one's self utterly into perfect rest.

We sink into immortality; we sink into incorruptibility.

Victory is the moment, in the twinkling of an eye, when our mortal frame instantaneously becomes immortal and when our corruptible soul instantaneously becomes incorruptible.

Let's think about this for a moment. All created beings are corruptible: ALL. All angels are corruptible, both those who have become corrupt and those who have not. That means all created beings are free of God; God binds no one to Himself. However, angels do not have physical bodies, thus corrupt angels know nothing about that realm of death. At the same time, the human spirit and the human soul tied to it continue on forever as an entity, continuing to live, move, and have his or her being inside of God, even though it continues corrupt.

Mortality and immortality relate only to the physical body. Thus those humans who are in heaven only, having lost their physical bodies, yet continuing to live inside of God as perfected spirits before Him, are not "immortal" because "immortal" is a term that must have a physical body to find its meaning. At the same time, the Scriptures do not allow us to assume that those who are in heaven only are in any way incorruptible. Rather, they are "dead" in Christ. That is, they continue on in the same condition as we do before God. They without us do not find Victory, and our Victory cannot precede theirs.

Victory comes to all overcoming believers on both sides of the veil at the same moment. Notice that those in the heavens rush to our side of the veil in order to know Victory, not the other way around.

Those who are in heaven only right now, though they are as much with Jesus as we are, yet they are NOT immortal and they are NOT incorruptible.

Mortal means capable of dying. Corruptible means capable of turning one's back on God. Adam was both mortal and corruptible BEFORE he ate of knowing God by the law. He could die, and he could turn his back on God even when he was completely innocent. Fallen man is dying and dies; fallen man is corrupt. Christians are yet corruptible; we can eat of life and we can eat of death. Fallen angels are corrupt, but they cannot cease.

Only the physical form can cease.

Jesus, when He walked this earth, was NOT immortal; His physical body was capable of dying. Jesus, when He walked this earth, was NOT incorruptible; He was tempted by the lusts of His flesh in all ways just as we are tempted.

God cannot be tempted by evil.

Yet Jesus was, in all ways, God-revealed.

When I say, "We must know Him as our weakness before we will know Him as His power," I am speaking primarily of the two sides of Victory, before and after, though it also has full meaning before that moment.

Declared to be the Son of God with power by the resurrection from the dead. Romans 1:4

Let's start with "incorruptible." We are to put on incorruptible. What does that mean? Victory IS the moment when you and I put on incorruptible. What does that mean?

Jesus said, **"Do not call Me good; only God is good."**

Only God is incorruptible. Only God cannot turn His back on God. God never denies Himself. The thought of denying Himself never comes anywhere near anything that is God.

In His resurrection, Jesus "became" incorruptible. When we say, "We are just like Him," we say it entirely inside the full knowledge of Seed—plant—seeds. That is, we understand fully that right now, we know Him in our weakness, that is, we walk just as Jesus walked. At the same time, because we know that God has already glorified us, though we see it not, we speak Christ as He is right now. We call that which appears "not" as though it IS. Thus we also say that we are just like Him as He is right now, though we know that the moment must come when the substance of our faith becomes the appearance of an immortal frame and an incorruptible soul.

Now, I started to say that Jesus "became" immortal, but I removed that because that could denote that Jesus remains alone in an isolated physical body. Then this word of Jesus came to mind.

Today and tomorrow I must do miracles, but on the third day, I will rise again.

Jesus was not talking about Sunday morning, April 17, AD 29. He was speaking of the Day of Tabernacles. Jesus does not consider Himself immortal until His entire body is immortal. Yet the immortality we PUT ON is Jesus' immortality. You see, this is a great mystery BECAUSE we are speaking of Christ and His church.

Seed—plant—seeds.

The Seed is complete in all ways, but in becoming the plant, in becoming the church, in becoming us, the Seed loses all of its Seed appearance and now looks nothing like a Seed. Yet that Seed, appearing now as the plant, continues to work through the plant until it has birthed and brought forth many more seeds exactly like itself. This is how we understand this great mystery. You hold to that pattern in your understanding and all things will find their place.

The moment the bean pod is broken open and the bean seeds are now ready either to be eaten or to be planted anew is called the resurrection of the physical body. It is called Victory. It is called the revelation of Jesus Christ, the removal of the cover.

Here is the definition of our becoming incorruptible.

That they all may be one, as You, Father, are in Me, and I in You; that they also may be one in Us, that the world may believe that You sent Me. And the glory which You gave Me I have given them (Victory), **that they may be one just as We are one; I in them and You in Me; that they may be made perfect in one, and that the world may know** (Salvation revealed) **that You have sent Me and have loved them as You have loved Me.**
John 17:21-23

You see that Jesus spelled the whole thing out precisely, yet we have never believed a word of it. We MUST understand why we have disbelieved and thus utterly ignored this whole scenario in our "theology."

This definition of our incorruptibility given by Jesus has ZERO place or relationship with the Nicene Creed or anything in it or anything coming out of it. Thus, this definition given by Jesus, should we actually subscribe to it, is utter, unrestrained, hideous BLASPHEMY!

Here is our dilemma. We know first, that this moment of Victory, this condition of incorruptibility, comes only by the swallowing up of our physical body into immortal life. Yet we also know that as seeds looking entirely like a plant in outward appearance, we CALL those things that "be not" as though they actually ARE!!!

Thus, on the one hand we speak these words as complete and total, our reality right now, but on the other hand, we know that all outward experience will change dramatically in one moment, the moment of Victory.

Seed—plant—seeds.

So, let me bring this incorruptibility into our present understanding with words that are personal to us.

First, both the Greek and the English have no positive word to denote the conditions of immortality and incorruptibility. The English in-corruptible means no-rotting, the Greek means no-withering. The English im-mortal means no-dying, the Greek is a form of *a-thanatos*, no-death, that is, *athanasia*, no-dying. Thus these conditions are presently denoted as the opposite of something bad, not the presence of the good with no idea of any existence of the bad.

In a sense, this is the only way these things can be known in human terms. The reason is that when we are immortal, we cannot know death, thus neither death nor no-death ever comes to mind. We will not be able to talk about "immortality" because there is no negative with which to compare the only Life we are.

Victory is the moment we become, in all experience, incorruptible.

To say that is to blaspheme the Nicene God for only God is incorruptible.

However, since we are just like Jesus, we know that Jesus' words in His kingdom-birthing prayer explain to us exactly how this Body works.

We are one with God in exactly the same way Jesus is one with God.

Union—Communion—Expression.

Father—Son—Spirit.

Filled with all of God, the Father—Christ Jesus living as us—the Spirit of God flowing out from us as rivers.

Jesus' words bring you and me as persons into the very Communion of the "Godhead."

That's why few preachers ever teach these words, and those few who do, try their best to explain how it is that they do not mean what they say.

Yet it is a simple thing, really; it's what we were created for. - We are filled full with another Person.

Let's define ourselves again.

First, the Holy Spirit FILLS our physical body, causing every cell and organ of our physical body to be the actual body of Christ, while at the same time, the Holy Spirit is working the resurrection life of Jesus' body all through every particle of our physical body, though we do not presently see it. Then, our spirit is poured out (baptised) into the Holy Spirit, and thus is "lost" into that Spirit that fills and sustains all things. Our spirit never becomes something separate from us, yet it is found wherever the Holy Spirit is found and flows out from us with Him as rivers. Wow, that's pretty cool. Our own spirit is inside all the rivers flowing out from us.

Then, Christ Jesus lives in our Hearts. Now, I take this to be that heart which is the central organ of our soul. Thus Christ has become our life, our psyche, our self. Yet the heart is one, and as heart, it is also the central organ of our body and the central organ of our spirit. Thus Christ is all that we are.

And inside this Christ Jesus who lives in our hearts, who is our only Self, who is all that we are, dwells the Father, all the fullness of God.

Now Jesus said: **That they all may be one** (UNION), a**s You, Father, are in Me, and I in You** (Communion); **that they also may be one in Us** (all of us together), **that the world may believe that You sent Me** (Expression).

The center of incorruptibility is Communion.

This Communion is found only inside of Union first, and it is always flowing out in Expression, bringing life and joy to all. This Communion is personal inside of each one of us, with both Father and Son. This Communion is also shared fully between us as brethren walking together in love.

But the Communion is the thing.

Incorruptibility, when all thought of death has ceased, will be known as communion, precious, precious Communion. *Koinonia* is the Greek word; fellowship is from the Saxon part of English; and communion is from the Latin part of English. They are all three the same word.

This Communion is first and foremost with the Father.

Here is how I said it in "Body."

– God's task is to so merge Himself with us that He might always be the One seen and known through us.

This merging of God and Jesus was complete, two Persons in One. Jesus is not just our pattern, but also our life, Christ as us. Thus Christ as us is already programmed to complete this full merger with the Person of the Father inside of us.

– God's consciousness must be in my full awareness inside of me and my consciousness in my awareness must be inside of God. Jesus said, "The Father has never left Me alone." We are always two persons together. –

My mind is the Father's mind, the mind of Christ, yet the Father's mind, His consciousness, also always walks together in sweet communion with my mind and mine is always in His in my full awareness.

My heart is the Father's heart, the throne of heaven, yet the Father's heart, the Mercy Seat, also always walks together in sweet communion with my heart, and mine is always inside of His in my full knowing.

The Father is the One always seen through me, yet I am also seen just as much. It's not me; it's the Father, yet it is me, for I am entirely alive inside of God. (Speak these things entirely as yourself; speak them by faith.)

In the resurrection, what is true of Christ now, becomes the same thing as the Father. Before the resurrection, all connection with the Father passes first through Christ. He is the only Way.

Jesus said this: **And in that day you will ask Me nothing. Most assuredly, I say to you, whatever you ask the Father in My name He will give you.** John 16:24

You see, here is how I understand it at present. Jesus is never "replaced" by the Father. Yet He, like us, always recedes into the background. Jesus is the Way, that means that all that He is, all that He does, is for the sole purpose of bringing you and me into total communion with the Father, into incorruptibility. Jesus is always right there inside that Communion, yet He always and only exalts the Father in us and towards us and never Himself.

As we are just like Jesus, we do the same for one another.

Greater love has no one than this, than to lay down one's life for his friends.

I'm talking about Jesus forever.

I'm talking about **and we also.**

Incorruptibility, now known to us as precious Communion with the Father in all that we are, is the center of everything, the ultimate value, our most precious treasure forever.

In Thy Presence is fullness of joy; at Thy right hand are pleasures evermore.

But immortality is where the excitement takes place.

God is big on excitement; He is all about ADVENTURE!!!

If you want to commune with God, get ready for the RIDE of your life!

When I was twenty, I hopped in my car and drove twelve hundred miles into a far country, landing among a bunch of people I had never known before who had carved a primitive Christian community out of empty wilderness and in the midst of Bitter, Icy winter, a people shouting about never dying and being equal with God! I loved it.

When I was twenty one, I hopped in my car (without enough money to get there) and drove three and one-half thousand miles across the country, landing among a bunch of people I had never known before who were building a Christian community and convention site in a very strange land, the American South, in Hot and Muggy heat, with zero air conditioning, a people who raised the roof in the power of the Holy Ghost dancing before God in hilarious exhilaration over the defeat of death!!! I loved it.

I like adventure too; you see, God made me just like Himself.

I have rushed into so many frying pans, so many raging fires, because I just can't stay away from this God who takes our breath away.

Yet in all standing upon the peak of Everest, in all discovery of the heart of Africa, in all circumnavigation of the earth, in all stepping out onto the moon, ain't nothing comes close to our physical body being swallowed up by life, ain't nothing compares with putting on immortality.

I want the whole deal, and I want it now.

Paul said that we GROAN for this very resurrection, that the Holy Spirit GROANS inside of us in the deepest of longing for this ultimate ADVENTURE. When was the last church service you were in when you alternated between dancing in Holy Ghost celebration over our defeat of death in one moment to groaning in the deepest Holy Ghost travail for that same resurrection in the next moment? Have you ever been to Church?

If by any means I might attain to the resurrection from the dead!

That I might seize hold of that very thing for which God has seized hold of me!

This immortality is not our body, but Jesus' body; we put on the Lord Jesus Christ, spirit, soul, and body. Yet it is our body, for the Holy Spirit causes our body to be His resurrected body, **flesh of His flesh** and **bone of His bone.**

Precious communion, always inside of total union first, always flowing out as exuberant adventure!

We are always and forever part of God; God always and forever is seen and known through us.

That sounds pretty exciting, something one would sell everything else to possess.

God has given us the Victory through Christ Jesus our Lord.

We already do possess; when we call Jesus our only Self, we already have sold everything else.

But what, exactly, is that full experience of putting on immortality? What will we feel? What will we do?

I'll let you know just as soon as I know, only I won't need to, because you also will be telling me.

But here is one thing I know. God is never "high and mighty." He is always meek and lowly of heart. He always carries the least and lifts up the lowest. He is always gentle and tender and kind. There is no greater joy God could ever experience than to take little children into His arms and bless them.

God desires the moment of our full entrance into Him and He into us in incorruptibility and immortality far more than we could ever know.

God longs to be seen. He wants to be known. He aches to touch and to be touched.

God desires us; God yearns for His Body.

If we could but glimpse, just a tiny little bit, the depths of God's longing for our immortality, we would never doubt again. We would be so caught by that Desire that we would instantly become immortal.

Father, I DESIRE that these, whom You have given Me, may be with Me where I am (in the Father), **and that they might see My glory which You have given Me.**

Now I see something I had not yet seen. Our bodies will become immortal, transformed into His same body, the very moment our eyes are opened and we see the overwhelming, unending, intense DESIRE in God to be seen and known through us.

When we see and know His heart.

This is eternal life, that they may know You, the only true God, and Jesus Christ whom You have sent.

We know that we shall be like Him for we shall see Him as He is.

~

I want, now, to conclude this series, and there is no better way to do so than the way I often have in the past.

If anyone loves Me, he will keep My word; and My Father will love him, and We will come to him and make Our home with him. John 14:23

Love is always the source FIRST; keeping His word is only ever the fruit, fruit that must by its very nature always proceed from the source, whether we presently see it or not.

The source of all things in our lives is the Holy Spirit abounding as love in our hearts. He is already there; He is already love; He is already working ALL in ALL. Our part is to believe with the same confidence in our Spirit as God believes, that is, the faith of Christ in us. We keep His word only out from knowing that it is true, that it is the only reality that we are.

Yet here is what I find, the more I speak His word made personal in me, the more I speak Christ and blessing to you, the more I find that same word, that same love, constraining my way, guiding my heart, keeping me.

Those who will not speak Christ ALL and ALL cannot know what I know.

My Father will love him. This love is found in our knowing. This is not Father's general love for all, but rather something extraordinarily personal and intimate. And you know, this is love, which means we are always free of it. This personal and intimate love of Father for me, just me, is mine if I say it is, if I know it is. But if I will not say and know that it is, then, it is not. Father will never force Himself on anyone; yet the moment you and I chose to KNOW His particular and personal love for us, watch out, for this is One exuberant Fellow.

I sit here in the knowledge of how special I am to Father, filled with Father, enveloped by Father, carried by Father, as I have never known. Yet it's just me, Daniel; just like its just you, Father-revealed.

May I suggest that you go back to my letter, "Father," and shout out the prayer of Jesus as it appears there, speaking your full name in the blanks. Speak it aloud in wonder and awe. Let the tears flow. It is true. I teach no theoretical gospel; I teach Father and you.

If ANY ONE – We will come to him/her.

This is not a corporate experience. The body of Christ, the kingdom of God, these are corporate experiences, but not this one.

This HOME is you, Jesus, and Father, just the three of you, together as one in your body.

Person with person with Person. Person inside of Person inside of person.

Our Holy Spirit is the *energia* of all of it.

"Our Holy Spirit." I said that in a prayer I included in an email reply this morning. I had to pause; can I say that? Our Holy Spirit.

I can and I do. Precious, precious Spirit. Our Spirit. Our holy, holy Spirit.

Our as in yours and mine. Ours as in mine and ours and Christ's. Ours as in mine and ours and Christ's and Father's. Our Holy Spirit.

This One in whom we ALL put our full confidence in all of our expectation with joy.

We will make Our home with him.

Why did God create the universe? Why did He lose everything? Why did He suffer all things Himself for all whom He lost? Why did He become us, carrying us all the way into life?

Why?

Home.

Father just wants to come home.

"But how will I know the way home?" – Little William Thatcher.

"Just follow your feet." – William's father.

"Did you follow your feet? Did you find your way home?" – William's father.

"Yes, father, you will never be alone again." – Grown William Thatcher.

(*A Knight's Tale*)

Home is NOT heaven, and home is not for us.

Home is us, the express image of God's Person to both heaven and earth, and Home is for Father.

Then they brought little children to Him, that He might touch them . . . And He took them up in His arms, laid His hands on them, and blessed them. Mark 10:13-16

Do you see God?

Do you know the desire of His heart?

Conclusion

What do you want?

Do you want His glory revealed through you more than life itself?

In these pages you have read a view of Christianity considerably different from anything you have heard in the mainstream. But you have also seen that this view is grounded utterly in Scripture, in what God actually says.

An honest heart, having read these pages not understanding, will stay before God in worship with one cry, "God, if these things be so, show me. Open Your word to me that I might see You as You really are."

God fulfills His Word through only a few, a glorious few, a happy few – at first. Yet their joy and the entire purpose of their lives is to hold the door wide open while many, many sons rush through to glory!

You have no ability for such a thing?

Good! If you did have some ability to accomplish something, you could not see or know the reality of abiding in Christ. God made us weak. We turn our backs on the sin of Adam, this hatred and rejection of the weakness of our flesh.

When I am weak, then I am strong.

His strength is made perfect in my weakness.

And thus we know Salvation, the true Lamb of God, and in knowing Salvation, we know that we abide in Him and He abides in us, carrying all that we are inside Himself, revealing God to all through us.

And we go forward filled with all the fullness of God filling us full, with the Spirit of God flowing out from us as rivers, carrying the lie to its destruction, defeating death and bringing glorious liberty to all the creation of God.

And she brought forth a male child and her child was caught up to God and to His throne.

THE JESUS SECRET
- Who I Am -

This book is meant to be a spiritual exercise of speaking what God says we are. God says that He is determined to conform us to the image of Jesus Christ and that our faith is effective as we acknowledge the good things of Christ inside of us. What are those good things of Christ? - All that God says about Christ in the New Testament.

I have often, through the years, lain on my bed awake in the middle of the night, tears streaming down my face, with a deep, deep, desire for God, for more of Him, for His perfect will in my life. Many times I have said to Him, "God, if You're doing anything in Your people that I am not part of, take me there; if it be possible, do it in me."

But I have known a lot of failure in my life. I am very weak. If this were up to me, I would have no hope. Why, then, am I filled with indescribable joy?

It is **The Jesus Secret**. The Jesus Secret has shown me Jesus like never before. If you want the Lord Jesus more than anything in the universe, it will reveal Him to you as well.

What do you want?

To be with Him. To stand by His side as He comes in His glory. To know that, in His triumph, He is counting on you; to hear Him say, "Well done, Friend, faithful and true."

All over the world, something phenomenal is happening in the lives of believers who want God more than anything. Hearts are being filled with glory; rivers of living water are flowing; darkness is shattering and falling.

What is happening? It is:

The Jesus Secret

OUR PATH HOME
1. Journey's End
2. Who Are We?
3. Into His Image

After writing *The Jesus Secret* in the fall of 2006 and learning to speak Christ my life, I sought to understand God's purpose for us. God says some mind-blowing things at the heart of the New Testament about the structure of our being and His purpose for us.

- **God is determined to conform us to the image of His Son.**
- **You are filled with all the fullness of God.**
- **Rivers of living water flow out of your bellies.**
- **They overcame the accuser, casting him out of the heavens.**

What do these things mean? If they are true, then how has Christianity become so side-tracked from these incredible assertions of God?

God makes the claim through both Paul and John, that we will be just like Jesus. What does that mean? How does it happen for us?

If we are to be like Jesus, then what are we? Who are we?

And if that is our end state-of-being, why, then, do we hear so little about the fulfillment of this vision in present-day Christianity?

The answer to that last question may surprise you. It will require a change of all your thinking about God, about the Bible, and about our walk upon this earth.

Christianity seems to have reduced salvation to going somewhere after we die! Where does God ever say that?

God is doing something incredible in His people on this earth right now. Don't be left out; the door is wide open. Discover what God really says in the New Testament about:

Our Path Home

THE GREAT STORY OF GOD

God reveals Himself to us through story, through a Man laying down His life for His friends. This volume weaves together a view of God's story told through Jesus, through the stories of the Bible, and through our own lives. It's primary focus, however, is on the climax, the proving, the final purpose of God's great story, revealed now in us.

God is story. God's story calls to the deepest recesses of our hearts. God says that we know Him only through the Story of a Man laying down His life for His friends.

There, in that act of Love at the heart of His Story, God shows Himself as He is – God ripped wide open for all to see.

In every story the hero leaves comfort behind and goes on a far journey. On that journey the hero gathers friends and companions; he battles enemies along the way and enjoys places of rest.

Finally the hero returns to fight for his people and his kingdom, to deliver them from the oppressor. His companions give their all out of the bond of love.

The hero faces the enemy at the point of the lie and defeats him. He restores the kingdom and brings joy and life to all.

God reveals His heart through the power and pathos of story. But story, to be real, must capture our hearts. For, though this is God's story, it is also very much ours.

At the heart of the Story are these words, spoken in our hearts.

> Greater love has no man than this,
> that a man lay down his life for his friends.

And so I give you:

The Great Story of God

THE KINGDOM RISING

It is time for the weak, the lowly, the incapable to shake the counsels of the mighty, to bring down kingdoms, and to overturn the ages.

The Jews of Jesus' day looked for a Messiah coming down out of the sky in power. When God sent them a man, just like themselves, weak and without influence; they could not see the Kingdom.

The Christians of today look for a Messiah coming down out of the sky in power. God sends them the weak, the lowly, the incapable.

The age of human folly is at an end. There is a knowing in the air that something must give, something must change; humanity on this earth cannot hold the present course. Certain ruin lies dead ahead.

Kingdoms of darkness are shattering and falling. Evil shows itself openly upon the earth because it's on its way out. The time of the accuser is finished.

Look to the cause. The Kingdom is beneath your feet.

The Kingdom comes, but it is coming where everyone least expects it. No one considers the crippled or the blind. No one looks to the autistic or the Down Syndrome. No one follows a little child without pretense or strength.

No one is looking for a God revealed through the inability of the weak and the lowly. Yet there is God, and there is the Kingdom.

The Kingdom is rising upon this earth and none can stop it or slow it down. No one will see it until it changes everything because all mankind have their eyes in the wrong place.

This is intended. If Christians, if non-Christians, knew where the Kingdom really is, they would kill it before it is born. But they do not see it and they do not know it, and thus it arises from beneath them and swallows them up, in Love, in:

The Kingdom Rising

THE COVENANT
Caught up in God

The New Testament is the New Covenant. What is that Covenant, binding in full upon all who sign it, both God and man? The completion of all that God does upon this earth will be found only in the fulfillment of that Covenant in our lives.

This volume weaves together three mighty strands of truth.

The first strand is the most important verses in the Bible, the central terms of that Covenant. God has a people who dare to read the Bible only through the terms of the Covenant and no other way.

What are the mighty terms of the Covenant we have signed with God and God with us? How must they be fulfilled in our lives?

The second strand is the one time and place God showed Himself as He really is inside of His creation. There God walked between the pieces of His own heart ripped wide-open in Blood upon the hillside.

That second strand is the Path of the Atonement, the steps of Jesus from Gethsemane to the right hand of the Father. That Path is the first and only time any part of creation has ever seen God.

The third strand is the central metaphor of the Old Testament upon which the New Testament is written, the Tabernacle of Moses in the wilderness.

The writers of the New Testament used the furnishings of that tabernacle to speak of believers in Jesus Christ in their walk all the way into the full knowledge and revelation of God.

We know God as the One who fills us with all of His fullness; we know God as the One who flows out of our bellies as rivers of living water.

The Veil is wide-open. But God does not command us to eat of life. We must boldly enter in. Faith alone, a heart of faith – the heart of God, seizes the full Bond of:

The Covenant

THE UNVEILING
As the Daystar Arises in Our Hearts

We are at the end of the limitation of God. They rejected Jesus BECAUSE He was a man living in mortal flesh. They killed Him because they could.

God reveals Himself in weakness, in a babe lying in a manger, in a man hanging naked upon a cross, laying down His life for His friends.

This is God; know Him.

He comes as the Daystar arising in our hearts. And He is as real in us as He was in Jesus.

That the life of Jesus also may be revealed – UNVEILED – in your mortal flesh.

The unveiling of Jesus Christ is upon us.

He is here; Jesus has walked this earth since the Day of Pentecost, June 5, AD 29. He has walked this earth hidden and unseen as those who belong to Him, filling their hearts with His Person.

Yet the time of His waiting is at an end. The cover is coming off. We are just like Him, for we see Him as He is.

God reveals Himself to all creation through us.

What do you want?

Are you available for His purpose? Is being with Him as He reveals Himself once again upon this planet, in tenderness and meekness, in truth and purity, in kindness and joy, in power and great glory, the only thing you desire?

To be like Him - Jesus - our Savior and our Friend.

For the sufferings of this present time are not worthy to be compared with the glory that will be UNVEILED in us.

The Unveiling

GATHERING TO LIFE
Eating and Drinking of Christ

The passion of the Lord Jesus Christ is extended with great desire over His Bride and over her gathering together unto Him.

That gathering together is to the fullness of the Lord Jesus Christ revealed now in our lives; it is a gathering to Life.

Jesus said, "**Eat of Me.**"

What does that mean?

A large part of eating of all that is Christ is life together.

The kingdom of God, the revelation of Jesus Christ, is multiplied little communities of believers, walking together as family, scattered all over this planet.

Every little member of the church is the Lord Jesus Himself in Person in them. When I give to you, I am giving to the Lord Jesus. When I receive from you, it is the Lord Jesus Himself giving life to me.

Community, family, the fellowship of brethren, men and women, old and young, brothers and sisters, fathers, mothers, and little children, sharing life together as God intended from the beginning.

As the revelation of Jesus Christ.

The Lord Jesus is preparing His ministry through whom He will send that word of life, that water of life, that will bring the full life of Christ into the experience of His church, brethren walking together in love. The revelation of Jesus Christ is community; it is family.

This book is written for the sole purpose of calling forth those little communities of Christ all over this earth. Whosoever will may come and freely drink. And the Spirit calleth, "Come."

That He might gather together in One all things in Christ.

It is a:

Gathering to Life

THE TEN MOST IMPORTANT VERSES IN THE BIBLE

(A Booklet)

The Ten —
Spoken as Christ
— Made Personal in Us.

1. From the very beginning, God determined to make me just like Jesus.

2. I am filled with all the fullness of God.

3. The Spirit of God flows out from me as rivers of living water bringing life and joy to all.

4. I cast down every voice that speaks against the Word God speaks, against Christ my only life.

5. Christ is my life; I have no other life.

6. I boldly enter the Holiest, the throne of God – with my heart sprinkled always with Blood, and with my body, flesh of His flesh, washed pure and clean.

7. I exult boastfully in all the victory of Christ revealed in me. I speak Christ; I keep the joy of my confidence high.

8. I love you; I lay down my life for you.

9. I set creation free.

10. Just as Jesus is IN the Father, so I am in Him and He is in me, every part of me in Him and Him in every part of me. I abide in Christ; He abides in me.

The Ten Most Important Verses in the Bible

THROUGH EYES OF FIRE

John's vision on Patmos has mesmerized Christians since it was written. But John's vision seems to speak of dark and terrible things. Much violence has been perpetrated because of things people imagined they read in it. Some say it should never have been written.

Why did God give this vision to John? And why do so few people find the precious Lord Jesus inside of His Revelation?

We desire to know Jesus as He really is, to be just like Him. How, in the midst of all the clamor, can we find our own place inside of Him? We know our place in God as we see all things out from Jesus' eyes, out from eyes of fire.

The Revelation of Jesus Christ God gave John by vision on the Isle of Patmos is a book in which so very few find Him because they do not seek for Him there. Instead, so many turn John's vision away from the salvation of Christ and onto the horrors of human thinking in this world.

In this study of John's vision, I seek to know Christ revealed as Savior and as Salvation – in and through us, His body, setting all creation free. I find Jesus in Revelation because He is the only One I seek.

I want to be with Jesus as He stands in His glory upon this earth. I want Him to place His arms around my shoulders and say, "This is Daniel; he is with Me." I want Jesus to reveal His glory in me.

But I am so incapable and weak. I have always failed at everything. Yet I cannot be, I will not be, I am not anywhere else.

So, in my weakness, in my desire, I have done something quite desperate. I have boldly entered into the Holiest Place in Heaven and seated myself upon the chair that is there. I have turned myself around. I see out, now, from that throne, I see all things through eyes of fire. I do so entirely by faith. I do so because no other possibility can exist for me.

We see through His eyes alone. (We say that by faith.) We see :

Through Eyes of Fire

The Two Gospels

If you would like more copies of this book, type, "The Two Gospels – Yordy" into an Amazon search. If you purchase more than $25 worth, there are no shipping charges.

If you would like to communicate with me out of a heart longing to know the living God as your very life, then go to www.dyordy.com, and click on "Send me an email."

Or write me here:

Daniel Yordy
7914 Fernbank Drive
Houston, Texas 77049

Those who wish to debate will likely not receive a response. Responding to debate is a gift God left out when He fashioned me inside His heart.

To those who love His appearing, I bless you with all the joy of Jesus.

Daniel Yordy grew up in the Mennonite church and in the Willamette Valley of Oregon. At the age of twenty, he followed his heart into the Canadian wilderness of northern British Columbia where he committed himself to a Christian fellowship known as the move of God and to eighteen years of living in the context of intentional Spirit-filled Christian community.

Although Daniel left that fellowship with his family in 1998, he remained committed to the vision of the revelation of Jesus Christ birthed in his heart through his years in community.

In 2006, he heard a word he had not considered before: "Speak what God says you are." Since God says that we are just like Jesus as we see Him as He really is, Daniel again committed his heart and life to know the furthest extent of what God means by what He speaks, and by speaking what God speaks, to call those things that be not as though they are.

Daniel Yordy has obtained a Masters Degree in Education and is by present trade a teacher of English and of writing. Although he loves to learn and the discipline that a college education brings to the mind, he gained primarily a further seeing of the emptiness of knowledge in this world.

At the age of 53, Daniel realized that he has lived inside the autism spectrum all of his life, in a portion of that spectrum known as Asperger's syndrome. That condition brings difficulty, yes, but also a particular ability – the ability to see patterns others may miss.

And so, with a quiet and humble heart, he offers to you the things God has taught him through 37 years of longing to know the Lord Jesus Christ with all his heart and through many tears inside the probing dealings of a holy God.

Made in the USA
Middletown, DE
24 July 2018